THE RISING OF THE RED SHAWLS

D1233053

AFRICAN STUDIES SERIES   43

AFRICAN STUDIES SERIES

THE RISING OF THE
RED SHAWLS

A Revolt in Madagascar 1895–1899

STEPHEN ELLIS

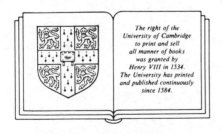

The right of the
University of Cambridge
to print and sell
all manner of books
was granted by
Henry VIII in 1534.
The University has printed
and published continuously
since 1584.

CAMBRIDGE UNIVERSITY PRESS

CAMBRIDGE

LONDON   NEW YORK   NEW ROCHELLE
MELBOURNE   SYDNEY

Published by the Press Syndicate of the University of Cambridge
The Pitt Building, Trumpington Street, Cambridge CB2 1RP
32 East 57th Street, New York, NY 10022, USA
296 Beaconsfield Parade, Middle Park, Melbourne 3206, Australia

First published 1985

Printed in Great Britain at the University Press, Cambridge

Library of Congress catalogue card number: 84–19887

British Library cataloguing in publication data

Ellis, Stephen
The rising of the Red Shawls. – (African
studies series; 43)
1. Madagascar – History – French invasion,
1985 2. Madagascar – Politics and
government – 1885–1960
I. Title II. Series
322.4'2'09691   DT469.M34

ISBN 0 521 26287 9

DT
469
.M34
E45

for

HILDA MARY ELLIS

and in memory of

DEREK HUGH JOHN ELLIS

also of

ISABELLE VACQUIE

Thus we have related briefly the main facts, but only the main facts, of this terrible rebellion; it would require a volume to give a full account of it and to tell the whole tale of woe and suffering which it brought in its train.

Reverend Richard Baron, 1900

Contents

Contents

Maps

Abbreviations

a.cl.	ancien classement
a.f.	ancien fonds
AAM	Archives de l'Académie malgache
AM	Académie malgache
AcSOM	Académie des sciences d'outre-mer
aff. étr.	affaires étrangères
aff. pol.	affaires politiques
Ann. Univ. Mad.	*Annales de l'Université de Madagascar*, série lettres
ANSOM	Archives nationales, section outre-mer
Ant. Ann.	*Antananarivo Annual*
Arch. And.	Archives de l'archevêché d'Antananarivo, Andohalo
Arch. dép.	Archives départementales
Arch. nat.	Archives nationales, Paris
ARM	Archives de la république malgache
ASEMI	*Asie du sud-est et le monde insulindien*
B. de M.	*Bulletin de Madagascar*
BAM	*Bulletin de l'Académie malgache*
bat.	bataillon
Bib. Nat. Tana.	Bibliothèque nationale, Antananarivo
Bib. U. Tana.	Bibliothèque universitaire, Antananarivo
cab. civ.	cabinet civil
CO	Colonial Office
col(s).	colonial, colonies
comm.	commandant
DAOM	Dépôt des archives d'outre-mer, Aix-en-Provence
ENFOM	Ecole nationale de la France outre-mer
FFMA	Friends' Foreign Mission Association
FO	Foreign Office
IRSM	Institut de la recherche scientifique malgache
JAH	*Journal of African History*
JME	*Journal des missions évangéliques*
JOMD	*Journal officiel de Madagascar et dépendances*

Abbreviations

La. p.	Laroche papers
LMS	London Missionary Society
Ly. p.	Lyautey papers
Mad(ag)	Madagascar
MAE, CP	Ministère des affaires étrangères, Paris, correspondance politique
MAE, M&D	Ministère des affaires étrangères, mémoires et documents
MDRM	Mouvement démocratique de la rénovation malgache
mi.	microfilm
mil.	militaire
min.	ministre, ministère
Mp-ts.	*Mpanolo-tsaina*
n. cl.	nouveau classement
n.d.	no date
n.f.	nouveau fonds
NMS	Norwegian Missionary Society
Nor. Miss.	*Norsk Missionstidende*
NRE	*Notes, reconnaissances et explorations*
ORSTOM	Office de la recherche scientifique et technique d'outre-mer
R. de M.	*Revue de Madagascar*
rés., res.	résident, resident
RFHOM	*Revue française d'histoire d'outre-mer*
SHA	Service historique de l'armée
SJ Ambositra	Archives of the Society of Jesus, Ambositra
SJ Tana.	Archives of the Society of Jesus, Antananarivo
SME	Société des missions évangéliques
SPG	Society for the Propagation of the Gospel
TA	*Tantaran' ny Andriana*
terr.	territoire
US Cons.	Archives of the US consulate at Tamatave
VVS	Vy, Vato, Sakelika

Introduction

William and Lucy Johnson and their baby daughter were killed on 22 November 1895.

They had met through Quaker work in the north of England many years before and had married at Tamatave, Madagascar's main port, in 1872. Since then they had worked for the Friends' mission in several parts of the island, but especially at Arivonimamo, a provincial centre some forty miles to the west of Antananarivo, the capital of the kingdom of Imerina whose queen and prime minister claimed all of Madagascar as their own.

The Johnsons had lived through some difficult times at Arivonimamo. From 1883 to 1885 the kingdom of Imerina and its subject provinces – over half of Madagascar – had been at war with France. For the French the war had been no more than a minor colonial distraction, but within Imerina it had caused a considerable breakdown of central government and a wave of anti-European feeling. The conflict had finished with the imposition of a nominal French protectorate which, although resulting in no French military occupation until 1895, marked the beginning of the end of Madagascar's independence.

Arivonimamo had a reputation as a difficult missionary district. Every missionary who worked there found the local people proud, aloof, difficult to convert, having a strong sense of collective independence and a profound attachment to the traditional cult of the ancestors which, to the missionaries, involved unspeakable forms of vice and idolatry. Throughout 1895, after French forces had landed in Madagascar in strength and in earnest to impose a real protectorate, the Johnsons had watched in dismay as the principal clan of their district, the Zanakantitra, abandoned churches and schools, brought into the open the talismans which they had revered in secret since Christianity had become the official religion of Imerina twenty-six years previously, and showed open hostility to the missionaries whom they thought to represent an alien form of government and a foreign religion. In the Arivonimamo area, as in many parts of Imerina, the entry of French troops into Antananarivo on 30 September 1895 and the submission of Queen Ranavalona III did nothing to pacify the country people. On the

1

contrary, through local family elders and village notables they began to organize an insurrection which would expel the Europeans and those Malagasy whom they held responsible for the French conquest.

November 22 was the most prominent date in the Merina calendar. It was the date of *fandroana*, the feast of the bath, the most holy day in the year when all Merina freemen gathered at their ancestral villages to celebrate the unity of their families and their loyalty to the queen. Given the degree of patriotic feeling after the French invasion, it was clear that 22 November 1895 would not pass without some demonstration by the Zanakantitra and many other villagers in Imerina. During the preceding fortnight William and Lucy Johnson had hardly been out of doors, feeling it would be better not to provoke the Zanakantitra by appearing in public. But their servants and the native evangelist attached to the Friends' mission had brought news that the Zanakantitra had held a series of mass meetings in which they had sworn to rise against the French and to drive away or kill all Christians, whom they believed to have betrayed the country to the French. After hearing of the largest such meeting to date, on 14 November 1895, William Johnson had sent a letter to the French commander General Duchesne warning him of the impending rising of the Zanakantitra. A party of Malagasy troops was despatched by the government to the village of Amboanana, the seat of the insurrection among the Zanakantitra. The soldiers were killed by a party of Zanakantitra insurgents on 21 November 1895.

The Johnsons had had the clearest signs of impending danger. Some days previously the evangelist from Amboanana, fleeing for his own life, had warned them that the people planned to come to the Johnsons' house to kill them. The missionary couple had resolved not to leave, but to stand firm and to demonstrate to the Zanakantitra Christian courage and faith. Both were pacifists. William Johnson had long expected a 'sifting time' as he called it, when the faith of the Malagasy would be put to the test and the Christian wheat separated from the pagan chaff.

Soon after dawn on the morning of 22 November 1895 word came to the mission house that a party of perhaps a thousand Zanakantitra were arriving from Amboanana. The Johnsons still refused to leave their house and kept their daughter with them. At breakfast-time the insurgents came, in a mood of patriotic and religious fervour and determined to rid the country of all foreign invaders, British, French or whatever. Some of the insurgents, many of whom were personally known to Johnson, came into his house. After a short exchange of words they demanded money. He said that he would have to go upstairs to his bedroom for that. Two or three men followed him and took the money he offered to them. One of the men struck Johnson, and within seconds his attackers had stabbed him to death. They threw his body from the first-storey window onto the lawn, where hundreds of people were now gathered. They set upon the body and mutilated it. The rising of the *menalamba*, the 'red shawls', had begun.

Lucy Johnson and her daughter Blossom were in the grounds of the house during the murder. The attackers discussed for some time what to do with them. One young man, declaring that from women would come forth future generations of Europeans, struck the first blow with his knife. Soon both mother and daughter were dead.

The Johnsons were the first European victims of the *menalamba*. Within days their deaths had been avenged dozens of times over by French troops sent to the land of the Zanakantitra to punish the insurgents and pacify the region. This they did by indiscriminate brutality. 'The punishment', wrote a participant, 'was terrible: we burned the rebel villages and cut off rebel heads . . .'[1]

The rising of the *menalamba* was one of the key events in modern Malagasy history. It helped to determine the pattern of French colonization and Malagasy attitudes to it. It also exposed some of the main elements and conflicts in Merina society. A study of the rising is also a means for examining the nature of Imerina in preceding decades. Insurrections, during which people consider and seek to reconstruct the fundamentals of their society and their politics, are a privileged point of observation for historians. It is the more so in the case of the *menalamba* because the Malagasy people had – and have – such an exceptionally keen sense of their own history.

My first aim in this book is to try and discover the causes, the nature and some of the consequences of the rising which began at Amboanana on the day of the feast of the bath in 1895. Malagasy society – for the rising eventually involved peoples other than the Merina – was the sophisticated and highly original product of several centuries of evolution, absorbing elements by foreign contacts or new waves of immigrants. Simply to describe the rising of the *menalamba*, and the aims and ideals of its participants, makes necessary an investigation of the 'customs of the ancestors', the Malagasy name for an accepted way of life and behaviour. I hope that in telling the story of the *menalamba* I will contribute to a wider understanding of Malagasy history.

1

The decline of Imerina

O Imerina, examine and read carefully the history of the customs received
from your ancestors.

The *Tantaran' ny Andriana*, passage translated by the Rev. James Sibree

OLD IMERINA

The fundamental unit of Merina society was, and is, a social group which
European travellers have often called a tribe or a clan. Every freeman
belongs to one of these groups, each of which usually takes its collective
name from whichever ancestor is regarded as its founding father. Everyone
who claims descent from the same ancestor is a kinsman. In the past, men
and women ideally married one of their kinsfolk, so that to a Malagasy it was
irrelevant to ask whether a child claimed descent from the common ancestor
on his mother's or his father's side. He claimed it on both, for both were of
the same blood. Maurice Bloch, an anthropologist who has made the best
study of this system, considers that the basic group is best called a deme, a
word sometimes applied to similar social units in Malaysia and Polynesia.[1]
This word will be used throughout the present study to describe the bilineal,
in-marrying groups which the Merina call *karazana* or *foko*.

The Merina are the most numerous of all the Malagasy peoples, constitut-
ing over the past two centuries somewhere between a third and a fifth of all
Malagasy. Even today, Merina of free descent consider that each individual
deme has a homeland where its ancestors lived and where their tombs still
stand. In the past it was normal for members of the deme to live in the little
territory which was their homeland, and they would still think of it as home
even if they had to earn a living elsewhere. The homeland is so important to
the social system as to be sacred. The only Merina without homelands before
colonial times were slaves or vagrants or bandits. The most basic Malagasy
religion, the cult of the ancestors, depends upon land, kinship and tombs.

Madagascar is usually reckoned to be inhabited by eighteen peoples,
although the number varies because it is difficult to say at what point an
alliance of demes becomes a people. Each one is a confederation of dozens
or hundreds of demes or similar groups which has at some time formed a
state. All speak the same language and have rather similar customs. In the
nineteenth century some peoples were ruled by one monarch while others
owed allegiance to numerous petty kings of one royal dynasty. Still other

4

Map 1. Madagascar in the nineteenth century

peoples had no kings at all and were composed of republics, or they were held together only by the memories of former glory, reflected in rituals and social habits. The image of political structures remained long after the reality had vanished, because the Malagasy traditionally look to their ancestors for models of ideal behaviour. 'The commands of a father or an ancestor', a missionary observed, 'are held as most sacredly binding upon his descendants.'[2]

The Merina (sometimes misleadingly called Hova in old texts) are immigrants to Madagascar, of predominantly Malaysian origin. According to their own traditions they arrived at some time during the Middle Ages and expelled or assimilated an earlier generation of inhabitants, the Vazimba. At an early stage of their history, probably before the seventeenth century, some Merina demes began to evolve a sophisticated system of agriculture based on intensive rice cultivation. They came to enjoy a reputation as artisans and traders too, although the Europeans who visited the coasts of Madagascar from the sixteenth to the eighteenth centuries only rarely met any Merina traders face to face.

The oral traditions of the Merina portray their history since the period of immigration as a story of demes settled around the tombs of their ancestors. But the traditions to some extent paint an ideal picture. There is evidence of constant migration, and it is apparent that some present-day Merina have changed their first homeland, while other descendants of Malaysian or Indonesian immigrants have gone to other parts of the island and have ceased to be Merina at all.

It would seem that the deme is not only the most basic political unit of Malagasy society, but also the oldest. As the centuries have gone by there has been an enlargement of scale. In very early times, neighbouring families in Imerina acquired the habit of forming village communes for the settlement of minor disputes and for mutual aid. These communes are so basic to Merina society that they have functioned through every change of government, and still thrive today. Some demes formed an allegiance to neighbouring groups. These federations grew so large, or gained such a notion of central authority, as to form kingdoms, which again was before the seventeenth century. This is what happened in Imerina, although it is not known whether kingship developed mainly from influences elsewhere in Madagascar or by a process which happened to occur at the same time as strong kingdoms were emerging among other peoples in the south and west of the island.

A Merina of the nineteenth century could describe himself or herself as belonging to each of several levels of allegiance. Imagine that a missionary from Leeds ventured north of the Merina capital at Antananarivo to collect oral traditions, to the land of the Zanakandriambe deme. In olden days the Zanakandriambe had allied with other demes to form a larger group, the Mandiavato. These had combined in turn with other federations in a league called Avaradrano, which was an independent kingdom in the eighteenth century. After the unification of Imerina, about 1800, Avaradrano became just one province of the kingdom of Imerina, which later claimed to be the sole government of Madagascar. If a Zanakandriambe were called upon to identify himself he could do so at a number of different levels from Malagasy downwards, just as the missionary who questioned him might describe himself as a European, a Briton, an Englishman, a northerner, a Yorkshireman, and so on.

Sovereigns arose in Imerina in response to certain needs, some of which would nowadays be called religious, others secular. A Merina of those times would have made no distinction between the two, and would have regarded them as spiritual and practical in equal measure. The system of irrigation which produced abundant rice harvests had to be built and repaired by a number of people beyond the resources of a single deme. Neighbours acquired the habit of working together under the direction of one sovereign. If political strife prevented the mobilization of labour, agriculture suffered. A competent ruler was one who could organize labour dues for the common good. At the same time as these larger units were taking shape, talismans called *sampy* were introduced from other parts of Madagascar. These were small constructions of animal remains or other charms which symbolized the unity of a deme or of a league of demes, and the power of the talismans was closely connected with kingship and the material benefits derived from labour dues owed to the sovereign. The talismans were not owned by the king, and might be considered local or royal in different contexts. But there arose a belief, with solid practical foundations, that the kingdom could prosper only in revering the talismans and the royal ancestors, just as a freeman could prosper only in paying proper respect to the ancestors of his family.

The Merina concept of the state, and even of its geography, was connected to beliefs in magic and astrology. The sovereign existed to uphold the cosmic order, which could be subverted by dark forces. If this order failed, so did the rice harvest. The early monarchs were not administrators except in their obligation to organize labour or perhaps in time of war, and even when they later gained great temporal power the relation between ruler and ruled remained extraordinarily intimate. Even the most powerful of the early kings might not be able to administer government in villages just a few miles from his capital. To see a map of the Merina kingdom in about 1700, when it was temporarily united, is misleading. It was perhaps the size of a large English county, but every village and district had its own rulers in the form of traditional deme elders or subordinate kings. It was a very parochial system. That adjective is used deliberately, for when Christianity was later adopted the parish proved to be almost tailor-made as a system of government.

The surest way of detecting witchcraft was by a poison ordeal whose application was controlled by holy men associated with the talismans. A king who had effective control of the talismans also commanded the poison

7

ordeal. Over two centuries, from about 1650, it developed steadily into a fearsome arm of royal power. From being used on animals, it was given to humans. From being used against witches, it was turned on any subject whom a king or queen saw fit to accuse of sorcery. It was generally tolerated because without the ordeal there was no defence against witchcraft, just as there could be no prosperity without labour dues.

There were times when no single monarch was stronger than neighbouring kings or queens, so that for decades Imerina was divided into what might be called city-states if that were not too grand a title for the little wooden villages of old Imerina. The people of every valley or village lived very close to their king. When he in turn owed allegiance to a greater lord in Antananarivo or some other town, the relative status of different provinces of Imerina was called into question. The king and the guardians of the leading talismans were supposed to pronounce on such things, and they could channel material benefits towards their supporters. In this way certain traditional privileges might bring access to new lands or lighter labour dues. A conquering monarch, like any politician newly arrived in office, had to be extremely careful to respect traditional rights as far as possible while adequately rewarding his closest collaborators.

Relative status was reflected in those categories which have been called castes,[3] a word which will be retained here for want of a better. Merina sovereigns liked to confer a special status upon their kinsmen. They gave them ritual privileges which included the right to certain forms of address, for example. This system is said to have been introduced in the days when probably the entire population was composed of farmers and part-time traders, although in the past some scholars have thought that Merina castes may originally have represented some sort of ethnic division. A king's deme was held to be *andriana*, which will be translated as 'noble', although it is essential to bear in mind that the nobles were unlike the aristocrats of medieval Europe. In one of the minor kingdoms of the seventeenth century a large part of the free population could claim to be related to the king and therefore noble. Other free demes were considered to be *hova* or commoners. The titles bore no relation to wealth or right to office. To describe men or women as noble in those days no more implied power than to say they were left-handed. At the bottom of the scale of freedom were certain demes called *mainty* (blacks), sometimes misleadingly translated as slaves but which will be called slave-demes in the present study. The origins of this category are obscure. It seems most likely that the oldest of them derive from demes which had been displaced by newcomers, perhaps at the time when the Merina overcame the Vazimba. The conquered groups lost their homelands and therefore declined in ritual status. At the same time it was recognized that they were the original occupants of the land, which was holy, and worthy of a certain respect on that account. In some cases they had important ritual functions in national ceremonies or special rights to approach the monarch. At the very bottom of the social order were *andevo*,

8

household slaves in a sense more familiar to Europeans. They were not numerous in Imerina before the nineteenth century. They would usually be prisoners-of-war or enslaved criminals, and had neither demes, nor home-lands, nor ancestral tombs, which were the marks of the free.

Historians are still not sure about the early history of Imerina but it is generally thought that the first kingdoms sprang up in the south-east of modern Imerina, in the district called Vakinisisaony. It was here that the castes of commoner and noble were first spoken of and some people think that it was here that the talismans first entered Imerina. Only later did Imerina's political centre of gravity move northwards to Antananarivo and the large and fertile plain which surrounds it.

On the rare occasions when one king succeeded in dominating most of the demes of Imerina, which seems to have happened three times before the nineteenth century, the victor promoted his kinsmen to the highest rank of the nobility, which pushed the older noble ranks nearer to the status of commoners. In time a noble deme could even lose its nobility altogether, either as a punishment for revolt or because its royal ancestor had lived so long ago as to be almost forgotten. By the same standard a commoner deme could be promoted to a higher rank within its caste, but it was very rare for a commoner deme to become noble purely as a result of faithful service.

These developments were incorporated into formal oral histories, which were the greatest art form produced by old Imerina. In an age of illiteracy prodigious feats of memory were made to remember the deeds of the ancestors and to recite them in support of present claims for status. One of the fundamental myths of Merina society was that every deme owed its status to a compact made by one of its forebears with a previous king. Normally the pact involved recognition of the king in return for confirma-tion of the right to occupy a certain territory and to perform certain roles in important ceremonies. Stories of past and present were woven into a beautiful seamless garment of words. By remembering the king with whom a covenant had been made, or some ritual associated with him, a deme could confirm the nature of the pact. A deme which had once been of high rank, but had since slipped down the social scale, was more likely to pay particular reverence to a sovereign of long ago and to the most ancient customs. History was the means of testing the legitimacy of government. For example, the Antehiroka deme, which was said to have originated among the Vazimba, had an important part in the old ceremony of circumcision. Any attempt to change the ceremony, or to obliterate the memory of the kings who had granted the Antehiroka their role in it, would be interpreted as an attack on their status. The only Merina deme which retains a clear memory of its arrival in Madagascar in the dim and distant past, the Zafimamy, is also the one with the most precise claim to have founded the institution of monarchy in Imerina. Conversely, the demes which enjoyed enhanced status in the nineteenth century were less inclined to remember the sovereigns before King Andrianampoinimerina (*c.*1783–1810), who raised them to new heights.

The customs of the ancestors were held to be the model for all that was right. The wise counsellor was the one who could refer to a relevant precedent. The best orator was the fluent speaker who could embroider his discourse with proverbs. The most skilful statesman was the one who could best use traditional symbols of power and rank. A ruler who could not provide a traditional claim was illegitimate.

If every deme claimed to have, or to have had, a special relationship with the monarchy, it follows that some of them must have been disappointed when they submitted to a new overlord with more urgent priorities. The earliest kings tried to placate these grievances by leaving conquered kings to administer their native lands or by installing their own relatives to receive the symbols of tribute. This was the origin of the *tompo-menakely* or fief-holders. There was no standing army and no civil service until the nineteenth century. The power of the paramount king lay in his control of the talismans and of the poison ordeal, or at least such control as he was able to exert, for the guardians of the talismans originated in the provinces and not in the royal household.

In spite of Imerina's early history of dynastic disputes and petty civil wars, every time the king of one little state became the overlord of his cousins another step was taken in the consolidation of central government, as the waves of an incoming tide recede only to travel further up the beach. It is said that King Ralambo, who probably lived in the sixteenth century, was the first to divide the nobles into a scale, with his own kinsmen at the top. The next great Merina king, Andriamasinavalona (*c.*1675–1710), went further in installing his family as fief-holders in some parts of the kingdom. Not only did his offspring pass to the first rank of the nobility, as was now the custom, but they became a lineage without any particular homeland. But Andriamasinavalona's sons quarrelled and Imerina split once more into rival states each owing allegiance to one of his family.

The little kingdom of Avaradrano whose capital was at Ambohimanga to the north of Antananarivo eventually passed to one of his descendants who took the name of Andrianampoinimerina. He came to unite all the Merina demes on a previously unknown scale, and he was later considered to have brought traditional practices to the height of their development. He acquired a means of coercion greater than that of any of his rivals by the skill with which he dealt with European slave-traders and acquired guns from them. Before his death in 1810 Merina soldiers had gone beyond their borders to subjugate the kings of another people, the Betsileo, and the independent demes of the eastern forest.

Imerina now needed to look constantly outwards for its prosperity. Being an inland state, it could trade with foreigners only if the routes to the east coast were kept open. The king established a central authority of a type which a European could more easily compare with the power of medieval kings. This was done, in the time-honoured fashion, by exploiting traditional practices for new purposes. Andrianampoinimerina gained closer control of the talismans than had ever been done by duplicating the more important of them and placing them in one of the villages where he had staunch supporters. Most of the leading talismans existed in several versions, a few of which remained in the provincial villages where they had been since time immemorial, others being near the king's court in Antananarivo or in a village of Avaradrano. An astute British missionary later observed that Andrianampoinimerina 'acted thus solely from political motives, having their foundation in the conviction that some kind of religious or superstitious influence was useful in the government of a nation.'[4]

During his conquests Andrianampoinimerina overcame a handful of major sovereigns and dozens of minor ones. Some resisted; others negotiated peace. Where a king had fought he was often replaced with a member of Andrianampoinimerina's family, who then ruled as a fief-holder. Kings who had negotiated terms were usually allowed to remain as hereditary fief-holders under the higher authority of the king of all Imerina and were entitled to the same marks of respect as those fief-holders who were members of the king's own group, the Andriamasinavalona. Alliances with local magnates were confirmed by marriages. At the same time there was the first attempt to create a civil service. There was a royal council composed of the traditional heads of provinces and the king's personal advisers. A body of fifty (later seventy) officials carried the king's orders to the provinces. Still, the essential work of administration was to be done as always by local elders and fief-holders. But the latter category had greater temporal power, and was more closely controlled by the king, than had previously been the case.

Where there were border-lands liable to attack from outside, Andrianampoinimerina installed garrisons of settlers drawn from his home province of Avaradrano. For ritual purposes and in the allocation of labour dues these statellite colonies were still considered to form part of the social groups from which they had come. Some northern colonists were even settled within Imerina proper, in areas where the loyalty of new subjects was unsure. This strengthened the king's military power and rewarded the land-hungry demes of Avaradrano who had carried him to the throne of Ambohimanga, and from there to Antananarivo. The king used the traditional rhetoric of ownership to explain the powers which were now his. 'The land is mine, and I am its owner', he declared,[5] meaning that the king was to Imerina as a freeman was to his homeland. He had a sacred and inalienable right to rule.

Guns, slaves and new lands on Imerina's borders were available to those who enjoyed the king's favour. The positions of real power, as opposed to formal or ritual office, went to the king's first and most loyal supporters from Avaradrano, and the majority of them were from commoner families. Certain of the commoner warlords occupied a ritual place to the north of the king's court and came to be known as the Andafy-Avaratra ('on the north side'). In time they were to establish themselves as the controllers of armed force and of the king's praetorian guard.

Andrianampoinimerina's reign created several problems which were to be near the heart of Merina politics for the next hundred years. The structure of power was monopolized by the demes of Avaradrano, especially by the families which composed the Andafy-Avaratra. This was felt to be particularly unacceptable in Vakinisisaony and southern Imerina. The southern demes, after all, claimed to have set up the earliest kingdoms and to have been granted special rights by the first kings. The feeling was shared by some nobles of other provinces whose high birth entitled them to be royal counsellors and who thought that the commoners of the Andafy-Avaratra held a position which was not theirs by right. There were even nobles of the highest rank who privately thought that Andrianampoinimerina was a usurper, since he was from a junior branch of the Andriamasinavalona and had taken power in Avaradrano by force.

Given the tradition of revering only what was granted by the ancestors, it was not possible to govern the new kingdom by any startling innovations, but Andrianampoinimerina sometimes modified old institutions to the extent that their very nature was changed. For example, the people of Ambohimanambola in Vakinisisaony were the hereditary guardians of the most famous of all the talismans, called Kelimalaza. They resisted Andrianampoinimerina's attacks for a year. But such was the king's anxiety to win the legitimate support of the talisman that when they submitted he promoted them to the nobility and to the status of honorary citizens of Avaradrano.[6] If one also considers the extent to which the king relied upon his kinsmen as fief-holders and officials, it becomes evident that he was changing the nature of nobility for service in an enlarged state. He seems to have tried to transform the nobility into an élite of service. Moreover, the sudden increase in the scope of central government upset the delicate balance between the scales of power and of rank, and it was never to be restored. The commoners of the Andafy-Avaratra were to be the power-brokers and king-makers in Imerina until 1895. They were astute enough to ally with other factions when it was necessary, including noble ones, but in the popular imagination and in the eyes of many nobles they represented an oligarchy of upstarts, 'the princes who came up with the pigs'.[7]

Andrianampoinimerina was succeeded by King Radama I (1810–28), who used the power left by his father to conquer perhaps two-thirds of Madagascar, although the Merina government only ever exercised an active control over half the island. Radama has been most celebrated for his alliance with Britain, dating from 1817 when he signed a treaty undertaking to stop Madagascar's overseas slave trade, a trade which seems to have enriched the magnates rather than the king in person. He encouraged the western education given by the representatives of the London Missionary Society (LMS) who arrived in Imerina in 1820 and he used graduates of the mission schools as agents of a literate bureaucracy. He held a census of Imerina, dividing all freemen into centuries which were liable for either civil or military service. These were innovations on a large scale, but they appear to have been determined in part by Radama's determination to undermine the oligarchy established by his father.

Radama was a strong-willed man, and one who had inherited great power, but his reign serves as a demonstration of the limits of modernization. Before his death there was such tension between his father's oligarchy and the new élite raised up by King Radama as to threaten political stability. Further, there was a weakening of government control in the country districts. In the newly conquered territories outside Imerina armed force had been only half consolidated by a permanent administration. Within Imerina proper the king could rely upon a greater measure of goodwill towards his government, but this was not enough to compensate for the strain placed on the traditional channels of government represented by the talismans of the older oligarchy. The talismans were of political importance because they represented a link between the magnates and their constituents or clients. Radama could therefore dismiss or ignore the talismans only at the risk of undermining local government. On the other hand, the expansion of the kingdom had created new needs which the ancestral religion could not satisfy, notably in the institution of a standing army and in the influx of domestic slaves which resulted from the abolition of slave exports. Both soldiers and slaves were largely unattached to the old talismans. The British missionaries noticed that among those who showed the greatest interest in Christian teaching was a high proportion of soldiers and slaves. From 1827 there was a cooling of Radama's European sympathies.

Radama's soldiers were Merina farmers who were required to drill regularly and to serve without pay in whatever part of the island the king needed them. The workshops where missionary artisans produced weapons and gunpowder, and the mines where Madagascar's mineral wealth was extracted, were manned by other farmers whose duties were civil. Certain of the king's subjects were required to attend schools. All these innovations were presented and interpreted as extensions of the traditional obligation to fight for the sovereign and to perform free labour for him, a personal duty invented in the days of tiny kingdoms, continued in the days of a national state. Subjects of every monarch after Radama I not only had to do forced labour on local canals, as they had done for two centuries, but also to perform a host of new and more onerous obligations. Ultimately the existence of forced labour stifled the development of wage labour which is essential to a modern state. It crushed the life-blood out of the state too. Imerina was to be ruled by the techniques of a city-state until its fall, and this was a fundamental flaw in its structure and a constraint upon its development.

Radama's death in 1828 was the start of a period of strife which came close to a civil war in the judgement of several observers, and in which Christian factions formed an important element. Although there were no baptized Christians until 1831, the thousands who had passed through the mission schools or who adhered to the party of Christian sympathizers were strongly represented in vital areas of the military and the civil service. The years of in-fighting ended only when the Andafy-Avaratra emerged again in the mid-1830s as the arbiters of power and the leading ministers of Queen Ranavalona I (1828–61). They restored the talismans of Andrianampoinimerina and expelled the missionaries from Imerina.

The government of Ranavalona I was not a revival of tradition but a horrible caricature of it. Where villagers were once obliged to give cattle as a ritual offering to the monarch, they were now forced to tend the herds of leading politicians free of charge. Where fiefs had once been a largely symbolic recognition of allegiance owed to the royal family, they now became private estates to be given to the wealthy. The traditional privileges of each deme became worth fighting for in a material as well as in a moral sense. The exemption from forced labour enjoyed by certain noble demes, for example, was clearly a most valuable prerogative. Several groups of nobles or privileged commoners recorded how attacks were made on the marks of their status, as the government tried to make of nobility a more exclusive caste. Every ritual obligation was a weapon in the hands of the queen's ministers and of their armies of private retainers. All of these used their positions quite arbitrarily to demand free service from those outside the ranks of the government. All who refused were liable to accusations of sedition, and therefore of sorcery.

Over a period of thirty-three years the Merina kingdom, which now called itself the sole government of Madagascar, was subjected to the most fearful purges. We of the twentieth century are accustomed to reading of such institutionalized massacres of enemies of the state. The purges of Ranavalona's kingdom were conducted not against those said to show oppositionist tendencies, or to be of inferior race, but against supporters of religious symbols which denied the supremacy of the twelve royal talismans, whether those symbols were Christian or other. Whole villages were given the poison ordeal for crimes of sorcery. The best available figures put the deaths from the ordeal during the whole of Ranavalona's reign at between 200,000 and 400,000, in a population which was probably not more than one million.[8] This is an even more startling figure when it is added to the number of those who died in the generals' ceaseless campaigns to keep their hold on Madagascar and to capture slaves. The freemen who were slaughtered in droves were replaced by slaves.

During the absence of missionaries, a sort of Christianity gained great influence. It was subject to occasional persecution, but considering the ferocity of the regime it is surprising that there were no more than about 200 Christian martyrs. Christianity had powerful patrons at court, most notably in the person of the crown prince, called Radama like his alleged father, who was sometimes hailed by Christians as a saviour who would lead his people to a happier kingdom. The queen's chief ministers were not averse to the cult surrounding the prince provided he remained within their control. Christianity was persecuted only when its patrons grew too bold or when the underground fellowship of the Christians seemed to express a wish for regional autonomy. Religion, whether Christian or traditional, was a medium of recruitment. As long as Christianity was espoused by literate civil servants and middle-ranking soldiers there was political capital to be made from patronizing it.

The most powerful families in Madagascar, that is the magnates originating in Avaradrano, were prepared for Radama II's accession to the throne when his mother died in 1861. But he acted with more independence and recklessness than they had expected. He surrounded himself with counsellors nicknamed the *menamaso*, many of them drawn from noble families of south Imerina and not from Avaradrano. They lightened labour dues and military service and attacked the system of patronage by which Ranavalona's ministers had controlled half of Madagascar. Foreigners were encouraged to trade and to preach even in Imerina. Radama refused to observe some of the rituals by which the conservative political factions rallied their followers.

But the traditional cults and rituals also bound the king to his people, and Radama II ignored them at his peril. There arose a possession cult, called the *ramanenjana*, whose devotees performed a grotesque, inspired dance through the villages of Imerina right up to the king's palace, claiming to be in communication with past sovereigns of Imerina. They mimed the rituals whose reassurance they craved, but which could not be performed without royal participation. The dance of the *ramanenjana* was a cry from the heart, a way of restoring the rupture of the old ceremonies by which a king should bring blessings upon his people. It served as a reminder that the most important role of a Merina sovereign was still religious. In May 1863 a faction led by leading members of the Andafy-Avaratra took advantage of the popular unrest to kill the king and his counsellors, although the rumour spread in some places that Radama II had survived the attempt and would lead the provinces in a counter-attack against the oligarchy. There was a serious rising in the west, and Imerina again came close to civil war. The system of government through religion had broken down, and the agitation was exploited by factions in the capital. Order was restored only in the middle of 1864. Henceforth the effective ruler of Imerina and of half of Madagascar was Rainilaiarivony of the Andafy-Avaratra, the son of one of Queen Ranavalona's leading ministers and grandson of one of King Andrianampoinimerina's commoner warlords. He was to call himself 'prime minister and commander-in-chief of Madagascar' until he was deposed by the French in 1895.

The return of European missionaries and traders in 1861 was a great stimulus to the Christian congregations which had survived and multiplied in the years of persecution. They won a growing number of converts, including

15

a high proportion of the rich and powerful. There were now several rival missionary societies working in Madagascar, but the adherents of the Congregationalist LMS came to represent the leading faction in the army, and the only one strong enough to combat the influence of the supporters of the talismans at court. Some of the leading magnates of the Andafy-Avaratra resigned their positions as officers of the national talismans and joined the Protestants. Rainilaiarivony, the most cautious of men, eventually decided that the only way to avoid either a Christian *coup d'état* or a new descent into civil war was to take personal control of the Christian faction. The Andafy-Avaratra always knew how to stay in power by riding with the tide. In February 1869 the prime minister and Queen Ranavalona II, husband and wife, were baptized. From then on Rainilaiarivony's hand was forced by the speed of events. Soon after the start of work on a royal chapel there was a threat of revolt by devotees of the talisman Kelimalaza, which was especially revered by some of the demes of the south who had first brought it to Imerina, and which was supported by interests at court.[9] The prime minister responded by ordering the destruction of all the chief talismans of Imerina, in September 1869. It was a reminder of the extent to which the fortunes of religious fraternities were connected with the manoeuvres of rival political factions in the capital.

The dramatic conversion from paganism[10] to Christianity greatly impressed the missionary authors who are the source of so many modern opinions on Imerina's history. But there is a continuity running through the history of all the reigns of the nineteenth century which makes it impossible to regard Queen Ranavalona I's rule as a fight against the tide of Christian progress, as it was invariably portrayed by missionary scholars. There was a steady development of the organs of central government, and Ranavalona's wars and purges of local resistance gave considerable impetus to the creation of a kingdom of Madagascar in the minds of her subjects. No government, not even that of Ranavalona I, could afford to dispense with imported devices which served central power, such as literacy. The essential debate through successive reigns was simply as to what form central government should take, and to what extent power should be dispersed outside the hands of the military and religious oligarchy established by King Andrianampoinimerina. This process was challenged only at times when the tensions of change brought the kingdom close to civil war, especially in the early 1830s and 1860s. It may be said that Ranavalona I's reign, far from being a frightened reaction to progress – meaning in this case the strengthening of the structures of central government – was highly effective in enforcing a vision of Malagasy unity by the energy and savagery of its policy.

CHRISTIAN IMERINA

The Christianity which emerged after the death of Queen Ranavalona I was based on the teachings of the first generation of missionaries, which had translated into Malagasy the Bible and *The Pilgrim's Progress*. Both books had come to be revered by Merina Christians as works of an authority to rival that of ancestral custom. The loosely organized congregations closely resembled the traditional form of society. That is, a congregation would normally be formed of kinsfolk. Meetings took the form of a series of sermons from prominent members of the assembly, rather like the oratory which the Merina loved to hear at family reunions. Both the missionaries who came to reclaim this legacy, and the politicians who sought to patronize the existing congregations, tried to organize the system more thoroughly, and were beginning to do so at the time of the queen's conversion.

All over Imerina the queen's baptism and the burning of the talismans in 1869 were taken as a sign that all loyal subjects should do the same out of civic duty, as it had earlier been a duty to revere the national talismans. The number of church attenders increased from about 37,000 to 153,000 between 1868 and 1869 as a result of the queen's conversion. The vast majority of these converts were Merina who were ignorant of every tenet of Christianity, and knew only that it was a cult favoured by the queen. The country congregations clamoured for guidance in the new and unfamiliar form of worship. The challenge was taken up by no fewer than six missionary societies, the chief of which was the London Missionary Society. In many respects it was the best adapted to work in Malagasy conditions, and it certainly made the greatest commitment to Madagascar in the 1860s.

The missionaries who worked among the Merina were faced with an overwhelming number of people who had formed congregations on the implicit order of the government but remained non-Christian in all but name. This is quite unlike the position of most missionaries, including those who worked in Madagascar outside Imerina where obedience to the queen was not automatic. The Church Missionary Society soon discovered that the LMS had excluded it from the most fruitful field, and abandoned the island altogether. An Anglican rival, the Society for the Propagation of the Gospel (SPG), worked mostly on the east coast, where only Merina settlers proved at all receptive to its teaching. Roman Catholic missionaries worked in many parts of Imerina and Betsileo-land but found that they were obstructed by the fact that the queen and prime minister were Protestants.

The three leading Protestant missionary societies agreed that they should divide the kingdom into territorial divisions for evangelization. The LMS was given the lion's share of Imerina and worked in Betsileo-land too. The Norwegian Missionary Society (NMS) was allocated the province of Vakinankaratra and also worked in Betsileo-land, while the Friends' Foreign Mission Association (FFMA) was installed in the west of Imerina. The missionaries themselves never decided at what point a pagan church-goer might be defined as a Christian, and therefore the figures for membership of each society are variable. Undoubtedly the LMS had the greatest number of adherents, perhaps 289,000 by 1895. About a quarter of these had sufficient knowledge of Christian doctrine to be regular communicants.

Possibly a better indication of a mission's real strength was the number of its scholars. The LMS claimed 74,000 in 1895, although only perhaps a quarter were literate.[11] In the same year the FFMA had an estimated 15,000 adherents, 2,500 communicants and 14,000 scholars; the SPG had 10,500 adherents, 3,000 communicants and 2–3,000 scholars; the NMS had 80,000 adherents, 30,000 communicants and 37,000 scholars. The Roman Catholics claimed 136,000 adherents and 27,000 scholars, although their claim for conversions seems rather optimistic in relation to the small number of scholars.[12] The figures for all the Protestant sects are particularly misleading in that they hide the number of congregations which were responsible to the Palace Church, and where missionaries had very little control.

A fair estimate is that in 1880 about one-sixth of the population of Imerina, which was probably about a million, attended non-conformist or Lutheran chapels regularly, while smaller numbers went to Anglican or Roman Catholic churches.[13] Of the non-Merina subjects of the self-styled queen of Madagascar, only the Betsileo went to church in significant numbers. These figures give no idea of the number of what the Victorians called 'earnest Christians', and they show only the relative strength of the various sects. To understand Malagasy Christianity it is more fruitful to regard religion as the Malagasy did, as the ritual form of the government of Imerina.

The conversion of the queen was part of a long tradition of strengthening central government by religious means. In both ritual and political terms, the construction of a Christian state was the most radical of successive measures of centralization, and certainly the most restrictive as far as country people were concerned. The talismans, after all, had been given by the provinces to the sovereign. Their attendant rituals enshrined a scale of rank, and of privilege, which had been built up over centuries. The new order destroyed the old hierarchy of rank along with the talismans, and gave the highest place to those who enjoyed power with the Andafy-Avaratra. There was something of a re-definition of nobles and commoners according to their functions in the Christian government. High religious office, such as leadership of the main city churches, often went to nobles, while political office more often went to commoners. The ancient families which had raised the talismans to greatness could expect no share of this new status if they were not associated with the present structure of power. Time was to show that Christianity was widely held to be the religion of the Andafy-Avaratra who ruled Imerina from behind the throne.

In the first euphoria of success, Protestant missionaries found themselves working easily with the government to organize Christian congregations more effectively, even if some junior officers proved regrettably over-enthusiastic in driving people to church by force. Missionaries and the prime minister alike agreed that the only way to evangelize the thousands of church-goers was to form an élite of church officials who could then be sent out to country parishes which a European could rarely visit in person.

Imerina and Betsileo-land were divided into congregations, each normally consisting of members of one deme or one commune. A village church was usually built with the villagers' own hands and money, serving 'in nine cases out of ten' as a schoolroom during the week.[14] It was a meeting-place for the discussion of local and national affairs, abstract or practical. Most often the elected pastor was 'someone looked up to because of his wealth and initiative', very likely a family head.[15] The church reflected faithfully the structure of politics. When a village was inhabited by families of different origin, or at loggerheads with one another, there might be two or more churches, or one family might refuse to go to church at all. This was how non-Christian families might 'lie interspersed with others that are truly enlightened . . . in the same village'.[16] Groups of eight or ten parishes were formed into a district under the supervision of an evangelist, who was often an outsider. The LMS missionaries' aim was to train as many evangelists and schoolmasters as possible at the LMS Theological College or the Normal School in the capital. They succeeded to the extent that by the end of the nineteenth century the type of Christianity found in country areas was primarily the work of the evangelists.

The prime minister was most willing to assist the building of this national Church, but it soon became apparent that his motives were rather different from those of the missionaries. The students at the Theological College and the Normal School almost invariably came from families living in or near Antananarivo, and in most cases they were relatives or clients of the most powerful families in the country. The two establishments became staff colleges for the ruling class of Imerina, whose graduates went on to careers in the Church, in government, or both. Furthermore in 1873 the prime minister began to appoint evangelists and schoolmasters personally in the name of the Palace Church, easily the richest and most influential parish in the land. Three years later he declared that the government intended to take all the mission-schools under its authority in order to establish a national system of education. There were no illusions as to the effect of this. 'King Radama [I], and Malagasy governments in later times', one missionary wrote, 'have alike sought . . . in patronizing and promoting schools, to strengthen their hold on the most serviceable and capable of their subjects.'[17]

Control of the state Church did not lie with the missionaries. But it was churlish for them to complain, for was not a vigorous and independent Church the ideal of non-conformism? And was not compulsory education a measure only recently carried out in Britain itself? The problem was that the Church was put to uses which the missionaries often considered to be secular and oppressive. Evangelists in particular used their position as a way of gaining a foothold in local politics. When compulsory military service was announced, it became common for older schoolchildren to be conscripted *en masse*. Parish registers were sometimes used to estimate levies for forced labour, and the unfortunate conscripts were occasionally assembled in the very churches which they had built with their own hands. The Church was also the most effective available means of raising money. There were frequent collections for missionary work or for building, and sometimes to buy rations for unpaid soldiers. This was certainly the cover for a great deal of corruption. The use of the Church as an organ of government increased greatly during and after the Franco-Merina war of 1883–5. Missionaries who travelled in the country districts in those days left an appalling record of the exactions committed by churchmen on their parishioners.[18]

It was unfortunate that the Protestant Church became an arm of the state at a time when economic and political changes were reducing many peasants to a state of misery. The financial pressure on citizens of Imerina was such that any minor office-holder had every incentive to resort to fraud or at least to gain access to capital at low interest rates if possible. Pastors and schoolmasters were often part-time traders, and could use their offices to sell exemptions from forced labour, or could borrow or steal Church funds to finance a trading venture.[19] By and large, the most convinced Christians were also capitalists. In a thousand homilies and sermons, pastors and preachers encouraged commerce, a reflection of the sturdy, practical Christianity favoured by the Protestant missionaries. Trade was good for the soul as well as the pocket.

To appreciate the relentless propaganda to which congregations were subjected in the name of Christian progress, it is sufficient to read the missionary or government publications of the day. The Protestant periodical *Teny Soa*, which sold over 3,000 copies per month and was read by many times that number, regularly carried articles in praise of trade and patriotism, or instructing its readers in the finer points of European civilization. The government gazette *Ny Gazety Malagasy* sold about 4,000 copies per issue, and was likewise read by state and Church officials. These are only the relics of a constant campaign exhorting Her Majesty's Christian subjects to build a modern Malagasy state whose perfection would be realized at some stage in the future.

For most people, the model of ideal government lay in the past, in the deeds of the ancestors, as it always had done. The number of people who adopted the new Christian and progressive ideology wholeheartedly and broke completely with the old ways was quite small. It included almost everyone in the higher levels of government in Church and state. It is interesting to note that their incomes came mostly from payments received in the conduct of their offices or from trade. They dressed in the European style, took tea with missionaries, and lamented the ignorance of the heathen masses. They were rich and thought themselves enlightened.

At a lower social level there was a significant number of people who assimilated some Christian teaching and who participated to some degree in Madagascar money economy, but who cannot be considered a part of the Christian establishment. Theirs was a popular brand of Christianity which drew its inspiration from a mixture of Bible stories, local history and folklore. This tendency was particularly associated with lay preachers, of whom there were officially reckoned to be 4,000 in 1880.[20] There were probably many more itinerant preachers whose numbers were not recorded. They were quite capable of using their smattering of book-learning to pose as leaders of popular radical politics, and were often accused of being troublemakers. 'Much of their teaching', a missionary complained, 'is of a most profitless character . . . Their aim is frequently not so much to do the people good as to please and amuse them.'[21] They were all the more popular for that. This type of Christianity, if Christianity it was, was the true legacy of the underground movement of Queen Ranavalona I's day.

The importance of these purveyors of easy religion, who often peddled cheap goods and liquor too,[22] was quite out of proportion to their numbers. Their very existence shows how deeply Christianity had penetrated Merina society, for they always had an appreciative audience in any market-place. They had a foot in two camps, the old and the new, and they were to play an important part in the anti-French resistance of 1896.

The numbers of such unorthodox Christians increased as the years went by. In 1869 it was easy for a person to be a pastor while retaining the substance of old beliefs. This became more difficult as a new generation of earnest young people, brought up in Christianity, emerged from the training colleges and demanded a complete break with old practices. They persecuted not only the old cults and divination, but also rum-drinking, divorce and sexual licence. There was a considerable purge of unsatisfactory Christians in the late 1880s, during which many junior Church officials were deprived of their offices, and therefore of their livelihoods, for sins which they regarded as respectable customs.

Many Malagasy who attended church after 1869, and certainly those who never went to church at all, were not convinced of the rightness of Christianity in the form presented by their evangelists. Some of the talismans which had been burned in 1869 were secretly restored and revered, and people continued to consult diviners.[23] Christianity could not meet the most intimate spiritual needs of the people. If the rice harvest was bad, or if witchcraft was suspected, the grave, frock-coated evangelists could offer no solution. Every year, at the time when the rice was ripening, there were cases of the possession cult which had proved so important in 1863. 'Now is the reign of the sorcerers', one villager explained, because there was no longer any proper defence against spiritual subversion.[24] This was one aspect of the sovereign's role as upholder of the cosmic order; people attributed any sort of calamity important enough to threaten social stability to a failure of royal power. It made no difference whether the cause of the disaster were plague or poverty, famine or Frenchmen. The greatest exodus from churches back to older and more reassuring cults occurred during a severe epidemic, and again when the country was threatened with foreign invasion in 1883–5. At one village, in 1878, there was a general administration of the poison ordeal to detect a case of suspected witchcraft. The entire deme was fined by the Christian government and the man who had given the poison was beheaded.[25]

After 1869 every national politician who had previously spoken for the devotees of the talismans either converted to Christianity or was dismissed from national politics. The conservative faction in the country went underground. Its symbols were outlawed, and its cults became the centres of a secret society. They came to attract all who were damaged by economic and social change, but who had not converted to Christianity in their hearts. The worse conditions of life became, the more people suspected a massive disruption of the social order, to be traced back to the queen's conversion to Christianity under the influence of her Andafy-Avaratra prime minister. The growth of the pagan opposition coincided with the history of economic decline. The underground opposition was usually led by traditional local notables, previously associated with the talismans, who had been excluded from government by the Christian regime. Many were from the older generation of fief-holders who had been by-passed by administrative changes in the capital. Many were nobles. A French diplomat, pointing out the convergence of religious, political and economic grievances, referred to the leaders of rural conservatism as 'small landowners, people receiving unearned incomes, all those who don't work and who are afraid of contact with foreigners and the rapid increase in prices'.[26]

It was among this sort of country dweller that suspicion of Christianity, and of Europeans in general, was deepest rooted. These were the people who formed the backbone of the conservative, isolationist school of thought, whom Europeans labelled the 'old *hova* party'. Missionaries in isolated areas sometimes reported that the people considered them to be traders of some description. All the missionaries wanted, the Reverend Benjamin Briggs was told, was money, and the country parishioners 'say they are unable to endure the pressure now put upon them'.[27] Most disturbing of all was the rumour, widely believed but only heard at times of great unrest, that all Europeans were thieves and consumers of human hearts. This myth probably had its origin in the days of the slave trade, but it was highly symbolic of how villagers regarded European innovation. The foreigners could steal a person's heart by making him or her turn from the customs which the ancestors had held dear.

Villagers who wished to escape the hierarchy of the official Church had a number of options. In some places they refused to build a church at all. They could intimidate an evangelist or pastor, or burn their church. In the last resort they could flee from their homeland. Cases of this sort were recorded before 1895. More often congregations went to great lengths to keep their church as the preserve of the local commune or deme, as a matter of local pride and material interest. Control of a church gave the pastor access to funds, both officially and through fraud, and exemption from the crushingly heavy forced labour. A pastor also had some power to decide exactly which parishioners were to pay the most in taxes or do the most labour. The same was true of schools, and as compulsory education became more widely enforced it became a matter of some urgency for a congregation to present its own school officials. They too acted as recruiting-sergeants.[28]

Struggles to retain local Church autonomy often focused upon the election of a pastor. It was not unknown for people to go to an election 'armed with knives, meat-axes and clubs' to ensure that an outsider did not get in.[29] If an evangelist proved overbearing, a congregation could transfer its allegiance to one of the smaller societies, the Anglicans or the Catholics. The latter were particularly popular with dissident congregations because the Jesuits were far less convinced than their Protestant counterparts that trade and self-finance were Christian virtues. In other cases congregations transferred their allegiance to a smaller sect to protect a family tradition. Where two demes lived side by side on bad terms, one might wish to have its own church so as to escape the stifling control of its rival. Protestant missionaries and Palace Church officials alike disapproved of such transfers of allegiance, but they were still possible. Certain magnates at court were known as patrons of one or another sect. Influence or bribery could be brought to bear to arrange things.

It would be wrong to discuss the matter in too godless a way. There were certainly cases of individuals becoming convinced of the rightness of one form of worship and educating their children in that tradition. The fact remains that mass conversions to Catholicism in particular took a definite pattern. The most numerous cases before 1895 were in the provinces of Betsileo-land, Vakinankaratra and Vakinisisaony. Within these divisions certain social groups proved keener than others to convert to Catholicism.

The construction of a state Church was not the only reform enacted by the Christian prime minister Rainilaiarivony in the name of the two successive Christian queens whom he married. But it was the essence of his achievement. It was the most effective way of placing centrally appointed officials in the provinces, and the Malagasy saw it as the ritual manifestation of every other change which took place. Compulsory education was intimately connected with the Church. Even military service and forced labour came to be organized through the Church more and more for lack of a suitable alternative.

Foreign observers, and the evangelical lobby in Britain, were often mightily impressed by Rainilaiarivony's modern superstructure of government. It included a written law code and government departments like those in Whitehall. The emancipation of imported slaves in 1877 was also hailed as a humanitarian measure, although there are reasons for thinking that it was done for hard-headed economic motives. Madagascar sometimes appeared to be entering upon a 'nobler and higher stage of its history', as one missionary put it,[30] and Imerina to be an oasis of light in a desert of heathen darkness.

Rainilaiarivony was a masterful politician, industrious, patient, intelligent and ruthless. Perhaps he really believed that European institutions were a recipe for economic and social progress. But most of his reforms were clearly aimed at the elimination of provincial structures of power. The destruction of the talismans was followed by a series of attempts to place officials responsible to the central government in every large village, culminating in the appointments of village governors in 1886–9. The governors fared better than the earlier experiments, but nothing could match the organization of the Church.

Like his predecessors, the prime minister was obliged to adapt traditional institutions to his own purpose where he could. He knew that a sudden abolition of the offices held by notables and deme elders would be unacceptable. Legal restrictions were placed on the rights of fief-holders, but this did not mean that they were eliminated in every province. Some might actually be given greater powers if they lived in an area difficult of access from Antananarivo. They could sometimes bolster their power in a new guise, by becoming village governors or pastors. But in general, a fief-holder could acquire great wealth and power only by going to court, neglecting his provincial power-base, and becoming one of the magnates of the Christian élite. The great inducement to collaborate with the Andafy-Avaratra, no matter how much they were despised, was their control of access to wealth and trade.

In many cases local notables, including fief-holders, were given judicial powers while administrative control lay with a governor, Church official, or military commander. Quite often the most respected offices were left with the most unpopular duties. Labour recruitment was still organized in many places by the local centurions whose forebears had been appointed for the task in King Radama I's time. People had to be reminded that forced labour, vicious though it may be, was an ancient and venerable custom.

Rainilaiarivony's method was to add new structures of government on top of old ones, as one photograph may be superimposed on another without obliterating it. In the same Merina village there were normally a number of minor office-holders whose existence represented one of the periodic waves of centralization which had marked the history of Imerina. Family heads took turns to preside over the village commune, noble and commoner alike. There might also be a petty fief-holder whose rights were more symbolic than administrative, and perhaps his family had once guarded the local talisman. There would normally be one or more centurions, a governor and his lieutenants, a pastor, deacons, and lay preachers, perhaps a schoolmaster and an evangelist if it were a big village. Over one half of the adult male population was classed as permanent soldiers. They had to report for drill every few weeks unless they paid a bribe, and might be called up for service in a garrison near or far. Sometimes one individual or family might occupy two or more of these roles at the same time. To get the most from his subjects, a senior administrator had to have a considerable knowledge of local history and politics. To raise money or labourers it might need a promise to one notable, a threat to another. In one village the task of

24

recruitment might fall upon the governor or pastor; in another, upon a centurion.

Forced labour in the later nineteenth century was a terrible burden. It penalized all enterprise. The most unfortunate labourers were simply worked to death. Labour dues fell unevenly and according to almost random factors. This was largely because of the manipulation of ritual obligations for economic purposes which had taken place in Imerina over a long period. It had made certain rights almost valueless, and had given other privileges a significance quite different from their original intention. This may be compared to the effect of monetary inflation in a modern economy. Just as rising prices may destroy the traditional status of certain social groups as they are reflected in wages, but are a source of profit to others, so in old Imerina traditional status was altered by the transformation of ritual rights and obligations. An example occurs in a group of nine hamlets near Antananarivo in an area which had relatively light labour dues. On the eve of the French conquest there were 360 inhabitants, of whom 3 were governors, 22 were officials of the commune, 22 were secretaries, 11 were teachers or Church officials, 58 were nobles. All of these claimed exemption from forced labour. When orders came for forced labourers, service was performed time and again by those who could not claim exemption on traditional grounds. In one hamlet of the nine, labourers had to work four days a week without pay, while in another they had to do only one day a fortnight.[31] Inflation, first of religious privileges and in the form of ever more extravagant ritual, and later of prices, was in fact a constant theme of Merina history in the nineteenth century.

The uneven distribution of forced labour was exaggerated by the fact that contingents were assessed according to the figures of a census carried out in the 1820s. The government would demand a certain number of man-days from each century. In some centuries the number of inhabitants had increased, so that forced labour was widely distributed. In others the population had fallen, to the detriment of the survivors. Migration was not always a solution, for both soldiers and labourers were assessed according to the traditional location of their deme. A citizen might have to report for service at Antananarivo or at his ancestral village, even if this involved considerable travel. He could not then go home until he had paid a bribe to some grasping official.

Naturally exemption could be secured by bribery or influence. The people with the most money, the most slaves and the best family connections lived near Antananarivo. The city came to be considered by many a nest of intrigue, corruption and decadence. So many people clung to the coat-tails of the grandees that the capital was reckoned to have 100,000 inhabitants by 1895, almost all of them officials, traders or slaves.[32] The class of person who endured the heaviest labour dues and in some areas was almost annihilated by them, was 'the small farmer, the day labourer'.[33] There were further distinctions even here. In some fiefs commoners still had to do labour for the noble fief-holder as well as for government officers. The people who suffered least from the heavy burden of unpaid labour, oddly enough, were probably household slaves. They were traditionally exempt from state labour, the origin of which lay in the obligation of a freeman to his lord. Nor could they be pressed too far because they had no homelands and were therefore far more ready than freemen to flee from oppression. Many slaves farmed or traded on their own accounts and even prospered.

Probably the most miserably ill-treated people in Madagascar in the later nineteenth century were those Betsileo and Betsimisaraka peasants unfortunate enough to live near a Merina fort. They were colonized peoples and had precious few rights. Within Imerina proper those who suffered the most from forced labour were likely to be poor country people with little monetary income and only one or two slaves. Commoners seem to have fared worse than either nobles or slaves. It was the commoners who had borne the brunt of Queen Ranavalona I's purges and campaigns, too.

It would be hard to overstate the corruption and viciousness of the Merina kingdom in its last years. The arbitrary summons for labour, which was the most oppressive remnant of tradition, was deeply hated and was the greatest hindrance to the establishment of a money economy. Modernity too had come in the most unpleasant of forms. 'It is not improbable', one missionary wrote, 'that . . . the extraordinary number of churches so rapidly put up in 1868–1870 and crowded with congregations was due, in greater or lesser degree, to the facility with which labour could be commandeered.'[34] There was no appeal against extortion, for justice was for sale to the highest bidder. When 3,000 silver dollars was raised from a congregation to build a church, all but thirty dollars disappeared into private purses.[35] Nor was construction of a church the end of such demands. Afterwards came calls for money for repairs, for charity, for expenses of all kinds. 'Any pretext is good enough', a Catholic priest wrote, 'since money is the main concern: prayers come a poor second.'[36]

Europeans and Malagasy alike came to recognize the decay into which the kingdom had fallen. Even the most optimistic missionaries saw through the façade of Imerina's progress to the shabby construction behind, although they kept their opinions private. 'I have known the Malagasy Government now for many years', the Reverend Richard Baron wrote in 1894,[37] 'and my deliberate opinion of them now is this: they are corrupt to the core; their one idea being to get wealth, they are the veriest oppressors and bloodsuckers . . . Everybody out here I think has lost sympathy with them.'

CHANGING ECONOMIC PATTERNS

The rise of Imerina enabled its rulers to exercise an economic ascendancy over most of Madagascar. They imposed this in the 1820s and 1830s. It depended largely on the military hegemony which enabled the generals who dominated public life after 1828 to use garrisons outside Imerina both as a means of government and as customs-posts. They enforced a monopoly of the most important import and export trades of the whole island. At the same time control of the machinery of government allowed the magnates of Antananarivo to build retinues of military clients called *deka*, who controlled on behalf of their masters the trade of the regions in which they served. The same magnates had a supply of cheap manpower in the form of slaves or forced labourers. With these advantages the members of a handful of families were able to exclude independent Malagasy traders from the most profitable branches of trade, that is to say the export of rice and cattle. The richest and most powerful of all was the great dynasty of the Andafy-Avaratra.

These essential conditions of control were under assault by the mid-century and in decline after the 1860s. Imerina's growing inability to capture slaves elsewhere in Madagascar was both a measure and a cause of this decline. A reasonable estimate was that Imerina acquired 200,000 prisoners-of-war as slaves between 1828 and 1861.[38] This figure does not include the smaller number of slaves acquired from other sources. The Merina army was growing ineffective, exhausted by decades of continuous war. Its soldiers were demoralized by the fact that they were unpaid and unsupplied. Slaves were imported from abroad, but this cost money. Traditional obligations of forced labour were exploited to the limit, but tens of thousands of free peasants, Merina and non-Merina alike, suffered impoverishment, emigration or death. The ambition of successive rulers after Radama I to turn Madagascar into a nation-state implied the need to spread a money economy into the villages, but this was made difficult by the abundance of cheap or free labour. Ranavalona I's ministers ruthlessly excluded from trade all who were not their clients. From 1828 onwards successive rulers maintained themselves in power only by recruiting an ever greater number of retainers who expected to make money from trade or extortion since they were usually unpaid. This was possible if the economy were expanding, but it appears that the profits of trade grew very little, if at all, after 1861. The pressure on those without access to office increased in proportion.

The reign of King Radama II, from 1861 to 1863, opened Madagascar to European traders and missionaries once more and gave them a foothold from which they could not be dislodged, since they now had consular protection. The newcomers settled all over the east coast, and some managed to obtain plantations there despite the disapproval of the Malagasy government. The richer and more ambitious among the traders had, by 1875, 'commenced establishing branch houses at the capital', which had not contained a single European trader from 1836 until 1863.[39] They competed with the Merina oligarchy.

It is true that the government could still regulate trade to some extent through its customs-posts. Under Ranavalona I it was usual for port officials to charge a duty of ten per cent in kind on imports and ten per cent *ad valorem*, in cash, on most items of export. During the 1860s Britain, France and the USA all negotiated commercial treaties which confirmed this scale of dues. But the income finding its way to the royal treasury decreased because of fraud and because some of the most distant ports were so weakly controlled that traders were able to ignore customs regulations almost with impunity. European and American consuls insisted that the treaties be interpreted to mean that the duty charged on exports was ten per cent of the value of the commodity at the time the treaties were signed. Since many products increased greatly in value during the late nineteenth century, the percentage of duty levied fell. The duty on rubber, for example, dropped from ten per cent of the export price in the 1860s to only about three per cent in 1885.[40] The levying of import duties in kind proved very discouraging to importers, as imports changed from being principally weapons and cash to consumer goods which took a larger share of the market after the 1860s. The governors who collected their share of imports usually auctioned them on the spot, thus undercutting the importer. Sometimes customs officers deliberately flooded the market with their stocks to keep prices low. This technique aggravated the fact that by the 1880s there were too many importers on the east coast competing for the existing market. The most enterprising firms tried to establish themselves on the west coast, which was a long way from the main overseas markets of Mauritius and Réunion but which was almost completely outside Merina control. The snag was that the existing Zanzibari and Indian traders in the west were unwilling to see their business shared by Europeans.

The most stable of the main Malagasy exports was cattle. Mauritius and Réunion bought bullocks throughout the last half of the nineteenth century at a rate of 12–20,000 head per year, although after the 1860s they were no longer obliged to pay the high prices demanded by the rulers of Imerina. Having by-passed the government's stranglehold on the ports, foreign traders were able to buy cattle at source for a fraction of the old price. Firms which equipped themselves with steamships were even able to buy bullocks in the cheap markets of the west coast where customs-dues also were lower.

A second staple export of earlier years, which held up much less success-fully than cattle, was rice. The Merina kingdom, once the principal supplier to Mauritius and Réunion, ceased to be a net exporter of rice by 1886 at the very latest.[41] The main reason for this was that the rice-growers of the east coast were so weighed down by labour dues and debts that they ceased to produce a surplus for the profit of their Merina governors. Betsimisaraka and Antemoro farmers migrated to places where Merina power was less in evidence or sought wage employment with European settlers. Merina and Betsileo farmers, who traditionally supplied rice for home consumption, seem to have suffered a fall in productivity because of the misuse of forced labour, but also because the canals were silting up. Rice prices rose sharply after the 1860s.[42]

The third and last of the great export trades of the eighteenth century, the slave trade, similarly ceased to be conducted for the benefit of the Merina oligarchy. When rich Merina were unable to capture slaves any longer, they took to buying imported Africans from the independent kings and traders of western Madagascar. This was one reason – but not the only one – for the rapid growth of the slave trade between Africa and Madagascar in the 1850s. Henceforth the import of slaves into Imerina at a rate of several thousand per year proved to be a considerable drain on the kingdom's currency reserves, because the Arab and Indian merchants usually demanded payment in cash. The price of slaves in Imerina increased rapidly.[43] At the same time, Imerina's demand for European imports was increasing. Guns and ammunition continued to be a necessity for the government, and to these were added bills for imports of cloth, liquor, and luxuries of all kinds. The Merina kingdom was running a balance of trade deficit by 1877 if not earlier, while at about the same time the independent west coast of Madagascar was overtaking the Merina-controlled ports of the east as the main forum for trade. Many British and French traders, ignorant of conditions on the west coast, were only vaguely aware of this.[44]

Furthermore the medium of payment was in the process of devaluation. The European traders who arrived during and after the 1860s brought with them French five-franc pieces which contained only twenty-five grams of silver. These were still cut into fractions, for small change, based on the old weight of twenty-seven grams which the traditional Spanish piastres had contained. The result was a loss for any holder of whole five-franc pieces who divided them for small payments, unless he marked up prices in proportion. This debasement of the coinage reflected the extent to which Madagascar was susceptible to changes in the international economy. Silver coinage in general, and piastres from South American republics in particular, were being devalued all over the world by changes in the money markets.[45]

These observations on currency might well provide an explanation for the emancipation of imported slaves decreed by Rainilaiarivony, himself the greatest slave-owner in Madagascar, in 1877. It was usually interpreted by Europeans as a humanitarian measure carried out under the influence of the Protestant missionaries. But there are also grounds for believing that the emancipation of the Mozambique slaves was a financial device designed to stem the flow of cash towards the Arabs and Sakalava and to make the freed slaves more useful as cheap labour.[46]

The Merina had a reputation as a nation of shrewd traders, and it was to be expected that they should adapt swiftly to the changing conditions of trade. The richest of them continued to export cattle, selling bullocks from the herds that they owned on Imerina's borders. They made vigorous efforts to restore the profitability of more prosperous times. Rainilaiarivony and a handful of his associates tried exporting agricultural produce to Réunion, Mauritius and Natal on their own accounts, in ships which they hired or bought. The prime minister even experimented with a joint stock company for the handling of general imports and exports. Other magnates set themselves up as importers of European goods on a large scale, sometimes handling lots of cloth of up to 30,000 piastres – 150,000 French francs – in value. Their command of forced labour and slaves gave them a decided edge over European competitors in this business. Once again, it is notable how greatly the rulers of Imerina depended on forced labour for their wealth.

Even before the Franco-Merina war of 1883–5, the richest Merina were already leaving the commodity trades and looking for safer ways of making money, from investment in land and from government service which, if exploited for all it was worth, could yield a fortune. Another outlet they favoured was money-lending, a traditional sector of the economy but one which grew more attractive after the intrusion of Europeans into other fields. They used the shortage of cash to lend to their fellow countrymen at very high rates of interest. Some was borrowed by peasants, for although most Merina were subsistence farmers they needed to spend: on weddings and funerals, to grease the palms of their rulers, or to buy rice in years of poor harvest. A good deal was also lent to small traders who wanted to bring imported goods to Imerina for sale.

Small independent traders became numerous only after the liberalization of trade under Radama II. The magnates were no longer able to exclude their subjects from commerce, or perhaps they simply found that growing competition by foreigners made such exclusion pointless. Many of these minor traders were part-timers, combining trade with farming or a minor government post. One or two demes were specialists in the cloth trade, and families of certain privileged villages traded on a very large scale. But normally a village would contain only a few people reputed as traders. This might well include a village schoolmaster or pastor, since their positions enabled them to borrow the capital entrusted to them by the Church. Any other petty trader had to borrow capital from professional money-lenders. All were victims of arbitrary government, liable to forced labour if they were freemen and having to pay internal customs dues from which Europeans were exempt. Usually minor traders combined with other members of their family to form small consortiums.

Some villagers would perhaps make just one or two trips to the coast to buy imported goods. But there was also a class of professional traders often associated with the very lowest level of the Church hierarchy. 'Engaged in trading, or in government service, during the week, they endeavour to seek the spiritual good of their fellow-countrymen on the Sabbath', a missionary said.[47] These small traders often appear to be the same people as the lay preachers whom missionaries found so troublesome. Many were partly educated, while their itinerant way of life gave them a wide knowledge of current gossip and a breadth of acquaintance far outside the ordinary.

As the state Church became more highly organized with the passage of time, and as commercial competition grew more fierce, there was friction between unofficial traders and those who also held minor offices, particularly in the Church. Missionaries who in the early days had spoken favourably of itinerant preachers found them more irritating as they expressed more radical and unorthodox sentiments. One of the main businesses of minor traders was rum-selling. The generation of trained Church officials which sprang up in the 1880s often persecuted rum-sellers, on the grounds of Christian temperance and perhaps too because a teetotal pastor found it convenient to dispose of a rival trader on this account. We hear of a dishonest evangelist confiscating rum from a trader and also absconding with church funds.[48] In Antshihanaka one rum-seller had such a grudge against the local church that he paid a man to burn it down.[49] Another incident involved a Lutheran teacher and a pastor who had been dismissed from their posts for selling liquor but continued to demand the exemption from forced labour to which they had previously been entitled.[50] It seems that there were many villages where the anti-government faction was led by disgruntled rum-sellers, many of them former churchmen purged by a more up to date pastor who belonged to the temperance movement. The Church and the market-place were connected in so many ways that payment appeared to many to be a Christian commandment. 'I see that everyone', said a Merina church-goer to a missionary, 'great or small, is seeking and is dreaming of one thing only: to acquire goods and money, a lot of money, by any possible means. Such are the fruits of the doctrines you have taught us!'[51]

EUROPEAN INTRUSION AND ITS EFFECTS

The college-trained officials who appeared in so many villages of the highlands were symbolic of the invasion of European commerce, religion and values. Ever since the Reverend David Jones had first set foot in Antananarivo in 1820 it had been the missionaries' ambition to see a church and a school in every village, and in that sense the missionaries were one agent of a European influence which had penetrated to the heart of Merina society by the 1880s. There were also European traders and settlers attracted by the opening of Malagasy trade after 1861 and by the growing taste for imported products, or simply forced out of the neighbouring French island of Réunion by economic depression. Réunion acted as a forward base for French imperialism, generating its own pressures, represented in Paris by deputies and businessmen. Grand strategy too was becoming more aggressive as Britain and France vied for influence in the Indian Ocean.

From the early nineteenth century the Réunionnais sugar-planters had looked to the nearby island of Madagascar for their supplies of cattle, rice and, occasionally, labourers. When Réunion's sugar economy became depressed after the 1860s by competition from European and American sugar-beet and by a collapse of credit, many small farmers, on the verge of bankruptcy, looked jealously at the wide-open spaces and low cost of living in the independent island of Madagascar. In support of their designs upon Madagascar Réunion's politicians could usually secure a sympathetic hearing from some of France's more aggressive military strategists, who

31

coveted the northern harbour of Diego-Suarez as a base from which to challenge British hegemony in the Indian Ocean. They could also count on help from the merchants of Marseilles in particular. Thus it was possible for the Réunion lobby to influence official policy in favour of an aggressive stance towards Madagascar despite the fact that the Great Island was not of paramount strategic importance and the volume of French trade and investment in Madagascar before colonial times was hardly enough to warrant military action in its defence.

On the whole, Madagascar may be considered to have fallen within the British sphere of influence until 1883, thanks to the activities of the London Missionary Society and the legacy of the treaty between Britain and the inland kingdom of Imerina signed in 1817.

In 1871 Réunion was for the first time represented in the Chamber of Deputies in Paris. There were several causes of dispute between France and the Merina government which claimed to speak for all of Madagascar. The majority of these grievances could be placed in the category of harassment to French traders and restrictions upon the rights of foreigners to buy land in Madagascar. At the beginning of 1883 an extraordinary combination of circumstances enabled the Réunionnais lobby to make more use of these grievances than ever before. Britain and France had recently argued because of Britain's unilateral action in Egypt, which was supposed to be a field of joint responsibility. In retaliation the French government sought to assert its rights wherever possible. For a brief period the French foreign ministry was prepared to throw all its weight behind the colonial lobby on Madagascar. Above all, for a few weeks at the beginning of 1883 the Réunionnais deputy François de Mahy was made temporary minister of the marine. It was he who, in response to continuing French complaints against the Merina government of Madagascar, ordered Admiral Pierre of the Indian Ocean squadron to impress the Malagasy with a display of force. It is impossible to say, of course, whether a minister more disinterested than de Mahy would have made a similar decision to open hostilities against the Malagasy. But in the event, the people of Réunion through their politicians played a leading role in the deterioration of France's relations with Madagascar and in the island's eventual colonization. Admiral Pierre duly proceeded to Madagascar, occupied the town of Majunga on the north-west coast and then, in June 1883, sailed to the main east coast port of Tamatave and bombarded it. The ensuing campaign, the Franco-Merina war of 1883–5, was conducted in a very half-hearted manner by the French. They made no attempt to invade Madagascar but blocked some of the leading ports, thus damaging the island's external trade which was not large but was crucial to the Malagasy government's fortunes.

No one would deny the historical importance of European designs on Madagascar, but for present purposes I seek only to emphasize that the internal collapse which European intrusion provoked was already well advanced before the war of 1883–5. The conflict ended with a treaty which recognized a nominal French protectorate over the whole of Madagascar and effectively marked Britain's abandonment of her Merina ally. There were also ruinous financial conditions. France was to be paid an indemnity of ten million francs, through a loan arranged by the Comptoir National d'Escompte. To the loan was added a further five million francs, to be repaid at the same time, for the use of the Merina government. As security, the Parisian bank was to supervise the customs revenues of six main Merina ports. The bank did not actually collect customs dues, but counted receipts before they were handed to the royal treasury.

This was the final blow to the finances of the Merina kingdom. Trade never returned to the eastern ports on anything like its old scale. To raise money for repayment of the loan the prime minister was obliged to tax his people beyond the limits of their endurance and to sell concessions to European mining or agricultural interests. Perhaps the most detested of all the new obligations was forced labour in government gold-workings, where conditions were often extremely harsh.

By the 1890s European traders and observers unanimously agreed that the trade of the Merina kingdom was moribund. The only people who were prospering were the Indian and Zanzibari traders of the west and their Sakalava allies who did a brisk trade in cattle and slaves stolen from Imerina. The traditional exports of Imerina had gone, and therefore it was widely held among foreign traders that Madagascar's commercial future must lie in the export of plantation crops. Many Europeans thought that only a massive injection of overseas capital and expertise could revive Imerina's ailing economy. And yet despite the stagnation of trade, the number of foreign traders in the island was growing. There were in fact about 3,300 European residents in Madagascar by 1894, of whom some 2,850 lived on the east coast.[52] Some considered transferring their business to the west, despite its reputation for lawlessness, or pulled out of Madagascar altogether. These options were open only to those with money. Others went bankrupt. For the growing number of creoles fleeing from poverty in Réunion and Mauritius, there was no alternative but to struggle for a living in the face of feeble demand and cut-throat competition.

It is not easy to determine the exact role of the Comptoir National d'Escompte in bringing about Imerina's final bankruptcy. Although the available figures are inaccurate, it seems that the revenue of the six ports controlled by the bank kept up quite well until 1891–2.[53] Without doubt many traders preferred to avoid these ports since the French authorities insisted that all dues be paid in French francs, which were now in desperately short supply. Le Myre de Vilers, the senior French diplomat in the island, even maintained that the Comptoir National d'Escompte was itself 'one of the principal causes of the complications which we have experienced with the Malagasy government', the reason being that the bank was both customs-officer and money-lender. In its official capacity it had to prevent smuggling. In its private role, 'it has every reason to encourage it in order to serve its clientele of importers and exporters'. He went as far as to claim that Imerina's trade had increased since 1885, basing his case on shipping statistics.[54] He was arguing against armed intervention, and his argument was disingenous to say the least. Exports were not increasing.[55] Imports may well have been growing, but that did not act to the profit of all importers. It was getting more difficult to take goods to inland markets because of fierce competition, lack of cash, the theft of goods in transit and the absence of porters, who were often taken by the government for forced labour or military service. The auction-bell rang at Tamatave almost daily, announcing another importer left with goods which he could not sell, and which had to be cleared to pay outstanding debts. The total turnover of the Merina-controlled east coast ports was probably slightly over one million pounds a year.[56]

The chronic shortage of coin and Imerina's balance of payments deficit both grew worse after the war of 1883–5. The government suffered a catastrophic fall in its customs receipts, which either went to pay the indemnity or were depleted by fraud. The Comptoir National d'Escompte faced difficulties in its role as a private bank. Some Merina traders had used the bank to borrow large sums, which until 1891 were always promptly repaid. But by 1894 there were over 100,000 francs outstanding in bad debts.[57] In 1892 a British bank in Madagascar, the New Oriental Bank, folded under the weight of unpaid debts. Most of the firms capable of leaving Madagascar, that is to say all except the minor traders who had staked their livelihood on the country's prosperity, decided that it was time to leave. There was a general move to call in debts. The same year saw the failure of a French bank in Réunion. It was a year of economic recession and of a collapse of credit all over the western Indian Ocean and an important date in the economic decline of Imerina.

Certain structural flaws made the Merina economy, or economies, unstable. Some of these have already been mentioned, notably the reliance upon forced labour which made economic sense in the small kingdoms of the eighteenth century but which became a great burden as time went on. Associated with this was the oppression and even elimination of freemen and their replacement in the overall population by slaves. These tendencies strengthened the grip of the military élite, the Andafy-Avaratra and their friends. It was a process which had its own logic, regardless of changes of sovereign or of religion, but which led to the extraordinary position whereby an ever greater burden of service was placed upon a shrinking free population. 'Free', it need hardly be said, is a ritual term in this sense. In many ways slaves enjoyed more real liberty from arbitrary government than their masters by 1895.

The ruthless centralization of power, trade and resources was essential to Imerina's imperial system, if one may so describe the method by which Antananarivo governed the conquered outlands. It was parasitic. The staple exports of rice and cattle were produced not in Imerina proper but in the subject regions, of the east especially. The profits of these exports, and of many internal transactions too, went towards Antananarivo, which became the main consumer of imported goods. The provinces were drained of their assets of wealth and manpower at the same time as the grandees of the court sent their clients far afield in search of new wealth. Central Imerina became heavily populated by slaves. The freemen whom they replaced had either been wiped out by the purges and wars of the mid-nineteenth century or had settled outside Imerina, especially in Betsileo-land and on the east coast. These two regions alone contained over 100,000 Merina settlers by 1895. The expatriates took with them their allegiance to masters in Antananarivo and the Christian religion with which they helped to maintain their identity after 1869. They retained close links with their native villages, visiting them for weddings and funerals and sending back money earned elsewhere.

Once Queen Ranavalona I's protectionist policies had been abandoned, Imerina's imperial economy became very vulnerable to the intrusions of European traders whose lines of credit sprang from London and Paris and Hamburg and Massachusetts. The traders established themselves in a state which had maintained a rigid control of cash, credit and commerce. Although cash certainly had a straightforward monetary function in old Imerina it was also an expression of political ties. The distribution of silver by the generals to their military clients, the *deka*, was one of the ways in which retinues were formed and the wheels of allegiance were oiled. Moreover the state periodically regulated the quantity of coin in circulation by taking ritual gifts of silver coin in recognition of allegiance and particularly for royal burials. Silver, however, was in chronically short supply overall, a fact which was obscured in the early nineteenth century by the policy of Andrianampoinimerina and Ranavalona I, who both fixed prices at artificially low levels.[58]

The quantity of coin in circulation, and the hands through which it was allowed to pass in significant volume, was thus strictly controlled under the government of the early nineteenth century. This was done partly for political reasons because, in crude terms, money could purchase military retinues. There was also an economic rationale: unrestricted access to silver would increase imports and encourage people to trade rather than farm. Moreover, the easy availability of cash would imply the paying of wages, which would undermine the forced labour so useful to the magnates. It would cause prices to rise since government price controls would no longer be enforceable.

All these things came about when Europeans began to trade and spend in inland markets. There was a spectacular inflation of prices in the late 1820s, under Radama I, which was halted only by Queen Ranavalona I's protectionism.[59] After her death in 1861 it became apparent that even a small number of free-spending Europeans could have a great effect upon the economy of the region where they lived. Thus one missionary wrote in a book published in 1870,[60] 'The relative value of money and labour has been

35

considerably altered since the death of Ranavalona I. The large amounts spent in the capital in the building of the memorial churches, the residences, school-houses, and other buildings belonging both to the Protestant and Roman Catholic missions, have raised wages and the price of many articles of food.'

Free trade was destructive of the master–client relations which were built on family, forced labour and slavery. There is suggestive evidence that similar effects came from European economic penetration in other African countries where indigenous élites controlled the economy in similar ways.[61]

Before 1895 Imerina already displayed some of the characteristics which are typical of so-called underdeveloped economies today. A significant number of labourers had left the land and were devoting their energies to trade or services, to the detriment of agricultural efficiency. The taste for imported goods became widespread. Rising imports and static or falling exports led to a balance of trade deficit and a drain on foreign reserves by the 1870s. But imported silver coin was also the country's internal currency, so that money was in shorter supply as demand for it was growing. Once it became evident to European traders that the credit accorded to their Malagasy clients was over-extended – that is, the amount of debt exceeded the country's productive capacity – then a crash of some description was to be feared. 'Everywhere', wrote a British trader in 1887, 'the merchants are asking their debtors for Money, Money! and the demand is passed on from the petty traders to the people for *Vola, Vola*! Yet the requests are fruitless, there is next to no money in the land. Trade is dying from the dearth . . .'[62]

The ruthlessness with which Antananarivo sucked wealth from the provinces provoked resistance, first in the form of banditry or in a sullen refusal to collaborate with the central power, and eventually in the great *menalamba* movement in which disenchanted small traders played a vital role. This process of central demand and provincial compromise or resistance affected Merina political ideology very deeply. Provincial citizens developed highly ambiguous feelings for their capital and the alien culture which had taken root there. Many country people, although awed by the opulence of Antananarivo, retained their affection for the older provincial capitals which had declined in importance since King Andrianampoinimerina had founded his capital at Antananarivo. Ambohimanga in particular gained a great reputation as a spiritual capital. There was a popular song which ran as follows:[63]

> Ambohimanga is the source of all goodness,
> Antananarivo is the jar in which it is kept;
> Ambohimanga is the town which has raised up our kings,
> Antananarivo is the town where the people were united.
> Ambohimanga has love in abundance,
> Antananarivo is full of worldly joys.

I will turn to an examination of the kingdom's constituent regions to see how the conflict between the capital and the periphery affected politics.

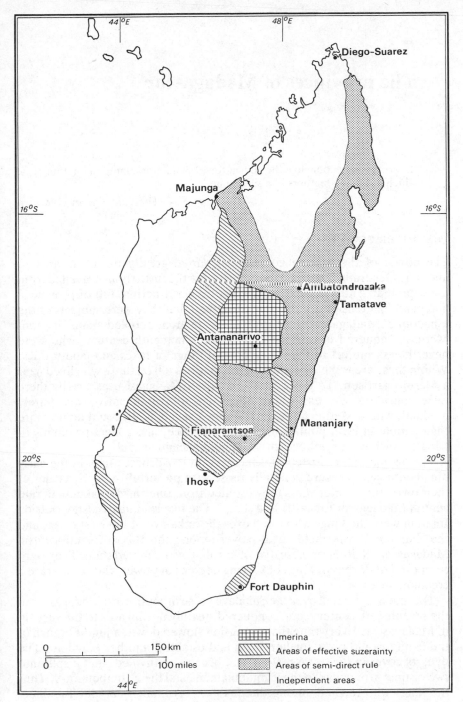

Map 2. The kingdom of Imerina, late nineteenth century

2

The provinces of Madagascar

'Imerina will become like the guinea-fowl,' said Andrianampoinimerina, '. . . which has many feathers of a single hue.'

The *Tantaran' ny Andriana*

THE OUTER CIRCLES

The power of the Merina government varied greatly from one area to another. Generally it became less perceptible the further one travelled from the capital at Antananarivo. At the centre was Imerina, full of provincial and parochial tensions, but where all agreed that they were subjects of the kingdom of Madagascar. Further afield were areas peopled mainly by non-Merina conquered in the first half of the nineteenth century, who were nevertheless subject to the whole hateful range of taxes and labour dues. Within these areas the most onerous obligations fell on those who lived near a Merina garrison. To the west and south of Madagascar especially there were considerable areas where allegiance to Antananarivo was purely nominal, where Merina governors, if they existed at all, could do no more than dabble in local politics, gather intelligence, and collect payments of tribute which were symbolic rather than financially useful.

The peoples who resisted Merina invasion most successfully in the early nineteenth century were generally those with powerful ruling dynasties of their own, and in later years they profited from Imerina's weakness to raid central Madagascar for cattle and slaves. The two leading dynasties outside Imerina were the kings who ruled over the Sakalava of the west coast, and the Zafimanely who held royal power among the Bara of south-central Madagascar. Neither of these dynasties ruled over a united state. They were composed of dozens of kings of varying degrees of power who could trace a common ancestor.

The line which ruled over the Sakalava arose in south-west Madagascar in the seventeenth century, and conquered steadily northwards to the very tip of Madagascar. Every time that expansion slowed down, a junior branch of the family would press further north and establish another kingdom. The dynasty covered such a large area, and became so divided, that it split into two distinct groups called the Zafimbolamena and the Zafimbolafotsy. Thus the kings who reigned among the Sakalava, Antankarana and Tsimihety peoples could all claim a common ancestor, but in every other sense were

38

utterly independent of one another. The most senior of these sovereigns was usually reckoned to be the king of Menabe, on the mid-west coast. He claimed the most direct descent from the founding ancestor, and he could prove it by his possession of the most revered ancestral relics. Generally his kingdom was also the most powerful in military terms. Further north lay the areas known as Ambongo and Boina, ruled by a number of petty kings. Those in Boina had been fairly effectively subdued by the armies of Imerina. In the far north of the island lived the Zafimbolafotsy kings of the Tsimihety and Antankarana. They were almost exterminated by the Merina invasions of the 1820s and 1830s, to the extent that one of the Antankarana kings had ceded the island of Nossi-be to France in return for diplomatic support. This was in 1841, when France was seeking a lever against the Anglo-Merina hegemony. Ever since that time the non-Merina peoples, and the northern Antankarana and Sakalava in particular, had had the reputation of being pro-French, and it is true that the Antankarana helped France in the war of 1883–5.

The far north of Madagascar in fact contained a fair number of Merina garrisons, relics of mightier days. But in most of these the troops were so badly armed and so dispirited that they were less powerful than might appear on paper. Merina governors of any ability intrigued with the local kings who were supposedly under their control and took money from taxes, from tolls or from trade whenever they could. They survived only by turning a blind eye to the flourishing but illegal slave trade. Later it became common to hear of Merina governors in the north tolerating or even assisting bandits because they were too weak to beat them. Malagasy of any origin would combine to keep Europeans from penetrating the lucrative cattle trade. All over the west coast, commerce became more lucrative in proportion as Imerina's hold on trade became less firm. The western kings welcomed the Arab and Indian traders who offered guns, manufactured goods and African slaves for sale, and who took in return cattle or slaves captured from Imerina. Many kings on the coast kept Arab traders at court, or intermarried with their families. Some of the Antankarana kings even converted to Islam.

The Zafimanely of Bara-land had a more recent tradition of unity than did the Sakalava kings. Most of the Bara demes had been united under one king in the late eighteenth century. After his death the ruling line split and, although the Bara were never conquered by the Merina, they came under great pressure from the flow of migrants escaping Merina expansion on the east coast. Although Bara-land as a whole grew richer on plunder taken from the Merina kingdom in its age of decline, the sway of the paramount kings was generally weakened by the unsettling effects of constant war and emigration. By 1895 there existed no fewer than three large Bara kingdoms, two intermediary ones and over two dozen minor ones.[1] Merina power was represented by the garrison at Ihosy, which was unable to stop raids into Imerina and Betsileo-land. The Merina commanders at Ihosy generally tried to shore up the oldest-established Bara kings against younger upstarts or breakaway groups, which were a menace both to Imerina and to the senior Zafimanely kings.

After the period of expansion, which ended in the 1850s, Merina provincial commanders generally found that it was in their interest to promote strong kings in the unconquered territories. Any area without strong authority was more volatile. This was especially true of Tanala-land, an impenetrable country covered with thick tropical forest which has been a sanctuary for fugitives since time immemorial. The Tanala in the nineteenth century were divided between two main kingdoms and a number of autonomous demes. One of the two kingdoms, that of Ambohimanga-Atsimo, had a tradition of co-operating with Merina overrule, and even accepted a school and eventually a Protestant evangelist. Its position in the forest protected it from the worst excesses of Merina government. It retained its own Tanala kings and had the status of a protected state, rather like an Indian princely state under the Raj.

The south of Tanala-land was dominated by the independent kingdom of Ikongo, the scene of many battles with Merina armies in the days when King Radama I and Queen Ranavalona I were conquering Madagascar. Its kings habitually gave shelter to refugees from Merina rule, whatever their origin. An entire province of Ikongo was composed of 'Merina political refugees, army deserters, runaway slaves, and escaped criminals'.[2] In the same way, the autonomous demes who inhabited the north of Tanala-land were joined by a constant stream of refugees from elsewhere.

The Tanala owed their independence to the forest which was their shelter in time of hardship. Those conquered peoples who were less favoured by the terrain of their land, especially if they owned some asset coveted by the rulers of Imerina, were less fortunate. The Sihanaka, the Betsileo, the Bezanozano and the Betsimisaraka may all be considered as colonized peoples. Antsihanaka received such a large number of Merina settlers in the nineteenth century that it came to resemble a Merina province in many ways, although the Sihanaka never abandoned the small, local cults which were the essence of their political coherence.[3]

Imerina's greatest feat of assimilation was among the Betsileo, whose traditional culture is very similar to that of Imerina. After their conquest of Betsileo-land at the turn of the nineteenth century, the Merina installed governors with large numbers of soldiers and officials in every important village. They even built a capital, Fianarantsoa, in imitation of Antananarivo. There were at least 40,000 Merina settlers among the Betsileo by about 1890, and perhaps as many as 100,000.[4] Many of them were government or Church officials or traders, or even all three combined in one person. They retained their family connections in Imerina even if they were born and bred among the Betsileo.

The paramount kings of the Betsileo collaborated with the Merina occupiers to the extent that in the years when Merina power was in decline some of them reached high positions in the local administration. The lower ranks of the administration, in the smaller villages, were filled almost entirely by native Betsileo. Nevertheless, both paramount kings and minor notables were remarkably successful in retaining the esteem of their subjects.[5] Betsileo farmers frequently eked out their subsistence economy by working as wage-labourers, either for Merina settlers or by seasonal migration to Imerina. Many were heavily indebted to Merina money-lenders. As time went by they became increasingly liable to demands for forced labour and military service.

All the colonized peoples of Madagascar were required to attend church as an expression of loyalty to the queen in Antananarivo. It was an unpopular duty and in most provinces the number of church-goers was small. But in Betsileo-land Merina power was so pervasive that many villagers were obliged to build churches and schools, which were widely used as recruiting-centres for the army. The Betsileo could at least count themselves lucky that their land was evangelized by three different missionary societies, which increased the scope for maintaining the independence of a given parish. Catholicism was often a means of escape from the exactions of the state Church because sponsorship by French Jesuits gave Catholic communities a certain independence from Protestant evangelists and a measure of protection by French diplomats. The Betsileo kings too were often instrumental in the establishment or protection of Catholic cults as a way of strengthening their own influence.

The frequent disputes between Catholics and Protestants among the Betsileo often took place when scholars were enrolled for school. Protestant officials would try to place them in a Protestant school, under close government control, while the congregation would wish to be registered as Catholics or to escape enrolment altogether. Not all Betsileo aspired to Catholicism, and not all Merina were Protestants, but it was often the case. Many Betsileo eventually became convinced church-goers, Catholic or Protestant, especially when they were allowed control of their own church affairs. By the 1890s there were even a number of Betsileo preachers who travelled the country practising and teaching a syncretic form of Christianity.[6] Christian missions had more success in Betsileo-land than in any other area of Madagascar except Imerina. To some extent this was a direct result of the number of men and the amount of money invested by the missionary societies, but perhaps the striking similarity of Merina and Betsileo culture included particular features which encouraged conversion.

On the east coast of Madagascar, where there was a rather less intensive missionary effort, the number of conversions by non-Merina was extremely low. The area was occupied by three main peoples, the Betsimisaraka, the Antemoro and the Antaisaka. Living among them, especially in the belt of thick forest which runs parallel to the east coast, there were a number of minor groups which had migrated from other parts of Madagascar. One such group, the Vorimo, had originally been driven from Imerina during the wars of unification around 1800 and had nurtured a deep antipathy towards central government ever since.[7]

The Betsimisaraka in the nineteenth century were rather hard to define. They had been united a century earlier under a noble lineage partly descended from European pirates. After the Merina conquest this ruling line had been almost annihilated by Ranavalona I's use of the poison ordeal, and the Betsimisaraka were reduced to a league of demes with no indigenous authority higher than their elders. The Antemoro and the Antaisaka, on the other hand, had ancient noble lineages which traditionally held purely ritual powers. These indigenous religious élites collaborated with the Merina conquerors, and were rewarded with a degree of temporal power which they used to acquire the best lands of the commoners. The nobles' sudden and illegitimate dominance and the brutality of Merina overrule provoked a series of revolts from the 1830s onwards. There were wholesale migrations which disturbed the stability of kingdoms hundreds of miles inland. By the later nineteenth century the Merina garrisons in the south-east were no longer strong enough to protect their allies from frequent disturbances. A rising of Antemoro commoners in 1882–3 resulted in the spilling not of human blood, but of that of thousands of cattle, as commoners forced nobles to eat beef which had been slaughtered by ritually impure hands. The profound upset in the structure of southern politics which dates back to the Merina invasions of 1820–40 was a process which reached its climax only in the anti-French risings of 1904–5.

All over the east coast, but especially among the Betsimisaraka who lived near the main ports, other problems arose from the number of Merina, creole and European immigrants who settled on the coast to trade and farm. Merina began to move there in the early nineteenth century and Europeans arrived in significant numbers during the 1860s and after. The newcomers competed fiercely for a share of the dwindling supplies of cash and manpower. The natives of the east were expected to work as forced labourers for Merina officers and as wage labourers for Europeans. It seems that until quite late in the nineteenth century the Betsimisaraka were deliberately prevented from trading so as not to provide still more competition. Many became indebted to Merina money-leaders.[8] Merina colonists, even more than Europeans, disturbed the tenure of land by buying estates or taking land as security for loans. For years the Betsimisaraka and the other eastern farmers resisted as best they could. Many refused to grow a surplus of rice only to see its profits go into Merina pockets, a fact which contributed to Madagascar's economic problems. Others took to the forest and hid, and there were even some minor insurrections.

The existence of a kingdom of Madagascar was not a popular idea in very many places outside Imerina. Still, it existed in international law. Britain recognized its existence as early as 1817. Several other European powers, and the United States of America, did so in the treaties which they signed with the Merina government after 1861.

THE INNER CIRCLES

In the Merina heartland, in Imerina proper, most people in the nineteenth century acquired a deep commitment to the ideal of Merina unity, even of Malagasy unity. It was presented by their rulers as an extension of the love of a freeman for his local homeland.

After 1869 the national idea was associated with a style of modernization which many people found unpalatable. As the apparatus of the modern state became more oppressive, country people without access to its benefits looked enviously at the relics of the good old days of the ancestors. There were still political offices or institutions which had been established before unification and which came to represent bastions of provincial freedom. The fief-holders and district elders who were descended from petty kings of old were often spokesmen for the conservative element in country life, the so-called 'old *hova* party'. They generally used their power less harshly than the newer generations of governors and evangelists. They were restrained, a diplomat said, by 'the traditions which bound a master's family to that of his servant'.[9] Fief-holders could still command free labour, but that was their undisputed right. And they normally required people to work close to their homes. It was only the magnates in the capital or their retainers who summoned villagers to travel for days to perform some duty of private interest. By the end of the nineteenth century provincial rivalries had become very bitter. 'In Imerina especially', observed a French official, 'people from different regions despise and detest one another; each province, as it is traditionally constituted, has its own narrow-minded chauvinism'.[10] It seems that one of the most important effects of the centralization of government was not to eliminate the bitterness of rival provincial allegiances, but to exaggerate it.

The matter is complicated by confusion arising from the fact that the traditional ideology assumed the territory and kinship of a freeman to be unchanging. This was the representation of an ideal, not of reality. The name Imerina is said to have been coined in the sixteenth century to denote the territory of a number of demes who lived on the central plateau. Since then there had been numerous migrations leading some of the original Merina to new territories. When people of the nineteenth century spoke of Imerina they generally meant the four provinces which had constituted the kingdom in the sixteenth century. If they wished to include the newer settlements in Vonizongo and Vakinankaratra they would speak of *Imerina enin-toko* ('six-province Imerina').[11] Sometimes people would even speak of eight-province Imerina, to include Merina-settled territories even further from the old heartland. I have used the terms greater and lesser Imerina to cover these meanings.

Each of the four provinces of lesser Imerina constituted an ancient political unit having one or more kings, which had been united by King Andrianampoinimerina. Each of them therefore contained at least one

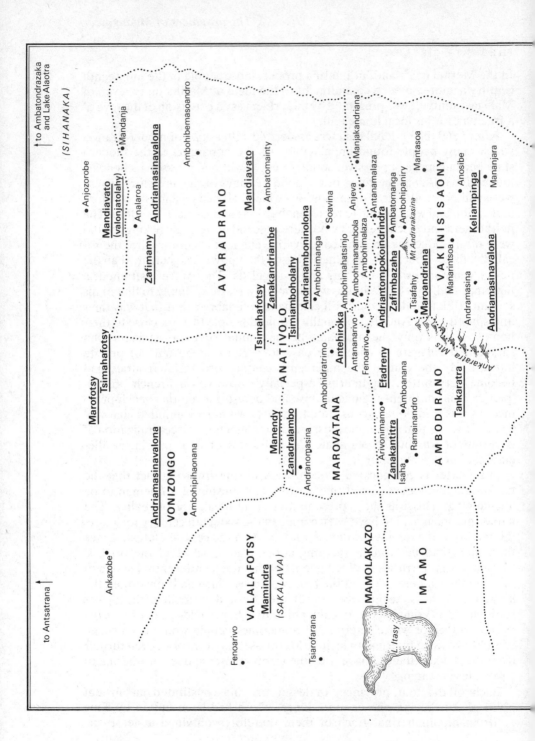

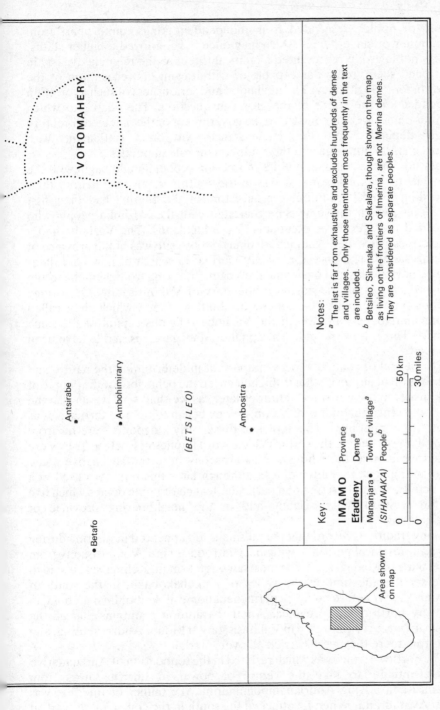

Map 3. The provinces of Imerina, also showing principal demes and villages mentioned in the text

Key:

IMAMO Province
Efadreny Deme[a]
Mananjara ● Town or village[a]
(SIHANAKA) People[b]

0 _____ 50 km
0 _____ 30 miles

Notes:

[a] The list is far from exhaustive and excludes hundreds of demes and villages. Only those mentioned most frequently in the text are included.

[b] Betsileo, Sihanaka and Sakalava, though shown on the map as living on the frontiers of Imerina, are not Merina demes. They are considered as separate peoples.

VOROMAHERY

● Betafo

Antsirabe ●

● Ambohimirary

(BETSILEO)

Ambositra ●

Area shown on map

group of nobles descended from independent kings, quite apart from commoner or slave demes which may once have enjoyed a higher status. Every noble group represented a political threat to the reigning dynasty in that each such group was capable of withdrawing its recognition of the government's legitimacy. The likelihood and seriousness of such a rejection depended on the status of the group in question. The degree to which various demes were reconciled to the government of the nineteenth century often depended on the circumstances of their settlement with Andrianampoinimerina and their subsequent role in politics.

A study of the regional politics of Imerina proper should begin with the province of Vakinisisaony. It was in the south-east of this territory that, according to oral tradition, the ancestors of the Merina had their first kingdoms, which for some time coexisted with the Vazimba people who preceded the Merina as occupants of the highlands. The Vazimba had a religious centre called Antananarivokely, whose site was in the province of Vakinisisaony. The ancestors of the Merina, in search of new land, later moved northwards and overcame the Vazimba, taking from them the fertile plain which lies on the northern boundary of Vakinisisaony. On a ridge overlooking the plain the conquerors built a village which they called Antananarivo, in imitation of the Vazimba religious capital of the same name.[12] This is how the modern capital of Madagascar is said to have been founded.

The period of conquest was so important in determining the nature and distribution of authority that it still influenced the behaviour of the people of Vakinisisaony two or three centuries later, as we shall see. It was also the time when the inhabitants of Vakinisisaony began to refer to themselves as nobles or commoners. The nobles of these early kingdoms were far from being a power élite of the sort which the word implies in English. They were so numerous that the whole of Vakinisisaony bore the alternative name Maroandriana, 'the many nobles', although later this term was used in a restricted sense to describe one particular league of noble demes which live in the west of Vakinisisaony and in the neighbouring province of Ambodirano.[13]

Many traditions record that the talismans too appeared in Imerina during this semi-mythical period, having been introduced into Vakinisisaony from other parts of Madagascar. The most famous talisman, Kelimalaza, is said to have spent some time in the valley of Ankobakobaka, in the south of Vakinisisaony, before finding a permanent home at Ambohimanambola, in the very north of the province. Another tradition maintains that all the talismans were concentrated in Vakinisisaony at Mount Andrarakasina, and that from there they were carried all over Imerina.[14]

The northward impetus which resulted in the foundation of Antananarivo was eventually to take the centre of power in Imerina away from Vakinisisaony. King Andrianampoinimerina, the unifier of Imerina, was from Avaradrano. When he attacked the south in the course of his wars, it was mostly the demes of northern Vakinisisaony which collaborated with him and helped him to conquer the south and east of the province. They were rewarded with a share in the power of the united kingdom. Many of those who resisted unsuccessfully not only lost prestige, but were sometimes obliged to concede lands to colonists from Avaradrano, so that the northern border of Vakinisisaony receded, while Avaradrano gained territory.[15]

The antiquity of Vakinisisaony in a system where power was justified by reference to tradition made it especially prominent in its capacity to confer legitimacy on a sovereign. Broadly speaking, prestige, power and wealth in nineteenth-century Vakinisisaony went to those who had collaborated with King Andrianampoinimerina or whose acquiescence had been rewarded with trade privileges by later national governments. But even these collaborators never accepted the commoner generals of Avaradrano, including Rainilaiarivony, as their superiors. The noble party at court, which was so bitterly opposed to the Andafy-Avaratra throughout the nineteenth century, largely originated in Vakinisisaony and Ambodirano.

Those demes of Vakinisisaony which were omitted from the political settlement of Andrianampoinimerina, and whose support was less crucial for the security of the government, fared worse. In general they lived in the south and east of the province, especially in the districts called Vakinampasina, Amoronkay and Atsimondrano. They continued to idealize the constitution in the form it had had when they themselves knew greater power. So the descendants of the first kingdoms of the highlands became divided not only by the degree to which they participated in government after 1800, but also by their whole conception of the type and scope of royal government.

Several villages in the south of Vakinisisaony recorded how their traditional fief-holders were replaced by outsiders imposed from Antananarivo. The nobles of Anosibe quarrelled with their old allies at Andramasina, while the latter profited from participation in government.[16] In the north-east of the province some old centres of nobility declined in the face of administrative centres settled by colonists from Avaradrano. Ambohipaniry and Ankadimanga declined in relation to Ambatomanga and Antanamalaza in the same way as medieval Lancaster has been succeeded by modern Manchester. Those who lived away from the new centres of administrative power probably suffered from heavier labour dues too, especially if their decline was accompanied by a loss of noble status. Southern Vakinisisaony was particularly heavily exploited for labour in the later nineteenth century, and there were even instances of entire demes fleeing to escape recruitment.

The competition for national power between the leading families of Vakinisisaony, mostly noble, and those of Avaradrano, mainly commoner, turned upon possession of Kelimalaza. In effect King Andrianampoinimerina had confiscated Kelimalaza in the name of Avaradrano and had bought off its hereditary keepers with a share of power. It remained in the hands of northerners during the revival of the talismans under Queen

Ranavalona I. During her long bloody reign, the only effective opposition was gathered around the crown prince, Radama. Some of the courtiers from Vakinisisaony, seeing that Kelimalaza, the symbol of their tradition, had been taken away from them, intrigued with the young prince's faction. When he ascended the throne as King Radama II in 1861, he rewarded those who had followed him in earlier years by choosing his leading counsellors from among the noble families of Vakinisisaony and Ambodirano, to the detriment of the Andafy-Avaratra and the northerners.

Thus the events of the 1860s may be interpreted as a struggle between rival provincial élites, as well as in the terms described elsewhere. For two years, from 1861 to 1863, the Andafy-Avaratra lost control of the machinery of national government. They won it back only by murdering King Radama II and his friends the *menamaso*. The victory was completed six years later with the burning of the talismans, the immediate cause of which was a threat of revolt by the southern partisans of Kelimalaza.[17] Rainilaiarivony made it plain that the people of Ambohimanambola could expect no favours now their talisman was no longer needed. They lost their exemption from forced labour and the chief guardian of Kelimalaza became the village pastor.[18]

Many people in Vakinisisaony were so attached to Kelimalaza and to all that it stood for that they refused to believe that it was burnt in 1869. They said that it had miraculously 'mounted aloft on the flames . . . and wafted himself [*sic*] southwards . . . to a little village on the borders of the Tsiafahy and Ankadibevava [mission] districts'.[19] In fact Kelimalaza was restored by a man named Rambinintsoa, a relative of the former chief guardian. He took the talisman to Ankobakobaka, from which it had come perhaps three centuries before. From there he travelled constantly and was visited by pilgrims from villages which had owned Kelimalaza long before King Andrianampoinimerina had taken it to Avaradrano. Finally Rambinintsoa settled at the village of Mananjara. His acolytes revived the old rituals of Kelimalaza which were so hateful to Christians. They practised the forbidden custom of polygamy and wore their hair long in the old fashion. The people of the south came in great numbers to revere their talisman, which had returned to them at last, and to remember older and happier days. It was a cult charged with overtones of opposition to the Christian government.[20]

It is hardly surprising to hear that the south of Vakinisisaony was generally regarded after 1869 as the most stubbornly pagan part of Imerina. As late as 1894, none of the evangelists there was college-trained, half the churches had no pastor or schoolteacher, and the missionary was able to visit only once a year.[21] People scarcely bothered to hide their devotion to the old cults despite the fact that they had been outlawed in 1869. Hundreds of people, even nominal Christians, still worshipped at Andrarakasina, the ancient holy site. Indeed they came from dozens of miles away to consult the astrologers who lived there.[22] All this may have seemed to missionaries to be a sorry state of affairs, but for the people of the south it was a means of resisting the intrusion of central government into their politics and of foreign beliefs into their tradition.

It was in the north of Vakinisisaony, where people generally collaborated with the government, that Christianity was strongest. But in the very north, around Ambohimalaza which lay on the border with Avaradrano, the population was deeply divided. Many villagers continued to revere Kelimalaza. Most village officials subscribed to official Protestantism, but there were pockets of firm Catholic support. Perhaps the main Catholic centre in the region was at Ambohimalaza, a village inhabited not only by the noble and highly respected Andriantompokoindrindra deme but also by a fair number of commoners and slaves. Among the thousands of Andriantompokoindrindra living around Ambohimalaza, one wealthy family was considered senior to the rest. And while the junior branches of the deme, together with the commoner families, became Protestants, this one family with its slaves invited the Jesuits to establish a Catholic church at Ambohimalaza.[23]

A similar sort of pattern took shape in several nearby villages whose nobles were traditionally allied to the Andriantompokoindrindra, certain noble families and their slaves converting to Catholicism while the commoners became Protestant. It is plain that there was a political motive in these conversions. Many of the commoners settled around Ambohimalaza were from families of Avaradrano which had arrived only in the wake of Andrianampoinimerina's conquest, and were very unpopular with the old-established demes. The first Jesuit converts included at least one *menamaso* who had escaped the massacres of 1863.[24] In 1869 the civil chiefs of both Ambodirano and Vakinisisaony, men of national stature, joined the Catholics, but were persecuted by pressure from the prime minister's Protestant family.[25] In other words, the feud between the nobles of northern Vakinisisaony and the Andafy-Avaratra which was at the centre of national political life between 1861 and 1863 became tangled with patterns of Christian conversion in 1868–70. Leading noble families of Vakinisisaony, so recently associated with the *menamaso*, refused to join Protestant churches in which they would be subject to the hierarchy dominated by the prime minister. Their expression of protest was closely connected with the dispute between nobles and commoners in the ruling élite.

The Catholic missionaries found a very similar incidence of conversion in Ambodirano, a province which had old and distinguished ties with Vakinisisaony. Some of the noble families of Ambodirano were among King Radama II's ill-fated *menamaso*, and again it was these same noble groups which showed the most interest in Catholicism.[26] The province also contained some demes which had been associated with the very earliest southern kingdoms, before the foundation of Antananarivo, and whose subsequent history caused them to view any form of Christianity with disfavour. The Zanakantitra, for example, had lived to the east of the Ankaratra mountains in the distant past, and they said that they had been nobles. They lost their noble status when they were defeated and forced to migrate to the foothills of the mountains, and even to drift still further west. But the main body of the Zanakantitra moved west only at the end of the eighteenth century. They were led by a man called Andrianjaza, the chief counsellor of a king who opposed Andrianampoinimerina and was defeated. From then on all the Zanakantitra lived west of the mountains. They were forced to perform heavy labour dues and once, about 1820, they mutinied because of this.[27]

The Zanakantitra were divided into two sections, one of which had its main village at Amboanana, the other at Ramainandro. The Ramainandro division was allied by marriage to a deme of Avaradrano, and this was the cause of a feud with the rest of the Zanakantitra, who were renowned for the strictness with which their members married only amongst themselves. This split proved to be decisive in the reaction to Christianity. The people of Ramainandro built a fine stone church by their own efforts, and enjoyed a large measure of control because they belonged to the Anglican SPG and not to the more highly organized LMS. A local man, Radaniela, became an influential governor over the district of Isaha.[28] The larger division of the Zanakantitra, on the other hand, never made more than a token conversion. The people around Amboanana had a deep suspicion of schools, which they thought to be a new form of extracting forced labour from them. They continued to revere their old talismans in secret. They displayed them openly whenever a catastrophe threatened, when there was 'a grievous sickness, and again during the . . . French wars'.[29]

Most of the western province, beyond a certain distance from the capital and with the exception of missionary centres like Ramainandro, was intensely opposed to Christianity. It was, said one Malagasy Christian, 'heathenish and lawless in the extreme. The only religion was idolatry or a kind of fetishism; the country was infested with robbers, men-stealing and cattle-lifting were common.'[30] Eye-witness accounts testify that the outlying areas were terribly misgoverned, and subject to murderous raids from the Sakalava after 1880.

To the north-west of Antananarivo lay the province of Marovatana, whose nobles were mostly Zanadralambo, descendants of King Ralambo who had been installed among the surviving Vazimba demes. The latter had then taken the status of *mainty*, or slave-demes. This illustrates very well the ritual rather than economic origin of Merina castes, for the noble Zanadralambo and the 'slave' Manendy were intimately connected over centuries. At the time of unification in about 1795, King Andrianampoinimerina met stiff resistance from certain groups of Zanadralambo and Manendy, particularly to the north of the village of Andranomasina.[31] As a punishment many Manendy were exiled to the unhealthy swamp-land of Anativolo.

The Zanadralambo who collaborated during the wars of unification were rewarded with the highest offices in the government of their province,

50

Marovatana. Some of their representatives held important offices at court, as their status required. They were free from labour dues apart from the highly symbolic obligation to provide the central pillar of the royal palace. But in other respects the Zanadralambo were closely controlled, for their ancestry entitled them to great respect and made them dangerous dissidents. A law code of 1828 forbade them, on pain of enslavement, from adoption into any higher rank of nobility and from forming social or political alliances with certain other noble demes with whom they had long associations.[32] This was intended to place the Zanadralambo in the lowest rank of nobility and to prevent them from uniting with any other groups in revolt. Although the Zanadralambo were not singled out for persecution during the reign of Queen Ranavalona I, they clearly did not approve wholeheartedly of the constitution of her government since they were prominent among the adherents of the underground Christian movement.[33]

The history of the Zanadralambo is a reflection of a process which was at work all over Imerina by which older élites were seduced from their constituents by the Andafy-Avaratra. Those who were appointed to high office on ritual grounds became extremely wealthy through their access to patronage and trade, while their kinsmen who remained in the ancestral villages achieved only modest prosperity. By the 1880s the head of the Zanadralambo lived in Antananarivo and made a lot of money from usury.[34] He owed his fortune to the fact that his presence was required to indicate that the Zanadralambo respected the legitimacy of the Christian government. His distant cousins who still lived in the country were mere peasant farmers or minor landlords. Thus did money corrupt the purpose of office and divide the old view of social classes from the new. It was exactly the same phenomenon which caused the Andriantompokoindrindra to profit from trade, and to accept Christianity, while most nobles in the south of Vakinisisaony remained non-Christian, and poor. The state was ruled by an élite of wealth.

East of Marovatana lay Avaradrano province. It was the people of Avaradrano who raised Andrianampoinimerina to the throne and he rewarded them by making them 'the senior of the six Merina provinces and the father of the population'.[35] Settlers from that province went all over Imerina and provided the garrisons on Imerina's northern and western borders. They had more lands, possibly more slaves, and were more likely to have family influence in the central government than the people of any other province since so many of the rulers of Imerina were originally from Avaradrano.

But in no sense did Avaradrano constitute the ruling class of Imerina. A very small number of families, most notably the Andafy-Avaratra, became extremely rich or powerful, and when they did they almost always left the traditional life of the village and moved to the capital. In the country areas the people of Avaradrano did not live very differently from their ancestors, nor from their neighbours. Only in a few areas where settlers from

51

Avaradrano were installed as colonists did they become involved in land disputes of a tribal sort. This was most notably the case in the northern division of Vakinisisaony, and was the root of many of the religious contests there. There are many cases in which colonists sent out from Avaradrano in the early nineteenth century quickly established reasonably good relations with older generations of inhabitants. On Imerina's northern border there were several hereditary garrisons of Tsimahafotsy from Avaradrano, put there in the 1820s to guard against raids from the Sakalava and to control a slave-deme called the Marofotsy, who were composed of fugitive slaves and were renowned for their lawlessness. But by the late nineteenth century the Tsimahafotsy colonies had grown too weak to defend either themselves or the part of the Marofotsy which lived in settled villages and was law-abiding. One Marofotsy, Rabezavana, formed a private army for the protection of his village. He was so successful in fighting off raids and in resisting extortionate demands for unpaid labour that he became the most powerful warlord on the northern march. In 1892, incensed with the failure of the garrisons, he went to Antananarivo and demanded an official appointment in return for restoring order. His wish was granted. Rabezavana returned to the north as governor of Antsatrana and took command of all the Tsimaha-fotsy garrisons. Though a Marofotsy, and therefore of low status, Rabezavana was able to command men of higher rank whose ancestors had been sent to his land three generations before,[36] and to enjoy good relations with them.

A similar alliance occurred among the Zafimamy, a nobility so ancient that a lot of people had forgotten the Zafimamy origin and called them commoners. They lived beyond the north-east border of Avaradrano. Like the Zanadralambo, they were subject to several assaults on their noble status in the nineteenth century, and they were obliged to share their territory with colonists from Avaradrano. Those who settled amongst them were known as the *valonjatolahy*, 'the eight hundred men', a branch of the Mandiavato of Avaradrano. Despite early friction between the Zafimamy and the newcomers, a settlement was eventually worked out between them and confirmed by a marriage between a leading family of the Zafimamy and the Mandiavato.[37]

Avaradrano suffered from changes in government during the nineteenth century quite as much as less privileged provinces. The elders who represen-ted each deme or each district at court became seduced by the wealth of the oligarchy. The channels of patronage became so clogged that little of this wealth ever left the capital. Traditional holders of office were often degraded to the profit of the central government. The people of Avaradrano were generally held to be better disposed towards Christianity than the people of south Imerina, and this is understandable inasmuch as Christianity was the ritual reflection of a political settlement which was most favourable to Avaradrano. But the country people of the province, as elsewhere, converted in name only in 1869.

52

Outside lesser Imerina were two provinces, Vonizongo and Vakinankaratra, which were peopled largely by settlers from central Imerina who had so detached themselves from their places of origin that they were considered to belong to autonomous areas. Vonizongo had submitted peacefully to Andrianampoinimerina, and he allowed the large number of fief-holders there to continue to govern under his hegemony. These noble fief-holders were often persecuted by Andrianampoinimerina's successors because of their renowned independence of mind. Many of the early Christian martyrs came from this class.[38] In later years, just before the French conquest, the territory suffered impoverishment at the hands of Rainibanona, a particularly ferocious governor-general and former evangelist.[39]

In Vakinankaratra the many villages originally settled by fugitives from Imerina were mixed with settlements of Betsileo origin. In the eighteenth century the population had been ruled by a multitude of small kingdoms whose ruling dynasties came either from Imerina or from Betsileo-land. Andrianampoinimerina conferred power on those kings who collaborated with him during his invasion of the province, and thereafter its history was marked by a broad division between those families which had access to the government, mostly descended from local rulers who had received Andrianampoinimerina favourably, and those who had resisted him and been degraded by Merina overrule. The governors of Vakinankaratra formed a local élite which depended upon Antananarivo for support but was independent enough to resist the kind of economic and political subjugation which overtook the princes of Vonizongo. The magnates of Vakinankaratra adapted to the Christian state by adhering to the Lutheran Church, which they then used as an organ of government. As Lutherans they had a certain freedom from the prime minister's personal control. The most important figure of the élite of Vakinisisaony on the eve of the French conquest was Rainijaonary, the military commander of the province and the only Merina general strong enough to defeat Bara and Sakalava raiders consistently.

Catholicism attracted a following in Vakinankaratra, although it was firmly opposed by the Lutheran government hierarchy. It took firmest root in areas which had not benefited from the political settlement of the early century, where villagers tried to establish Catholic churches as a means of escaping the official Lutheran hegemony. This is broadly true of the region of Ambositra, for example.[40]

On the borders of six-province Imerina were several buffer-states having the constitution of autonomous provinces. Voromahery, on the edge of the eastern forest, was 'a sort of little independent republic' which owed no labour dues beyond the obligation to herd the sovereign's cattle. Its immunity encouraged a number of bandits to use it as a hiding-place in the later nineteenth century. The most famous bandit-chief was Rainibetsimisaraka, once a rich farmer in Vakinankaratra who had fled after incurring the wrath of the local Lutheran pastor. Since then he had waged almost a private war against the government of Vakinankaratra.[41] The province of Valala-fotsy had a similar independent status, its population being composed of refugees from all over Imerina. Further north the Marofotsy, also a group of very diverse origin, had broad exemptions from labour service. All the border provinces were eventually subject to attacks on their traditional privileges by the central government. In Valalafotsy officials from Antananarivo were sometimes able to obtain forced labour by naked force. The Marofotsy were obliged to do heavier labour by Rabeony, the governor-general of Antsihanaka and a man notorious for his ability to extort money.

The diverse nature of Imerina meant that the various reforms decreed by governments at Antananarivo fell very unevenly, in proportion as a prov-ince was able to resist the capital's tendency to strip the provinces of their resources of wealth and manpower. The assault on traditional fief-holders was probably most effective in Avaradrano and Marovatana. Among the Mandiavato of Avaradrano, for example, there were 146 traditional fief-holders in 1896 of whom thirty did not actually have a fief any longer. Most of the others were no more than rich farmers. Only half a dozen lived in Antananarivo and could be considered members of the ruling oligarchy.[42] Similarly in Ambodirano most fief-holders lived quite humbly, except for four who had gone to Antananarivo and two who were considered tradi-tional heads of the province. Only one was a major politician, and that was Prince Ramahatra, a pillar of the Catholic faction at court.[43] The general impression is that those few fief-holders who survived Rainilaiarivony's reforms with their power intact did so in one of two ways: either they came to an understanding which confirmed them as collaborators in areas where central power was weak, as in Vakinankaratra; or, nearer the capital, certain of them managed to prosper by finding a place at court. This was the solution available to representatives of groups whose recognition was considered essential for the security of the government. These observations are true not just of fief-holders but of holders of traditional office in general.

The institution of village governors, the last of Prime Minister Rainilaiarivony's centralizing reforms, also fell unevenly according to the traditions of each province: 215 governors were appointed in Avaradrano; 57 in Vakinisisaony; 64 in Ambodirano; 51 in Marovatana and Vonizongo together; and apparently fewer still in Vakinankaratra.[44]

A fundamental division in Merina politics of the late nineteenth century was between the capital and the provinces. The skyline of Antananarivo was dominated by the palaces and neo-gothic churches which had been designed by British missionary architects. The supreme arbiter among the élite who lived in the upper town was Prime Minister Rainilaiarivony, the head of the Andafy-Avaratra. He was constantly threatened by plots even from within his own family. Queen Ranavalona III, who reigned from 1883, had political ambitions of her own. Many noble courtiers heartily detested the commoner upstarts and sought to undermine their influence wherever possible, although they recognized their essential community of interests as members of an oligarchy.

Quite often these factional divisions were expressed in religious terms. The Andafy-Avaratra and their retainers were Protestants of the LMS persuasion, while many of the noble magnates whose original family lands were in the south of Imerina were Catholics. A few people espoused an independent native Church, the Rush Church or Tranozozoro, which had little following outside the capital. The Protestants at court were usually educated by British missionaries and were considered pro-British in foreign affairs, whereas Catholic grandees were more likely to have been educated by French Jesuits and thus to be considered pro-French. There were even some educated Merina who were genuinely convinced, such was the corruption and decay into which Madagascar had fallen, that a period of European rule would be good for the country. But this was the view of a tiny minority.

Religious differences among the élite had implications for more humble citizens, since the churches were channels of patronage. All Imerina's LMS congregations were subject to a certain amount of interference from the Palace Church, where Rainilaiarivony worshipped. Similarly, Catholic congregations in Imerina and Betsileo-land frequently looked to the Catholic nobles at court for protection. But outside the capital country people saw little difference between British and French, but only between Malagasy and foreigners. Antananarivo was widely held to be corrupt. 'Ambohimanga and Antananarivo have no love of money', Andrianampoinimerina had declared, promising his subjects that they need not fear extortion from his government.[45] That compact had been broken, visibly, as the glitter of the capital and its inhabitants' insatiable demands for money showed.

The prime minister, in creating the Christian state, had rejected the system of legitimization connected with the talismans. Europeans rarely perceived the depth of Rainilaiarivony's unpopularity. They saw only his dictatorial powers. His illegitimacy was unannounced, hidden in traditions which could not be recited and talismans which could not be displayed, obscured by the sacred principle of obedience to the sovereign.

THE MARGINS OF THE KINGDOM

The colonized peoples of Madagascar, the Sihanaka, Betsimisaraka and Betsileo for example, had little affection for the sovereigns of Imerina who ruled them. But within Imerina proper there were sharp differences of outlook and of attitudes towards government between different demes, even neighbours. The determining factor was very often the circumstances under which a certain group had settled the land. This aspect of tradition was so crucial that it could cause a deme to split into factions having different customs or religious traditions, as happened among the Zanakantitra.

Throughout several centuries whenever there was a strong government in the heart of Imerina it sent a new wave of authority into the provinces. By the same token, political strife or economic misfortune in central Imerina produced waves of fugitives towards outlying lands. Each movement of migrants from the centre encountered older generations of settlers in the provinces. Certain parts of Imerina therefore came to form a living record of the past, like the layers of an archaeological site, recorded in the traditions and customs of various settlements. Generally speaking, the longer a colony had been established the more antique were its customs and its concept of the national constitution.

Concentrations of population which were in some way marginal to the mainstream of Merina life could be constituted in a number of ways. Throughout the nineteenth century there was, apart from the settlement of relatively affluent Merina colonists in Betsileo-land and the east, a constant flow of refugees from central Imerina to the periphery: impoverished peasants, army deserters or fugitive slaves. They settled in the thinly populated marches of the north and west in particular, in Valalafotsy, Antsihanaka and elsewhere. Within one generation the newcomers would often establish a new identity by taking the name of the existing inhabitants. It was relatively easy, for example, to adopt the identity of a Marofotsy or a Sakalava whereas it was practically impossible to become a member of a deme which still enjoyed occupation of an ancient homeland. Other marginal settlements on the frontiers of greater Imerina had different origins. Some magnates owned so many slaves in the nineteenth century that they housed them in entire villages in the border grazing-lands. In time the slaves might begin to form a new deme and to start the long rise to freedom. Sometimes the borders of Imerina were deliberately used as places of exile for political offenders.

The territory of a particular deme was in many respects a microcosm of the whole kingdom, and was called by the same name, *tanindrazana*, 'the land of the ancestors'. Just as displaced elements moved towards the national periphery, so they did on a local scale. Even in central Imerina margins were constituted by the frontiers between different demes, where there was a no man's land.[46]

If a group or deme was considered marginal in some way, it was generally for one of two reasons. It was either because of a previous migration, a memory of the loss of a homeland and the loss of status, or because a deme had lost status for political reasons, declining in the face of promotions given to others who lived nearer the seat of power in central Imerina. It was thus possible for a deme living fairly close to Antananarivo to be marginal to the Christian state after 1869, because of the profound upset of tradition which the new constitution represented. The Zafimamy and the Zanakantitra of Amboanana may both be regarded in this light. Margins existed not only on the edges of the deserted tracts which surrounded Imerina, but also within the central provinces.

The number of fugitives from central Imerina heading for sanctuary in the border provinces where there was some immunity from the law increased in the nineteenth century. The most spectacular incidence before 1895 was provided by the rising of 1863–4, when many people of western and north-west Imerina refused to do service for the Andafy-Avaratra and rebelled against them. Although the rising was brutally suppressed, the western border continued to be marked by the troubles. Some of the insurgents who escaped the government's revenge fled west to join the Sakalava, and from then until the end of the Merina kingdom the west was subject to heavy raids by Sakalava bands mixed with Merina refugees.[47] The number of slaves who had been acquired by Imerina during the early nineteenth century also came to pose a problem of control. Slaves, like bandits, could not be intimidated by the ultimate threat of expulsion from their ancestral lands, since they had already lost contact with the tombs of their ancestors. Moreover, Merina freemen who were subject to heavy labour dues often encouraged their slaves to travel widely in search of trade when they would usually split the profits. The number of itinerant slaves without firm roots in a given homeland hastened the breakdown of law.

A good indication of the growth of disorder on Imerina's frontiers is in the evidence of a shift in the slave and cattle trades, both of which were increasingly the preserve of peoples outside Merina control, and were often stolen from the plateau in the first place. After the emancipation of the Mozambiques in 1877, the slave trade took two main forms. The west coast continued to export fairly small numbers of slaves to the Persian Gulf or to Réunion. The vast majority of these were either re-exports of Mozambiques brought from Africa or captives from the central plateau. At the same time, the Sakalava and Bara peoples bought or captured slaves for their own use. Cattle exports too were increasingly made from non-Merina ports. So plentiful was the supply of cattle stolen from Imerina that the herdsmen of the north and west often slaughtered cattle for their hides alone and left the carcasses to rot. The boom in the hide trade, which peaked in about 1880, was eventually to lead to a considerable decrease in Madagascar's population of cattle. The Franco-Merina war of 1883–5 made matters worse for the Merina by further weakening their defences and adding considerably to the number of army deserters who joined the bandits. By 1889, it was reckoned by a missionary author that external raids were the most important phenomenon of the year.[48]

By the last two decades of the century there were large concentrations of population outside Imerina whose main livelihood was plunder and who had established trade-routes for the disposal of their booty. Raids into Imerina and Betsileo-land were very heavy. Moreover the raiders were often of Merina or Betsileo origin themselves, allied to independent kings by the social mechanisms available to fugitives. In northern Imerina and Antsihanaka the most notorious raiders were the Marofotsy and the Marofelana, the name given to robber-bands of diverse origin. Both contained considerable numbers of Merina who had fled from forced labour or similar injustice.

To the north-west of Antananarivo the once-prosperous province of Vonizongo was subjected to annual raids from the small Sakalava kingdoms of Ambongo, which had sheltered many Merina fleeing the repression of 1863–4. Raids on western Imerina were similarly conducted largely by people who called themselves Sakalava, but included the Bemihimpa, 'the many scattered ones' who were of Merina ancestry.[49]

The independent peoples most closely associated with attacks on the plateau were the Sakalava and the Bara. There was also a concentration of bandits in the eastern forest, consisting of Antemoro and Betsimisaraka fugitives from Merina rule and independent Tanala groups. They took slaves less often than the peoples with access to the west coast ports, but they plundered traffic from Tamatave and Mananjary. A few Bara and Sakalava kings were able to profit from this state of affairs. The best example is probably King Toera, one of two claimants to the throne of Menabe, who used the movement of refugees from the plateau and the revival of west coast trade to build a strong anti-Merina league. He had good relations with Indian and Zanzibari merchants who bought his captured slaves and cattle and sold him guns. But the fragmentation of kingdoms in the west and south of Madagascar was such that the disorders frequently threatened the kings there almost as much as they menaced Merina rule. In Bara-land a traveller found 'continual evidence of the unsettled condition of the people', and thought this to be a cause of raids upon the Betsileo.[50] Even King Toera's authority was disturbed by the influx of immigrants to his lands with no tradition of allegiance to his dynasty.

Many of the Merina fugitives, although under the nominal control of Bara or Sakalava kings, still considered themselves to have some attachment to Imerina. The Bemihimpa, who were called Sakalava, kept alive even into the present century the memory of their expulsion in 1863 and of their last Merina king, Radama II. Many citizens of the frontier regions were distantly related to the raiders. Rabezavana, the governor of Antsatrana, had a brother who led an important band of Marofotsy bandits.[51] Rabezavana, though, was known to punish bandits even if they were his relatives. Other marcher-lords sometimes conspired with the bandits in raids. The Bemihimpa had two usual routes into western Imerina for raids, one of which passed through Tsiarofarana. This was one of the main villages of their kinsmen the Mamindra, 'the wanderers', Merina subjects of Sakalava ancestry who had also been participants in the rising of 1863 but had later returned to Imerina under amnesty. The fief-holder of Tsiarofarana, a chief of the Mamindra, was a man named Rajamaria. He and his cousin Laimiza, the lord of Fenoarivo, were Merina government officials. This did not prevent them from collaborating with the bandits. They even organized a tax-revolt and tried to assassinate a governor sent out from Antananarivo.[52]

The frontier districts had networks of alliances which in some cases bound them to groups who were not recognized as citizens of Imerina. Agreements were formed without reference to Antananarivo. Indeed, so utterly corrupt was the central government that it was not unknown for high officials in Antananarivo to grant immunity to certain robbers in return for protection money.

Europe made an important contribution to the growth of banditry. The traditional French policy of supporting the subject peoples of Madagascar in order to unhinge the Anglo-Merina alliance helped to encourage the aggressive tendencies of the Sakalava kings in particular. The war of 1883–5 also provoked a wave of anti-European and anti-Christian feeling within Imerina, a precursor of the events of 1895, which was partly because churches were used to raise money and conscripts for the defence of the state.[53] The peace treaty of 1885 required the payment of a large indemnity which ultimately had to be paid for in increased demands by the Merina government upon its subjects. Rainilaiarivony, knowing that his country was sinking under the weight of foreign debt, invented a harsh and unpopular new form of service which consisted in panning for gold in auriferous regions. He also signed mining rights away to a number of foreign companies, most notably the Suberbie Company in the north-west. The suffering caused by the gold *corvée* was representative of much that had gone wrong in Imerina. Most of the gold panned by forced labourers went to line the pockets of officials or was taken out of Imerina by smugglers or foreign adventurers. Thousands of peasants were uprooted from their homes and had to leave their rice uncultivated. Many labourers deserted to join the great robber-bands.[54] The turmoil and the forging of new alliances in the border-lands threw up many of the men who were to lead anti-French resistance in later years. Rainibetsimisaraka succeeded in organizing labour deserters into robber-bands. Ratsizehena led an entire village into the wilds to escape the gold-*corvée*. Rabezavana, having acquired a military following through his own efforts, became popular in the north by resisting bandit raids and refusing to allow recruiting agents from the Suberbie Company.

The growth of banditry and its political repercussions on Imerina's borders was the most spectacular sign of the growth of opposition to the Merina government. In central Imerina there was also a hardening of opposition among marginal demes, that is to say among those who still occupied their homelands but doubted the legitimacy of the Christian government. This tendency was closely involved with the history of the talismans, which were the visible symbols of the constitution. Kelimalaza was not the only one which reappeared after the burnings of 1869. Many demes continued to revere their old talismans out of the sight of missionaries and Palace Church evangelists. Sometimes devotees of ancestral religion moved their talismans to a new site on the border of two mission-districts or in an isolated region where evasion of Church officials was easy. Every missionary came to recognize the existence of certain districts, villages or families which maintained a stubborn adherence to traditions of ancestral religion. Generally these corresponded to marginal groups, noble, commoner or slave, whose history provided them with specific reasons to suspect

59

the intrusion of central power and the denial of tradition which Christian conversion represented.

In some cases local notables could be persuaded to collaborate by the material benefits associated with Church office, but they were unlikely to retain their local popularity if the deme was generally convinced that Christianity was the tool of an upstart regime. In every deme which was divided in its allegiance – and that describes the majority – old and new political traditions had distinct focuses. Quite often the traditional capital of a deme, or the place where the talismans had been kept, became a centre of administration for the Christian government after 1869, and the devotees of the talismans had to meet elsewhere. This is precisely what happened to Kelimalaza. In other areas a talisman stayed in its traditional home and was secretly revered, while a rival village became Christian and prospered through its administrative advantage. Thus the main talisman of the Mandiavato stayed at Ambohibemasoandro, the place where the people had sworn allegiance to King Adrianampoinimerina. But the village receded in importance before Ambatomainty, where there was a mission station.[55] An administrative map of Imerina, showing the centres of government, gives the impression that every important village was Christian. But non-Christians continued to hold in highest regard the places which were important in their tradition, even if those villages consisted of no more than a couple of huts. Religion stood for two versions of geography, Christianity recognizing the importance of certain sites, ancestral religion of others. Very often sites which were of crucial importance to the underground adherents of the talismans were not even noticed by European travellers. The old traditions were opaque to anyone not versed in them, and this helped the talismans to survive as the symbols of an outlawed political opposition. Those who continued to serve them after 1869 included those notables and elders who had stood for something in the old order, but who could not or would not find a place in the Christian hierarchy.

Christianity and the talismans also represented different versions of history. In the more isolated country areas, precisely those least touched by Christianity, oral histories were still composed and recited in the old manner, which has been so beautifully described by Alain Delivré.[56] These histories were full of political significance. They were the means of expressing every reflection on society, on politics, on continuity and change in human affairs. After 1869 oral histories which were significantly different from the versions countenanced by the magnates of the church were suppressed.[57] 'Each person speaks to himself', Père Callet was told, 'and keeps what he thinks to himself.'[58] It frustrated a means not only of political but also of religious expression. For many peasant farmers, the great majority, Christianity was not a satisfactory link with the land, it did not smell of the earth like the older cults.

The disparity between the official and the unofficial versions of history is often quite staggering. To read the collection of transcribed oral traditions published under the title of *Tantaran' ny Andriana*, which has been used over and over again by modern historians but which was collected mostly from Avaradrano, is to be as unaware of other versions as a car driver is unaware of an underground train beneath him. In Vakinisisaony traditional-ists continued to flock to the hill of Andrarakasina to consult the astrologers and to make sacrifices, and to remember the kings who had reigned in Vakinisisaony when the plain of Antananarivo was still a marsh. In the northern traditions, Andrarakasina does not even figure as one of the sacred hills of Imerina.

The two philosophies, Christian and non-Christian, even measured time by different scales. Traditional life was governed by the lunar calendar which was closely connected with magic, astrology and the concept of public order itself. Its greatest feast was the day of the sovereign's ritual bath. Its holiest day was not Christmas or Easter, but the first day of the lunar month of Alahamady. The rulers of Imerina preferred to use the Gregorian calendar.

In every type of religious activity there was a growth of passion dating from the 1880s as the Christian regime showed serious signs of disintegra-tion. Missionaries noted that the devotees of the outlawed ancestral cults were becoming far more daring and assertive. Catholicism grew stronger, and was taken to be a challenge to the Protestant establishment. There was also a considerable born-again revival in the strong Protestant Churches, a movement which produced a new generation of earnest Christians. Church-men sent out from the LMS training colleges launched a head-on assault on the strongholds of Satan, the drinking and the adultery of rural church members.[59] A considerable number of pastors dismissed for immorality in the wake of these purges swelled the revival of ancestral religion. There was a growing expectation among Christian and non-Christian alike of a final combat between opposed forces, a cosmic battle between good and bad, light and darkness. The missionaries described it as a 'sifting time', when the Christian wheat would be separated from the pagan chaff.[60] The devotees of the talismans saw it as a time for weeding out sorcery and decay.

The opposition of marginal groups thus took two forms. On the frontiers it could be measured by the growth of banditry. Among the ancient demes of central Imerina it took the form of a refusal of Christianity, which was in essence a refusal to underwrite the constitution of the government. All that restrained the bandits and their external allies was the ramshackle Merina army. All that held back the dissidents of the interior was the knowledge that the queen, whom they revered deeply, had herself rejected the talismans.

3

The fall of Imerina (November 1894 to November 1895)

This land . . . is the land of Andrianampoinimerina. But today it is deeply humiliated.

The guardian of a national talisman, 1895

THE FRENCH INVASION

France fought a war against Imerina in 1883–5 in order to destroy the British hegemony in the island and to establish that Madagascar was within her own sphere of influence. Thereafter, some policy-makers advocated supporting the Merina government wholeheartedly – and taking the place formerly occupied by Britain – while others proposed supporting the Sakalava and others in order to alter profoundly the balance of power within Madagascar. The French foreign ministry chose the first and less radical of the two courses. It was supported by most of the Frenchmen of standing who were interested in Malagasy affairs. They knew that the island was neither an El Dorado nor a vital asset to French strategy. There were people who disagreed, notably in the colonial ministry. Some of them advocated a further choice, of annexation. Most of the French in Madagascar too were in favour of a more forward imperialist policy, naturally enough, and the existence of the protectorate gave them a means of applying pressure. But the chief support of the annexationist lobby lay in Réunion and the deputies who represented it in Paris.

So, although opinion among French strategists and politicians was divided, the dominant view from 1886 to 1896 was that of the conservative element who advocated a protectorate in Madagascar. This acted as a restraining influence on the Réunionnais. French economic interests in Madagascar, after all, were not numerous. They included three shipping companies which were concerned with the volume of trade rather than its origin, and the Comptoir National d'Escompte, which wished to safeguard the loans which it had already made. The leading French companies working inside Madagascar were financed mostly by small investors and not by any of the businessmen represented in the Parisian colonial party.[1] For the most part French interests could be safeguarded by a working protectorate. The problem was that the financial and political levers which had been designed in 1885 to give overall control of Madagascar were applied to a Merina government which was so weak as to be unresponsive to control. French policy in this period thus suffered from major deficiencies. There was constant disagreement between rival lobbies, while both conservative and annexationist groups consistently over-estimated the power of the Merina government. The protectorate of 1885, designed to prevent the need for a costly occupation, proved an intolerable burden on the Merina economy and eventually caused it to collapse.

The presence of a French resident in Antananarivo after 1886 also split still further the politics of the Merina élite. For years all the politicians in Antananarivo simply waited for the death of the prime minister, who was now reaching senility. Those who manoeuvred for his legacy included two main factions. One, consisting of his family and retainers, was mostly Protestant and commoner. The other, taking an opposite line wherever possible, was predominantly noble, pro-Catholic and allegedly pro-French. In fact as Rainilaiarivony began to lose his grip, Queen Ranavalona III acquired more real power than any sovereign since 1863. It was tempting to Europeans to see in these two factions potential supporters of either Britain or France. On the level of party politics there was some truth in this. But such an analysis ignored the fact that the basic division in Imerina was between court and country. The ruling class in the capital was so utterly alien to its citizens that discussion of these factions pales into insignificance beside the overwhelming divide between rulers and ruled, rich and poor, urban and rural.

After the commercial crash of 1892 it became almost impossible to trade, although the Merina government continued to pay interest on the French loan until the very end. The number of attacks on European citizens rose alarmingly, which was all the more embarrassing as France claimed to be the protector of Madagascar. The prime minister was called upon to put his house in order. He could not do so, although many Frenchmen suspected that he would not do so. When finally it came to the question of a military expedition to assert the rights of France, the Chamber of Deputies on 13 November 1894 voted credits of 65 million francs in a mood of outrage at the indignities committed on French nationals. The breakdown of law and order in Madagascar threatened everyone, regardless of nationality.

The main French expeditionary force, which was fitted out in late 1894, landed at Majunga in north-west Madagascar in January 1895. It was beset with difficulties of its own making in the form of poor organization and equipment. The journey of 200 miles to Antananarivo took nine months. Of the 20,000 troops which assembled on the coast at the beginning of the year, more than 5,000 were lost from disease, and only a handful from Malagasy action. The disasters of the expedition caused quarrels in Paris and led to a demand for firm treatment of the enemy.

Most of the British and Norwegian missionaries in Imerina decided to stay in the capital during the French advance so as to strengthen the Christian resolve of the Malagasy. They were worried by the abundant evidence that the country was on the verge of revolution. The news was dominated by

63

mysterious plots and assassination attempts worthy of cheap fiction. At the end of April 1895 seditious notices were fixed on church doors in the capital, and even on the doors of the queen's palace, calling upon the people to revolt and welcome the French. Attempts were made on the queen's life. It was no secret that there was a faction among the oligarchy which was resigned to the fall of the kingdom and was actively plotting to collaborate with the invaders. From June 1895 onwards the prime minister kept a force of 10,000 men, his best troops, on the plain outside the capital to guard against such treachery. Even at the last moment, when the French gunners bombarded Antananarivo, the front line was starved of guns and ammunition for fear of a *coup d'état*.[2]

The pro-French party consisted of a faction among the oligarchy, many of whom were members of those distinguished noble families which had long detested the Andafy-Avaratra and had expressed their independence by becoming Roman Catholics rather than Protestants. The leading lights of the pro-French party were the queen's cousin, Prince Ramahatra, and the prime minister's secretary Rasanjy, a commoner, a man of limitless ambition and unscrupulousness.

Only once did the British missionaries become alarmed by the threat of anti-European violence from the city poor and the common soldiers. A leading Quaker called Andrianony, a man the Protestant missionaries had known and respected for twenty-five years despite his reputation for independence of mind, addressed the troops outside the capital and encouraged them to attack the British. He called them 'white rats', who 'were all the friends of the French, and therefore their enemies'. The news of this speech spread 'like wild-fire' among the troops. The British vice-consul complained to Rainilaiarivony. A few days later Andrianony died, probably poisoned on the prime minister's orders.[3]

Malagasy resistance to the invasion was crippled at every level. Few generals were willing to fight on behalf of a faction they detested. Those who were willing had no weapons. The correspondent of the London *Times* described well the conditions of the lower ranks:[4]

> The Hova commissariat arrangements are very simple. The soldiers are expected to supply their own rations, and to enable them to do this many, when called out at the beginning of the war, had to sell their little rice plots and all their worldly possessions . . . But how could these poor fellows be expected to make any sort of a stand against a European foe, half-starved as they were, receiving no pay, robbed and betrayed by their officers, and in many cases unprovided with ammunition? How, moreover, could they fight with any loyal ardour in defence of a government that so shamelessly oppressed them, and threw away their lives with such criminal callousness?

These impressions are confirmed by a study of Merina documents on the government's military preparations, or rather its lack of preparations. In most country areas the schools were used as centres for conscription. Rakoto, the minister of education, 'has been fleecing the people to a terrible extent', said one missionary, and he had sometimes done so with the co-operation of evangelists and schoolmasters.[5]

The capital fell to the French on 30 September 1895. General Duchesne, the chief of the army, and Ranchot, the civilian delegate of the foreign ministry, carried out instructions which had been drafted in different circumstances and did not fit the present necessities. On 1 October 1895 a treaty was signed establishing a full protectorate. The old prime minister, Rainilaiarivony, was arrested and replaced by Rainitsimbazafy, a puppet. The strong men of the native administration which the French now established were to be the new secretary of the government, Rasanjy, and the minister of the interior, Rainandriamampandry. As soon as Antananarivo had been taken Duchesne and Ranchot ordered their officers to reinstate the provincial officials of the old regime and to disarm all Malagasy, including local governors. In fact disarmament was enforceable only among those officials nearest to the capital and most loyal to the royal government. About 8,000 out of 30,000 breech-loading rifles were recovered from government arsenals, and those that were left in circulation were often in the hands of the most hostile part of the community.[6] Hence the French inadvertently weakened their collaborators in the provinces, that is, officials who obeyed instructions from Antananarivo. All this was done in accordance with the opinion of foreign minister Hanotaux that the protectorate in Tunisia was a suitable model for an occupied state which, like Madagascar, already possessed the institutions through which the French could work a system of indirect rule. The protectorate policy was enforced despite extensive criticism stemming from the scandalous losses of the expeditionary army.

Most Merina, especially in the country districts, were terrified of the prospect of French rule. Stories of French atrocities passed by word of mouth. Two-thirds of Antananarivo's would-be defenders fled to the countryside on the eve of the French takeover, and only a few trickled back during October 1895. Of those who remained, most of the Protestant magnates of the older generation felt only shock that God and Great Britain could allow them to be colonized. Only a small number of Merina were active enthusiasts of French rule, notably Rasanjy and the Catholic factions in the capital. The French, though, could have profited from an administrative inertia which was all to their benefit but which they steadily wasted. That is to say, most Merina government officials, especially in central Imerina, may not have wanted French administration but thought it wise to collaborate. They were after all part of the government machine which the French now controlled. Some recognized that if France did not underwrite the government there would soon be no government to speak of at all. Others realized the power of European arms. In any case there was little choice: village governors were dependent upon help from the government in Antananarivo, whatever its political colour, to protect them from the bandits and army deserters who were roaming the countryside, and who in some cases were inveterate opponents of successive regimes. In a conflict between the centre and the periphery officials of middle rank and above had little option but to side with the centre.

The French rapidly wasted this advantage out of dogmatism and ignorance of rural conditions. Ranchot discounted the stories of panic reported from villages all over the highlands. He considered that Rasanjy and Rainandriamampandry were satisfactory collaborators, and that seemed to be what mattered most.[7] For at least six months after the fall of Antananarivo political discussion among French officials was limited to administrative questions: on the merits of direct and indirect rule, on the exact responsibilities of civil and military authorities, on the extent to which Merina officials should be employed on the coast. Most village officials in Imerina continued to try and govern in the old way but were deprived by disarmament of the means of coercion.

The French expeditionary army began to disband and return to Europe as soon as the capital had fallen. By 15 January 1896 General Duchesne had at his disposal only 1,786 European troops, 828 Algerians and 1,811 Malagasy regulars. He had a further 3,800 Malagasy irregulars, remnants of the old royal army, of doubtful efficiency and loyalty, with the option of calling up the citizen militia.[8]

THE REVIVAL OF ANCESTRAL RELIGION

If there was one sentiment which all Merina had in common, it was a passionate patriotism, both for their local homeland and the kingdom at large. All, that is, except cynics like Rasanjy. It could be dressed in traditional garb or in the rhetoric of Christian nationalism. Already, as the Merina army crumbled before the French in mid-1895, many soldiers spoke about keeping their weapons, if they were lucky enough to have any, and of continuing the struggle against the French once Rainilaiarivony's government had fallen.[9]

In the meantime there was a spontaneous movement to restore some sort of order in place of the Christian government which lay in ruins. It took the form of the 'sifting time' which had been predicted, beginning in earnest slightly before the French landings at Majunga in January 1895. This was when Imerina, Betsileo-land and Antsihanaka were being scoured for army recruits. Wherever there were freemen in possession of their ancestral lands the sifting implied a restoration of ancestral religion. It formed a ready-made framework for reconstruction. Most Merina considered that the invasion had taken place because the Christian government lacked the supernatural force which could come only from observing ancestral forms and rituals. This feeling was summed up by the guardian of a talisman who quoted the words of a famous speech by Andrianampoinimerina:[10]

> This land . . . is the land of Andrianampoinimerina. Today it is profoundly humiliated. The reason for that is that the power of our royal talismans has

66

been destroyed by the Prayers brought from across the sea [i.e. Christianity]
. . . Let us now restore the talismans so that Andrianampoinimerina's words
should not be in vain: 'This land is mine, and I will permit no other to take it.'

A return to the customs and rituals of the ancestors promised to restore
not only the effectiveness of the central government but also the unity of
those demes which had been split by feuds between Christian and non-
Christian factions. The process of purifying each deme of its unwanted
elements began perhaps in 1894. There were several cases of a possession
cult similar to that which had preceded the downfall of King Radama II in
1863, and which was an unfailing sign of a deep and dangerous spiritual
uncertainty. Reports came from parts of the country which were widely
known as strongholds of ancestral religion. Western Imerina was curiously
subject to the cult in 1894.[11] In the pagan far south of Vakinisisaony too,
'when the natives were very upset by the political circumstances of the
country, there was a great revival . . . of the Ramanenjana, or the Dancing
mania'.[12] At Andranomiantra in Anativolo the people said the possession
was to keep away demons.[13]

As the French advanced towards the capital, reports of religious agitation
took on a more warlike and overtly political form. It was in July of 1895 that
Andrianony roused the troops outside the capital with his oratory. Nor was
his an isolated case. Much of the agitation of mid-1895 in central Imerina was
conducted by Protestant preachers, although by men of a lower standing in
the church than Andrianony. The *Times* correspondent reported in July
1895 that stories of European atrocities, not just French, were being spread
by 'mischievous agitators – *native pastors some of them*'.[14]

The talismans were seen in public for the first time since 1869. During the
week before the fall of Antananarivo, in late September 1895, the mighty
Kelimalaza reappeared, brought back from exile by Rambinintsoa in an
effort to save the kingdom. Again, many of those who encouraged a return
to the talismans in September and October of 1895 were former Christians.
'There is no doubt about it', one missionary observed, 'the whole of this
disturbance is nothing more nor less than the old heathen anti-European
spirit reasserting itself. It has been silent for a long time, and has even been
wearing Christian garments, but it has never actually been laid in the
grave.'[15]

The sort of agitators who had previously worn 'Christian garments'
appear to have been unofficial preachers of the type which had often been
identified as trouble-makers in the past. Many, we know, were also traders.
The most troublesome were rum-sellers, a class of trader which had good
reason to dislike the Church.[16] Reports dating from 1895 often refer to
traders or lapsed Christian preachers as though the two categories were
almost interchangeable. Markets, being places for gossip and the settlement
of local affairs, were frequently reported as centres of agitation. 'The most
of the lies and the false reports were brought to Anativolo and spread',
wrote a Merina evangelist, 'by wicked traders from Imerina.'[17]

As soon as Antananarivo had fallen the revival of ancestral religion was given considerable impetus. The Christian government had been found wanting and there was therefore no longer any obligation to attend church out of obedience to the queen. Furthermore there was no administration worthy of the name, and many people were convinced that order could lie only in the unity of their own family or commune. This view was reinforced by the disarmament of native governors, which put many local notables into an impossible position. Pastors found themselves shouted down or even attacked. Governors were disobeyed. All village officials were regarded as agents of the government which had fallen. Some were also convinced Christians, and some were highly unpopular because of their previous conduct. They were faced with a dilemma: to seek French help was distasteful for any patriot, and would incur the wrath of the villagers. To join the pagan revival was an act of insurrection by the standards of the old government, and might imply association with hostile families in those frequent cases where villages were split into pro- and anti-Christian factions.

Just as opposition to the old government had taken different forms in central Imerina and on the frontiers, so now did two distinct types of agitation appear. In most of the border districts, where Christianity was not strong, the collapse of government was hastened by the activities of bandits who could raid unchecked now that the French were disarming loyal officials. The bands of the Bara and Sakalava kings and the robber-chiefs were swollen by thousands of deserters from the royal army who had no home to go to. In Antsihanaka, for example, life had been disrupted even before September 1895 by the conscription of the whole male population in some villages. Everywhere people were in 'constant dread' of the raiders from the west: Marofotsy, Sakalava or nameless bandits. 'Village after village on the west border of the lake [Alaotra] have they swept away', one missionary wrote. Some Sihanaka villagers slept in the rushes by the lakeside to hide. The conviction was widespread, here too, that the old regime was at an end, and Christianity with it. By the end of October 1895 most Sihanaka had abandoned Christianity and reverted to the religion of their ancestors. The evangelists in Antsihanaka, all of them Merina, had gathered in the administrative capital of the province at Ambatondrazaka for protection. Amparafaravola and its church were burnt to the ground. Former preachers, like their counterparts nearer the capital, 'have openly interrupted the work in the Country Churches, going to the service on Sunday, and disputing with the preacher, denying and blaspheming the religion of Christ and ascribing all the nation's calamities to the cause of Religion'.[18] By the end of the year the road to Antananarivo had been closed by robbers.

There are several known examples of movements for the revival of ancestral religion in Imerina, having a distinctly violent anti-European and anti-Christian character, which simmered during September and October 1895.[19] When these occurred on the frontiers of Imerina they were often associated with bandit raids against Christian officials. On the other hand the places most often reported as centres of disturbances within lesser Imerina were either the sites where the talismans were traditionally kept or else the borders between neighbouring demes. The government had broken down so disputes between such neighbours were settled by force, often in rural market-places. Any deme which was not dominated by its Christian element restored the holy days of the talismans and all the panoply of the old astrological calendar.

The religious revival rose towards a climax as people prepared for the major feast of the year, *fandroana*, 'the custom of the earth and of heaven, the custom of the kingdom and the new year'.[20] This was the time when the ritual bath of the sovereign symbolized the renewal of the unity of each deme and its relation to the queen. Tradition required every Merina freeman to assemble at the tombs of his ancestors in the capital of his deme. Since 1883 the feast had been fixed on 22 November every year.

Many of the dissident movements reached their highest pitch on the day of the feast of the bath. More than one resulted in fierce disputes between Christians and non-Christians and between rival Christian sects representing hostile interests in local politics. One such dispute in Vakinankaratra province resulted in the death of a senior Lutheran pastor and about sixteen of his followers, caught in an ambush by rivals who adhered to an LMS congregation.[21] There were many similar incidents which have left little record. To understand the way in which the religious revival and the growth of banditry were transformed into an insurrectionary movement requires a detailed study of local politics in each case.

Many of these incidents were reported to the French authorities but only one attracted serious attention from officials, because it was on the scale of an insurrection and because it resulted in the deaths of three Europeans, the Johnson family at Arivonimamo, whose death is described in the introduction. It took place among the Zanakantitra, one of those old and proud demes which had such good reason to distrust the Christian government of Imerina. They were one of the many groups which began to revere their old talismans openly during 1895. When the news arrived that Antananarivo had fallen, the Zanakantitra were terrified by the rumours they heard. The reaction of most of them was to strengthen the unity of the deme, which meant restoring the rituals of the ancestors and affirming possession of their homeland. The Christians among them were treated with a hostility bordering on violence. The reason was largely ideological, but it was also aimed at particular officials. Some of the leading Church officers among the Zanakantitra had been heavily involved in administration of the gold-*corvée*,[22] while the pastor who warned the Johnsons of their forthcoming fate was a dishonest man who had been dismissed from one church for fraud.[23]

It was a dispute over land which led some settlements of the Zanakantitra into a dispute with their eastern neighbours the Efa-dreny, who regularly traded with them at the weekly market near Amboanana. Throughout the month of October 1895 there were clashes between the two demes every market-day, culminating in a full-scale riot on 30 October.[24]

The Zanakantitra were divided into two branches, whose traditional capitals were at Ramainandro and Amboanana. The leaders of the agitation at Amboanana were two brothers, Rainizafivoavy and Ibenahy, aged only twenty-five and sixteen. They were descended from the heroic ancestor Andrianjaza by a junior line.[25] Both had been pupils at the local Friends' school and had been conscripted to fight the French. They had deserted shortly before the fall of Antananarivo and had returned home to gather a band of dissidents, against whom the village governor was powerless. The Christian element among the Zanakantitra was led by Governor Radaniela of Ramainandro, who was a direct descendant of the same Andrianjaza. There was therefore competition between the two branches of the same deme, one predominantly Christian, led by Radaniela, the other non-Christian, led by the two brothers.

During October the agitation turned into a full religious revival. The two brothers changed their names to Rainisingomby and Ilaitangena, 'the father of the tethered ox' and 'the poison-man', both names evocative of old rituals. They held a series of mass meetings in honour of the talisman Ravololona, and sought ritual experts among their distant kinsmen the Tankaratra, who were renowned as diviners. By early November they had patched up the quarrel with the Efa-dreny and agreed that the real enemy was the Europeans and the Christians. On 14 November 1895 a meeting of all the eastern Zanakantitra swore to kill all foreigners and their allies. The evangelist of Amboanana, Rajaobelina, had by this time fled to seek refuge with the missionaries William and Lucy Johnson at Arivonimamo, two hours' march away. William Johnson sent a note to Antananarivo asking for troops to come and quell the disturbance. A party of twenty Malagasy soldiers led by the governor of Arivonimamo and a high-ranking officer duly arrived at Amboanana. There, on 21 November, they were killed by Zanakantitra dissidents. On 22 November 1895, the day of *fandroana*, a crowd well over one thousand strong arrived at the mission and killed the Johnsons and their little girl.

The rebels then turned west towards Ramainandro where their targets were the Reverend E. O. MacMahon and Governor Radaniela. They were met by Rainivazaha, a leading Zanakantitra official of the Isaha district in which Ramainandro lay. According to MacMahon, Rainivazaha had for some time been an associate of robbers and 'unsatisfactory characters' and had made an attempt on Radaniela's life two years before.[26] He had arranged in advance to meet the party from Amboanana and 'his spies', said MacMahon, 'had kept watch near my house for some days previous . . .' MacMahon was warned by Radaniela's brother-in-law, who knew of the conspiracy, and fled towards the Ankaratra mountains. There he and his family were captured by another party, probably of Tankaratra, who were heading to join the rising but had not yet heard of the Johnsons' death. MacMahon managed to escape on 23 November 1895.[27]

The rising did not last long. For two days the Zanakantitra scoured their lands for Christians, until they heard that there was a French force coming from Antananarivo. They rallied to fight at Antsahavola, on the slopes of Mount Fandravazana, a holy place of their tradition which was sacred to the talisman Ravololona and where they were joined by some Tankaratra kinsmen.[28] On 24 and 25 November the insurgents were defeated by the French forces. The rebels were inspired to great bravery by the blessing of Ravololona, but their knives and axes were no match for guns. For three weeks the French detachment hunted down and killed all connected with the rising in the belief that a show of force would stifle all thought of resistance in the rest of Imerina.

Clearly the rising was premeditated. It was openly discussed among the Zanakantitra from early November. Some said that the plan was to go to Antananarivo shortly after the feast of *fandroana*, but that it backfired because of the killings at Amboanana on 21 November. This possibility was certainly debated, but in fact the insurgents showed themselves far more concerned to cleanse their territory of Christians and other undesirables, as they considered them, than to precipitate a national rising. Whether it was planned to start on the day of *fandroana* is less clear, but that was evidently the most auspicious day to begin such a thing. One source said it was due to start on 25 November, another that the signal was to be the death of the first European or royal officer.

Almost every witness agreed that the insurrection was chiefly an affair of the Zanakantitra. Elements of other demes, such as nearby settlements of the Maromena and Zanakambony, or distant kinsmen like the Tankaratra, had also played a part. The Efa-dreny had participated rather unwillingly. Almost every Zanakantitra outside Ramainandro had joined in, including village officials.[29] But of the 600 Anglican communicants at Ramainandro only three participated in the burning of the church, while the rest 'suffered severe persecution from the rebel leaders'.[30] Where there is sufficient evidence to draw a sharp distinction between insurgents and loyalists, the crucial division is between demes or groups who had settled the land at different times or in different circumstances. Such is the case of Ramainandro and Amboanana. But even the Christians of Ramainandro could hardly be called French collaborators. Their patriotism was simply expressed in terms acceptable to Christians, for there the rumour spread that the French would be driven out by British troops led by MacMahon, Radaniela and Rainijaonary, the Lutheran commander of Vakinankaratra![31]

It is notable that the Zanakantitra insurgents did not threaten to drive the Europeans from Madagascar but had the far more limited aim of purging their lands of foreigners and their allies, that is to say Christians. The same is true of other movements in Imerina which came to a climax around the time of the feast of the bath. The Zanakantitra were not clear about whether they were taking part in a local or a national rising; or, to be be more accurate, the question was not relevant. One of the insurgents later said that Rainisingomby 'had intended to proclaim the independence of the region and to have himself proclaimed King of Ankaratra'.[32] The best account of their aspirations was given by an anonymous participant in the rising when he described the position after the massacre of the royal soldiers on 21 November 1895 but before the murder of the Johnsons:[33]

> After their death, Rainisingomby spoke as follows: 'Here are the words of the Queen. The population of Avaradrano is ordered to kill Europeans, evangelists, pastors, school-masters and all who call themselves Christian. The same orders apply to the people of Marovatana and Sisaony. The people of Antananarivo are to kill all enemies in their district. We in Ambodirano are ordered to kill all enemies whom we find in our province. Those who do not obey this order of the Queen will have their goods confiscated and their lives forfeited.'

This is the first suggestion that the Zanakantitra had any intimation of activities in the other provinces of Imerina or of orders from the queen. It reflects closely the traditional ideology of Imerina, which portrayed the kingdom as a federation of autonomous demes whose unity lay in their common allegiance to the monarch and the national rituals. If the old order were to be restored, then it was the duty of every deme to purify its own territory. Every province would thus participate simultaneously in the movement of national renewal. The ties of kinship could co-ordinate activities in one area but could not raise the whole population. Only the sovereign could perform such a function, and Rainisingomby therefore presumed that it was her wish. Some rebels tried to persuade a loyalist governor to join them by saying that they were 'carrying the queen's orders to kill Europeans', and that 'those at Antananarivo will kill the foreigners there'. When the governor asked to see these orders he was told that 'there are no written orders, but messengers came from high up'.[34]

The principal military threat to the French authorities in late 1895 came from the banditry on Imerina's frontiers. Most administrators dismissed it as a recurrence of a familiar problem, which indeed it was, but they failed to notice a new element which had been brought by the army deserters. Many bandits, it should be recalled, were originally Merina who had fled from the Christian government. They now saw a chance to reclaim the lands and status which they had lost in earlier years, and to replace the government which had humiliated them. It gave them a greater degree of political consciousness than in previous years.

The rising of the Zanakantitra however was indicative of a different type of agitation, that which took place in lesser Imerina on the homelands of the old-established demes who sought to revive an authentic ideology. All the dissidents arose from a spontaneous movement. They acted with what they hoped was one accord but without central direction, like dancers without music. They took as their common timetable for action the traditional calendar and the rhythms of the agricultural year. This was the most important aspect of the religious revival from the 'point of view of an insurrectionary organization. There was no need for any conspirator to fix a date for patriotic demonstrations, because it was obvious to any Merina in contact with his or her traditions that the feast of the bath was an ideal time.

MOVEMENTS OUTSIDE IMERINA

French administrators had hardly begun to consider the implications of the Zanakantitra rising in western Imerina before another threat to their policy had arisen in a very different form. Many of the non-Merina peoples who were under the yoke of Antananarivo took the impending fall of the capital during 1895 as a signal to rise against Merina authority. While the French were still advancing on Antananarivo some Antankarana and Tsimihety kings who had long flirted with both France and Imerina decided that the time was ripe to attack the governor of Vohemar, the main agent of the royal government in the far north of the island. In other parts of the far north revolt was sparked off by the demand for conscripts to fight against the French. These were affairs of minor skirmishes and cattle-raiding.[35]

In Betsileo-land the independence movement took a religious form, although there was no significant revival of ancestral religion. In some parts, Betsileo seeking to escape the Merina-dominated churches followed a Christian syncretic movement. The fall of Antananarivo was hailed almost as though it were a Betsileo victory. Soldiers returning home spread the word that the French would allow a large measure of self-government. There was a wave of pro-Catholic and anti-Merina feeling especially among 'the poor ignorant country folks', as one Briton put it, who reasoned that since the French were now in control, they would surely rule through the Catholic Church. Some went as far as to burn down Protestant temples or to raise the French flag in their churchyard. At Ambositra it was said that the French would kill or exile all Protestants, and that Roman Catholic church-men would be exempt from government service just as the Protestant officials had been under the old regime. Some Betsileo schoolteachers flouted the authority of their Merina evangelists to the extent of forming their own police forces to maintain the independence of the local congregation. Such reactions were caused largely by the Merina governors' and evangelists' attempts to force their subjects to attend state-controlled churches and schools as before.

A good example of the problems created by Church disputes is provided by the village of Ambohimahazo, on the borders of Imerina and Betsileo-land. The people here had for years been under the supervision of an unpopular LMS evangelist, a Merina. In October 1895, as soon as news arrived that the French had taken Antananarivo, the congregation promptly declared itself to be Catholic, and therefore outside his control. They claimed the right to keep their church building. The case was referred to the

Merina minister in Antananarivo responsible for Church affairs. He ordered that the building should be given to those who had constructed it. The governor of nearby Ambositra, a pillar of the old state Church, decided that this meant he should give charge of Ambohimahazo church to the same LMS evangelist. The decision was not popular with the parishioners.[36]

It was apparent that in hundreds of Betsileo villages the old government had functioned almost entirely through the churches and schools. If the French were to have enforced their protectorate to the letter, they should logically have continued to use the Protestant establishment as an organ of government. No French administration could do this, especially when the Protestant churches were so closely associated with British influence. Besides, there was a thorny legal problem. The church at Ambohimahazo, for example, had cost twelve piastres to build, of which seven had been given by one local notable. It had been built by forced labour. Did the church then belong to the evangelist in whose district it lay, as the governor of Ambositra claimed? Or to the person who had subscribed the most to its construction? Or to the congregation who had built it, probably unwillingly, with their own hands?[37]

Yet another scene of unrest in the closing months of 1895 was the eastern littoral of the island, from Maroantsetra in the north to Farafangana some 300 miles further south. Among the Antemoro and Antaisaka the long-standing dispute between nobles and commoners flared up once more in the early months of 1895. Ill-feeling was equally directed against the system of forced labour and compulsory attendance at church. All over the east coast the fall of Antananarivo was a signal for the settling of old scores. Among the Betsimisaraka there were attacks upon Merina settlers and officials and their henchmen, including church officers. British missionaries realized for the first time 'how fully we have been associated with Hova [i.e. Merina] in the minds of the people'.[38]

Most observers considered these troubles to be an anti-Merina rising which began spontaneously when news arrived that the old government had fallen. But the risings among the Betsimisaraka and Vorimo can be traced to one incident.[39] In early October 1895 Ramanivorahona, the Merina governor of Ambodinivato, was robbed of 25,000 francs. He complained to his superior officer, Governor Rainisolofo of Mahanoro, who had an unrivalled reputation for rapaciousness among Europeans and Malagasy alike. He was said to have under his command eight lieutenant-governors, plus a personal retinue of 120 soldiers and eighty merchants and money-lenders. He had amassed a fortune by controlling all the retail trade of his province. Some of his unfortunate subjects were forced to do unpaid labour on fields that Rainisolofo had taken from them in the first place. He thus employed up to 200 unpaid labourers on his vanilla plantations alone.[40]

Following his complaint, Ramanivorahona returned to Ambodinivato. It was a village inhabited by the Vorimo, who had a well-established tradition of opposition to the government. He began torturing the villagers to discover where his money was. They rose in revolt, and the movement spread very rapidly among all the Vorimo, the inland Betsimisaraka and the outlaw bands around Anosibe-an-Ala. In less than a month it had taken hold of the entire east-central coast. The troubles continued virtually unchecked until the arrival of French forces and the astute civilian administrator Dr Besson in mid-December 1895.

In some places the insurgents included Merina army deserters. Of thirty-eight rebel leaders named at Anosibe-an-Ala, two were Merina.[41] The rising was so unorganized and so dependent on local conditions that reports were often contradictory. Some bands attacked under the banner of Queen Ranavalona, while others carried the French tricolour. Some killed church-men indiscriminately, while others spared non-Merina.

Only among the Antemoro and Antaisaka, where the indigenous social hierarchy was under attack, were the bands almost always led by hereditary notables. Elsewhere the leaders were of very diverse backgrounds. They certainly included many village headmen, but also the leaders of outlaw bands which had existed in the forest before 1895.[42] There were reliable reports of participation by French and British creoles. Foulpointe was occupied for a time by a band led by Bakary, a native of the French colony of Mayotte who had served with the police of the French vice-residence at Tamatave. He used his impressive-looking official papers to convince the illiterate Betsimisaraka that he had orders from the French to lead them against the Merina. His colleagues included a French citizen of Saint-Marie and another former policeman and trader from Mayotte. Near Mahéla the insurgents were led by two French mulattos, Jean-Régis Behr and Joseph-Paul Befalaka. They were in league with a full-blooded Frenchman called Desmarez and another French citizen, Pervanche, later to be an official interpreter. This motley crew was said to have encouraged the original Vorimo rising against Rainisolofo. The French-language newspapers of Tamatave hailed such men as nationalists.[43]

Many other bands thought that their actions were approved by the French authorities. One man claimed, perhaps even believed, that he had received a letter from Dr Besson ordering him to kill the Merina.[44] Others too were misled by 'a few Merina and Betsimisaraka who showed them letters bearing the stamp of the Residency – any letters would suffice – containing spurious orders to raise taxes in our name'.[45] But the insurgents were not averse to destroying French plantations as well as Merina ones. The old Madagascar hands among the French knew that this was more than just a tribal war.

The climax of the rising on the east coast coincided with the arrival of the first permanent resident-general of the new protectorate, Hippolyte Laroche. He immediately and consistently reported to the colonial ministry that the eastern insurgents were pro-French, 'always claiming allegiance to France and claiming to be under orders from French agents, scrupulously respecting white men and their property'.[46] Many French soldiers found it most distasteful to have to punish the insurgents whom they considered to be performing a useful task in clearing the corrupt Merina administration off the coast. Laroche was aware of the pressure to dismantle the old Merina colonial system, and he tried just a little too hard to appear fair to this shade of opinion.

Already there were poor relations between different groups of French policy-makers, military and civil, Catholic and Protestant, both in Madagascar and Paris. These disagreements became sharper as a result of an incident on the east coast which became a minor *cause célèbre*. A certain Captain Freystatter ordered the execution of forty-nine insurgents who had surrendered to him under a promise of clemency on 17 January 1896. Laroche, newly arrived but already disturbed by the brutality used in putting down the rising at Amboanana, lodged an official complaint about Freystatter. It was transmitted to the minister of war in Paris in person.[47]

Clearly the east coast was in a state of anarchy and, as the experienced vice-president Ferrand at Tamatave remarked, there was little choice for the moment but to confirm the Merina administration while trying to curb its worst excesses. Conflicting views on the subject contributed to the continuation of the eastern rising well into 1896, and to a notable cooling in the pro-French sentiment of the Betsimisaraka.

The risings among the Antankarana and the peoples of the east coast, and the troubles in Betsileo-land, were quite different in character from the agitation in Imerina which is the principal subject of this study. In some cases their main aim was to destroy Merina power, while in others the movements were really civil wars waged around local issues. These events deserve studies of their own. They took place in the outer circles of Merina power, in places whose political traditions and dynamics outweighed any sentiment of loyalty to the government in Antananarivo. At this early stage, the only agitation which aimed to restore power to the sovereigns of Imerina took place further inland, led by those who were soon to choose for themselves the name *menalamba*.

4

The rising of the *menalamba* (December 1895 to October 1896)

Shall we always live under the rule of these Nebuchadnezzars? People of Madagascar, will you always be like the grass-snake which is crushed under foot?

Anonymous Merina itinerant preacher

THE APPROACH OF ALAHAMADY

The risings on the east coast in late 1895 caused French officials to look again at the idea of a protectorate policy. The popular French interpretation of the Zanakantitra rising at Amboanana was also to the effect that the Merina oligarchy was not to be trusted. This opinion was widespread because people had heard echoes of Rainisingomby's claim to have received orders from the queen. 'Everyone', a French priest wrote, 'thinks that the real leaders of the revolt are in Antananarivo.'[1] This was not quite true. None of the British missionaries believed that the leaders were in the capital. More importantly neither did Ranchot, nor Laroche who replaced him at the head of the civil administration in January 1896.

Most Malagasy seem to have understood instinctively the nature of the rising of the Zanakantitra. Unlike most Europeans they had a deep knowledge of the traditions and symbols which Rainisingomby had invoked. Agitators all over Imerina observed the progress of the insurrection and took its message to heart. East of the capital a French priest saw a letter addressed to the Zanakantitra telling them that 'no action should be taken *yet*', as though something were being planned. He thought that the leader must therefore be 'a magnate'.[2] At the holy town of Ambohimanga some people said openly that the Zanakantitra should have waited for some sort of indication of a general rising. There were other rumours and letters in circulation elsewhere saying that the time was not yet ripe.[3]

Discontent began to assume a more organized form in accordance with the two main strands of opposition which had emerged in the previous decades. The warlords on Imerina's frontiers, who had assembled private armies for self-defence against outlaws, found that the recruitment of deserted soldiers left them in a position of strength in relation to regular government troops. This was true of Rainijaonary and Rabezavana. But it was not yet clear whether the marcher-lords would use their military power for or against France. When a government emissary toured Valalafotsy in November 1895 he was courteously received by the leading notables,

Laimiza and Rajamaria, although they were gathering large numbers of soldiers.[4]

In central Imerina, where there were fewer weapons in circulation, isolated pagan movements began to combine as the religious revival gathered momentum. Anti-Christian and anti-European disturbances in the south of Vakinisisaony were motivated by Kelimalaza, the talisman which Rambinintsoa had faithfully guarded since 1869. The holy man and his talisman made a brief appearance in the capital in late September 1895, shortly before it fell to the French. Rambinintsoa then returned south to gather support for the restoration of Kelimalaza. In December 1895 he was reported to be only fifteen kilometres from Antananarivo, and he addressed a meeting of 500 people. 'Rakelimalaza', he declared to the talisman in front of the multitude, 'now is the time to show your strength as the French are going to take the land of our ancestors.'[5] Everywhere that Kelimalaza was shown in Vakinisisaony, gatherings swore anti-European oaths.

It was also in the closing months of 1895 that the cult of Kelimalaza took on a more warlike aspect. Many villagers from the south who had fled the gold-*corvée* in recent years had sought refuge with the outlaws Rainibet-simisaraka and Ratsizehena. The two chiefs seem to have joined forces some time early in 1895. Ratsizehena, although he was now a fugitive, was related to some of the most venerable demes of Vakinisisaony. The fall of the Christian government enabled him to approach his former kinsmen once more since the regime which had outlawed him had fallen. It was probably through his mediation that Rambinintsoa and Rainibetsimisaraka met in 1895 and swore the oath of brotherhood of blood. In the eyes of the traditionalists in Vakinisisaony the robbers now had a new status. They were no longer outside the pale of the kingdom since they had been blessed by none other than Kelimalaza. Rainibetsimisaraka and his followers, said to number 2,000 by early 1896, now had a network of kinsmen and allies from Betsileo-land to Ambohimanambola, which was within sight of Antananarivo. They were more than strong: they were possessed of holy power.

So great was the threat from the former outlaws in the south that by December 1895 the road from Antsirabe to the capital was almost impass-able. The vital supply-route from Tamatave to Antananarivo was likewise threatened, in this case by Betsimisaraka insurgents moving inland in search of plunder. Most of the Merina governors were without troops or weapons. In the north too the road to Ambatondrazaka was 'really dangerous'.[6]

Northern Imerina in general showed less widespread evidence of the pagan revival. It did not possess a talisman of the same universal appeal as Rambinintsoa's version of Kelimalaza. When there were attacks on churches or churchmen in the north they were usually in areas settled by demes who were in some sense marginal, such as the Manendy of Anativolo and the Zafimamy. In the mission district of Ambatonakanga many churches were troubled, but only one had disbanded entirely by the end of 1895. The trouble here arose from a hereditary fief-holder who was 'one of the "leaders" of the small congregation'. This man was conscripted to fight the French in early 1895,

> and on his return from the 'Front' after the defeat, he set on the pastor, struck and wounded him and drove him bleeding from the church along with his small congregation, and then unroofed the chapel, broke the pulpit to pieces, tore the Bible to pieces and threatened the life of the pastor . . . or of anyone who dared to set up the 'White man's religion', which, he said, had been the cause of all their troubles, there again.[7]

The most significant religious revival in the north took place among the Mandiavato. In November 1895 there were persistent reports of the restoration of talismans in all the villages around Ambohibemasoandro. The ringleader in November was said to be Randriantsimahatahotra, a village governor who kept a talisman in his house and was threatening to poison all the Frenchmen in Antananarivo. He was shortly arrested, along with a rich and unpopular man called Ramahafinaritra of Analaroa, who had been accused of extortion. The people of Analaroa were overjoyed by the removal of Ramahafinaritra, and ransacked his property. But the agitation among the Mandiavato continued, led by the guardians of talismans and by some governors. Village officials who recommended calm were shouted down. The governors who carried the people with them were those who argued that they should resist the interference of central government, exemplified by the arrest of Randriantsimahatahotra. They said that an acceptance of the new government would certainly result in heavier labour-dues. Again the dissidents claimed to have high-level contacts in the capital, although they showed no interest in the new prime minister appointed by the French and agreed that Rainilaiarivony 'well deserved the punishment which he has received'.[8]

The agitation in northern Imerina soon produced strong leaders who were able to unite the disparate local movements. Unlike in the south, where the leaders were mostly outlaw chiefs or traditional holy men, the northern organizers included a fair number of royal officials. The most prominent in the north-east was Rabozaka, one of the children of that marriage alliance between the Zafimamy and the Mandiavato which had united several generations of settlers. Born in about 1870, Rabozaka had received a church education in Antananarivo and had for some time been a preacher and 'apparently earnest in promoting church work'.[9] By 1895 he had become a middle-ranking army officer of his native village of Mandanja. During the French advance on Antananarivo he was ordered to join a party of more senior officers sent to raise conscripts, and in this capacity he toured north-east Madagascar from June until October 1895. Perhaps it was then that he first considered organizing his own resistance to the French. Some reports say that he stole cattle belonging to Ramahafinaritra who, it will be recalled, had been arrested, and that he entered upon a revolt when ordered to return the animals. Certainly at the end of November 1895 Rabozaka refused to surrender his weapons to a government emissary and instead contacted two other dissident officials further west, Rabezavana and Ratsimamanga. A trader who had come from the southern Mandiavato heard at Christmas 1895 that 'there was a national movement to the north of Anjozorobe. I saw people buying guns.'[10] It may therefore be presumed that Rabozaka was actively organizing an insurrection before the end of that year.

It is not recorded whether Rabozaka had ever met Rabezavana before 1895 but he must have heard of him. Rabezavana was born in 1852 into a senior family of the Marofotsy, a wild and lawless people. He had risen to power by his ability to organize and protect his kinsmen both from bandit-raids and from unscrupulous administrators. In 1895 the royal government ordered Rabezavana to join an army sent against the French. Refusing to serve under any of the magnates of Antananarivo, he led his own contingent to the front. He was so utterly disgusted by the corruption of the royal army that he returned to his headquarters at Antsatrana, where he welcomed deserters into his private army.

By early December 1895 Rabezavana was in contact with yet another of the future northern leaders, Rafanenitra, who was a noble of the Zanadralambo, born and bred at Andranomasina in the province of Marovatana. Before 1895 he was at one time a trader on the east coast but had made little money from the venture. Shortly after the feast of the bath in 1895 Rafanenitra left his village to organize resistance to the French among the Manendy and Zanadralambo in particular. He met Rabezavana, and they agreed to organize an insurrection together.[11] Rabezavana's contribution to the partnership included a considerable military force and expertise, his followers being equipped with Snider breech-loading rifles. He had relatives among the Marofotsy raiders and great influence with the Tsimahafotsy garrisons of the frontier, which were to join the rising almost to a man. His wife was from Anativolo, probably a Manendy. Rabezavana also had useful contacts with the royal house of the Sakalava kingdoms of Boina.

The names of Rabezavana and Rafanenitra were frequently linked with that of Ratsimamanga, fief-holder of Analaroa and a vital link in the chain of the nascent confederation. It was reported on 23 December 1895 that Ratsimamanga was already in league with Rabezavana and was planning to attack the French at the end of rice-planting.[12] Analaroa was significant because it was the northernmost village of Tsimahafotsy proper, forming a frontier with the *valonjatolahy*, the Zafimamy and the less settled areas of the north. Ratsimamanga was an elder of a northern branch of the Andriamasinavalona, a distant descendant of the dynasty of Andrianampoinimerina, a man with family connections all over the north. His rival for influence in Analaroa was the same Ramahafinaritra whom the government had arrested in early December 1895 to general satisfaction. Thus when the government tried to reclaim Ramahafinaritra's cattle from Rabozaka and from the people of Analaroa, the effect was worse than if they had left him in place. The arrest had given Ratsimamanga a free hand in

Analaroa while the reclaiming of the cattle dissipated any goodwill from which the government might have benefited.

The insurrectionary organization in the north had two main sets of organizers, represented by Rabezavana and Rafanenitra on the one hand and Ratsimamanga and Rabozaka on the other. They seem to have prepared independently of one another until December 1895. It was inevitable that the two elements should eventually make contact, for throughout the later months of the year all the north-east was subject to very heavy depredation by the Marofotsy raiding for cattle and by roving bands of army deserters. The only person in the north with sufficient military power to control them was Rabezavana. Throughout December 1895 and January 1896 he worked to recruit the wilder of the Marofotsy in the national movement. His technique was to promise them booty and the opportunity of revenge on Rabeony, the governor-general of Ambatondrazaka, who was very unpopular for his exactions.

In late January or early February 1896 Rafanenitra, Rabozaka, Rabezavana and Ratsimamanga met at Analaroa. It was here that they decided on a programme for the rising. They swore the oath of brotherhood, and henceforth they sometimes addressed one another as kinsmen.[13] They decided to attack Rabeony in Ambatondrazaka, because he was the most powerful loyalist influence in the north and because this would be the best way of recruiting the outlaws and the independent Marofotsy to the patriotic cause.

The decision had the desired effect. In early February 1896 Ramenamaso, the most important of the independent Marofotsy chiefs, told two French gold-prospectors that he could no longer restrain the headstrong young men in his village. There had recently been a great meeting of all the Marofotsy, he said, and they had agreed to go and join Rabozaka at Mandanja.[14]

Governor Rabeony, meanwhile, had decided to nip the rising in the bud, knowing that Rabezavana was heading east against him with a force of several hundred Manendy, Sakalava, Marofotsy and army deserters. Rabeony's son defeated Ramenamaso in one engagement. At the very beginning of March 1896 Rabeony sent another force towards the rebel concentration at Mandanja. It was defeated, leaving thirty dead on the battlefield.[15] There could be no turning back now.

An insurrectionary organization developed very rapidly in the closing months of 1895. The dissidents of every province in Imerina had re-established the old channels of kinship and ritual through which a rising could be organized. In most cases people thought that by purging their deme of undesirable elements they would restore the harmony of olden days. Sometimes they attacked Christians and swore solemn oaths to keep the homeland pure, both the local homeland and the national one. This movement eventually produced leaders who were able to use the religious revival in the service of a broader strategy. The nationalist confederations of north and south were essentially a junction of religious dissidents with outlaws. They were held together by patriotism. The outlaws and deserters brought weapons and the experience of guerrilla warfare. The talismans and religious leaders provided the guarantee that the insurgents were not bandits but patriots, as they were frequently at pains to point out. The extent to which the patriotic cause involved rejecting Christianity and European influence varied considerably from one social group to another, as did the popular conception of the nation and the state.

One theme common to all the insurgents was their revival of traditional astrology, closely connected with the talismans. The leaders had therefore to seek a date for their rising which would be both suitable for campaigning and judged to be auspicious by the diviners. Many people thought it natural that a full-scale rising should begin after the end of rice-planting, about the end of March. French intelligence reports from as early as January 1896 maintained that some holy men, guardians of provincial talismans, were urging a rising on the first day of the lunar month of Alahamady.[16] Although it is rare to find such precise evidence that a rising was being planned for a specific date, it is nonetheless plain from later events that in dozens of places agitators were urging that action should commence on the first day of Alahamady. In the Merina system of divination Alahamady is both the name of the first month of the year and also of an astrological destiny, rather like a sign of the zodiac. Such a destiny might prevail over a person's life by reason of the time and place of his or her birth – as was the case with King Andrianampoinimerina, said to have been born on the first day of Alahamady – or over an event. Alahamady was clearly the most auspicious period for a movement of national renewal. For, according to tradition:

> Alahamady is a noble period, the time of the sovereign, the time dedicated to the *fandroana* of monarch and people, when the sovereign may accomplish his projects . . . It is the period of the most powerful destiny, and that is why the sovereigns have chosen it. Alahamady is the most auspicious of all destinies, and is also the one which gives dignity and strength, thanks to which any task may be carried out.[17]

In 1896 the first day of Alahamady was due to fall on 14 March by the Gregorian calendar.[18]

THE RISING IN THE NORTH

Incredible as it may seem, the agitation in Imerina before February 1896 was not considered serious by the senior French officials in Antananarivo. Ranchot's final report to Paris, written on 16 January 1896, concluded that 'in general, the situation in Imerina is fairly satisfactory', but that changes were needed in the administrative structure of the Betsimisaraka and Betsileo.[19] Laroche, his successor, hardly had time to learn his job before being caught up in administrative and personal quarrels. General Duchesne too left in January 1896 and General Voyron, his replacement as chief of the army, used the same unfortunate expression: 'the political situation is fairly satisfactory'.[20] One has the impression that they were almost the only people in Madagascar who thought so. Certainly many Frenchmen thought that their chiefs were being deceived by the Merina, who were generally held by Europeans of the day to be a cunning and deceitful people.

Most of the leading Merina politicians were indeed aware that a rising was in the air, but they were concerned above all to turn it to their own advantage. The atmosphere was already thick with stories of conspiracy when on 14 February 1896 the queen and a group of courtiers including Rainandriamampandry showed Laroche a treacherous letter, soon dubbed 'The Ambohimanga letter'. It was written in the queen's name and called upon the governor of Ambohimanga to organize a revolt. The letter was undoubtedly forged by one or another of the rival factions in the capital, but Laroche's dismissal of the episode did nothing to improve his reputation for gullibility among the French.[21]

Among the Merina, the sifting time was now at hand. In loyalist areas churches began to fill again in February and March 1896, often because local governors had warned that they would suppress the talismans by force. The faithful were comforted by sermons based on Exodus, Jeremiah or Isaiah, telling how God's chosen people were undergoing a time of trial. The themes could be interpreted as having a more political meaning. When the Reverend Richard Baron took as his text in March 1896 the story of the raising of Lazarus it was vilified by some Frenchmen as 'anti-French propaganda', 'hate-filled diatribes' or 'calls to revolt', which was how it was seen by some Malagasy too.[22]

The rising erupted in full force in mid-March 1896. On 11 March Rabezavana captured 1,200 of Rabeony's cattle which were being driven to Imerina for safety. His men, over 2,000 strong, advanced to besiege the loyalist stronghold at Ambatondrazaka and on 22 March 1896 they killed ninety of Rabeony's troops in a pitched battle. A Frenchman trapped in Ambatondrazaka realized that 'we are no longer dealing with bands of brigands, but with insurgents who declare plainly that they do not recognize French sovereignty and who wish to expel all foreigners. They have a rudimentary command structure and are well armed.'[23] Many other Europeans also noted the sudden entry of a sophisticated political element into the activities of former outlaws. This is what distinguished those who came to be called *menalamba* from the other resisters encountered by the French in their conquest of Madagascar. The *menalamba* may be defined as those who fought in the name of the kingdom of Imerina or the kingdom of Madagascar in the aftermath of the invasion. They were mostly, but not exclusively, Merina.

The transformation from disorder to a national rising centred upon the first day of Alahamady, 14 March 1896. An evangelist in Anativolo saw his village surrounded by insurgents on 12 March, but much to his surprise they waited until after the start of the month of Alahamady to attack.[24] Among the Mandiavato, Rabozaka's people, word spread from the beginning of

March that Rabozaka would rise at the beginning of Alahamady, and that schools were to be destroyed and patriotic oaths sworn at that time. On 15 March 1896 Rabozaka duly held a mass meeting near Mandanja, attended mainly by people of the *valonjatolahy* and the Zafimamy. Loyalists and insurgents alike saw it as the start of a national rising. Rabozaka called his followers *tia-tanindrazana*, 'lovers of the homeland'. They were also called *menalamba*, 'red shawls', because they stained their clothes with the holy red earth of Madagascar. They swore oaths to serve no ruler except a descendant of Andrianampoinimerina, to reject Christianity, and to spurn what Rabozaka called '*ny sivilizesona Frantsay*' ('French civilization').[25] Among other assemblies of the Mandiavato the oaths sworn were rather more specific. They included the restoration of the talismans at the expense of Christianity, and a refusal to attend school, do forced labour, or perform military service.

If there can be said to have been an immediate cause of the rising of Alahamady it was the rumour that labour dues would be increased and that people would be dispossessed of the land of their ancestors and enslaved or killed. Some said that the new government would also abolish slavery and suppress the institution of fief-holders. The French were puzzled by these rumours since the army had behaved very correctly in the early months of the protectorate, and there had not yet been any opportunity to enforce sweeping changes. The only explanation seemed to be that these rumours were 'planted among the people by the chiefs', perhaps even by British agents.[26] The French could not believe the truth, which was that the most prominent motive in the mass meetings of Alahamady was patriotism, pure and simple.

Estimates of Rabozaka's strength varied between 1,000 and 5,000 people, although one evangelist thought that 'not a fourth part of the people have really any sympathy with the rebellion, but only assented from fear of being killed'.[27] Contingents from each village were led mostly by the guardians of local talismans and by minor officials, and included a number of former LMS preachers. Their armament was said to include a cannon and at least 750 breech-loaders, plus some old flintlock guns. Rabozaka's plan seems to have been to head for the capital in concert with Rabezavana, but he also had to deal with Ambatondrazaka which was both a threat from the rear and a prize which would keep the Marofotsy and the other less disciplined elements with his cause. Accordingly, for most of the next six months his forces were divided, one section besieging Ambatondrazaka and the rest pushing south towards Antananarivo. Rabezavana was faced with the same problem. It was only his Tsimahafotsy allies who were keen to drive towards Ambohimanga and Antananarivo, which were central to their idea of the state.

While anarchy reigned in a hundred northern villages the northern triumvirate of Rabozaka, Rabezavana and Rafanenitra did their best to co-ordinate the encirclement of Antananarivo. They did this by making contact with leaders in other parts of Imerina who had not yet committed themselves to the resistance, or who had acted in isolation.

There was no hope of a close siege of Antananarivo. A blockade could be achieved only by cutting the capital off from the rice-growing provinces and from the port of Tamatave. Here they met with encouraging success. By May 1896 Rabozaka had established contact with other dissidents south of the capital and was to harry convoys from the coast so successfully that in June 1896 Antananarivo received only one-tenth of the volume of imported goods it needed. At Ambatondrazaka government troops were deserting to the *menalamba* at a rate of over fifty per day. Rabezavana and Rafanenitra moved west to raise the province of Vonizongo in perhaps the best-executed movement of the campaign. They began by raiding the province to burn churches. Laroche described the plan:[28]

> [Rabezavana's] invasion revealed the strategy of a calculated plan, speedily carried out. Handwritten proclamations, pinned to walls during the night or slipped under doors by anonymous messengers, were distributed and called for a show of patriotism . . .'Woe to the Malagasy who, seduced by sweet words, or corrupted by French silver, makes himself the accomplice of these foreigners.'

It was the noble fief-holders who provided the backbone of the *menalamba* in Vonizongo. Only one of any importance refused to support the rising. Of a total of about 235 fief-holders in the province, all but seventy were still with the *menalamba* as late as February 1897.[29] On Thursday 11 June 1896 a force of insurgents which had just killed four Frenchmen invaded the main market at Ambohipihaonana, the capital of Vonizongo. They sought out the unfortunate man who had replaced Rainibanona as governor-general and killed him and his officers. This was done close to a French garrison which responded to pleas for help with an order to go home and remain calm. Forty or fifty churches were burnt 'and all evangelists and pastors hunted for their lives'.[30] The last loyalist stronghold between Antananarivo and Majunga was in the hands of the *menalamba*.

The fall of Vonizongo opened up new possibilities for the northern confederation. On 20 July 1896 the governor-general of Marovatana was shot dead in a crowded market, and the whole province was on the verge of rising. Rafanenitra travelled west to make contact with the western notables Laimiza, Rajamaria and Rataizambahoaka, who had valuable connections among the Sakalava. They had already gathered considerable numbers of followers but had not so far moved onto the offensive. They in turn moved east to enlist the unarmed Merina of Mamolakazo, their opponents in many a cattle-raid. Such was the strength of the patriotic ideal that it was thus possible 'to see allied . . . the traditional pillagers of the region and their habitual victims'.[31] They were joined by none other than Rainsingomby, the veteran leader of the 1895 rising at Amboanana. They were stopped from raising all the country west of the capital only by the militia led by Governor Radaniela of Ramainandro, one of the few native officials to be entrusted with arms thanks to his loyalty during the Amboanana affair. Rainijaonary and his brother gave crucial help to Radaniela. It was not the first time that they put down a rising almost unaided, because a sympathetic French civilian administrator allowed them a free hand.

It was in the north that the rising was most successful in enlisting the old administration and in combining the revival of traditional cults with a vision of Malagasy nationalism clearly influenced by European techniques. It had, wrote Paul Bourde, the secretary-general of the government, 'a much more clearly defined political character than the rising in the south'.[32] Thus when the evangelist captured in Anativolo was taken to a rebel camp, he found that the leader's son was 'an old friend of mine before the rebellion'.[33] He and his brother found that 'it was urged by some of the leaders, who were secretly friendly to them, that the brothers should be employed as secretaries, to send out the commandants' letters and orders to the other camps'.[34] The same leaders told the two brothers that the pagan ceremonies were purely a formality, and that they could keep their Christian beliefs in private.

The northern movement did not have a talisman of the stature of Kelimalaza, nor a holy man of a political influence to equal that of Rambinintsoa. The northern guardians of the talismans had a role as ritual experts rather than warlords. The essential religious ceremonies consisted in invoking the power of the ancestors and in swearing allegiance to the royal line of Imerina and the sacred earth of Madagascar. Many who joined the movement changed their names, as was the custom when an important event took place. Most chose names evocative of old rituals or of prowess in battle. Rabezavana and Rabozaka were known after the first day of Alahamady as Ravaikafo and Ramasoandromahamay, 'Mr Glowing Ember' and 'Mr Burning Sun'. Others adopted less traditional names such as Ramasiaka, 'Mr Fierce'. Randriamisaodray, a former LMS evangelist from one of the leading noble families in Imerina, was unique among the *menalamba* for his high position in the old state church. He became 'Mr Free-of-remorse'. Names of this type may well have been adopted in imitation of the characters in *The Pilgrim's Progress*, second only to the Bible as a work of devotion among Merina Protestants.

Rabozaka and Rabezavana, to use their more familiar names, both had large numbers of guns retrieved from government arsenals or delivered by army deserters. They managed to buy a few from British Indian or creole traders on the north-west coast. They had at their service the Zandramalana, a deme of specialized blacksmiths who repaired guns and manufactured ammunition for them. Both these leaders were anxious to convince onlookers of the legitimacy of their movement and to provide a degree of central control by finding a suitable royal leader. Already a week before the first day of Alahamady Rabezavana had sent a letter to Prince Ramahatra in Antananarivo, asking him to be their king.[35] This prince was of the royal line, a known opponent of the Andafy-Avaratra and one of the very few courtiers who was popular. Ramahatra in fact used the letter to ingratiate himself with the French and to cast doubt on his enemy Rainandriamampandry, but it is significant that the northern *menalamba* were in search of a royal leader. Time and again the northerners sent orders to one another in the name of the queen or of imaginary courtiers called Ratiatanindrazana or Ratsitiavola, 'Mr Patriot' and 'Mr Does-not-love-money'. Again, both names were probably inspired by *The Pilgrim's Progress*. The second also refers to a famous speech of Andrianampoinimerina in which, reassuring his subjects that his government would not make excessive demands upon them, the founder of Merina unity had said that his kingdom did not love money.[36]

Most Malagasy with any experience of politics knew that the device of the queen and the mythical directors of the rising was a means of gaining popular support. But to judge from the number of *menalamba* who, under interrogation, told the French that they had allies in high places in the capital, it seems that it succeeded in convincing the rank-and-file that their rising had the queen's approval. 'It is not we alone who are waging this war', the *menalamba* declared to the defenders of Ambatondrazaka, 'it is the whole people.'[37] None of the northern leaders ever took the title of king for himself, but they referred to themselves as viceroys or ambassadors of the queen. Rabozaka styled himself 'governor-general of the eastern army' or even 'of the army of Madagascar.' Colleagues were addressed as part of a military command. Ramenamaso was 'governor of Antsihanaka', Rafanenitra 'governor of the west', and so on. Each leader had his staff of junior officers and secretaries, and other subordinates called only by their civil titles. Some leaders rose from almost nowhere. The best example is Rainijirika, a lowly household slave who had made money in trade on the west coast. He became a *menalamba* general and was accepted as an equal 'or as a leader of both *hovas* and *andrianas*. The case is a rare one.'[38]

Much of the northern organization was not of a traditional type. Some of the titles used were Malagasy versions of names which had been introduced from Europe quite late in the nineteenth century, by a government which the *menalamba* professed to despise. Furthermore, as the year of 1896 went by the northern *menalamba* became increasingly ready to use all sorts of innovations in order to defeat the French. When Père Berthieu was captured at Ambohibemasoandro in June 1896 he was told that if he renounced Christianity 'we will make you our leader and our counsellor'.[39] As it became known that French and British were on bad terms, and when the *menalamba* recalled that the British missionaries had at least never attempted to colonize the country, the attitude towards Europeans became still more equivocal. An English trader captured in August 1896 was told that 'the queen has ordered the leaders of the rising to spare the English'.[40] Rabezavana was soon using this idea of a British connection as a subtle means of winning the support of Malagasy Protestants. He may even have seriously hoped to enlist the help of Lord Salisbury in Westminster, ignorant of the fact that Britain had long since written off Madagascar as within the French sphere of influence. In time the less sophisticated of the *menalamba* and the more gullible of the French came to believe that Rabozaka really did have British military advisers living in his camp.

THE RISING IN THE SOUTH

One of the things which distinguished the *menalamba* from mere bandits was their attempt to form an alternative government. They had to have some sort of administration, no matter how rudimentary, to organize the considerable tracts of land which were under their control. They had an important ideological motive too. The *menalamba* could justify their revolt only by saying that they were restoring a pure form of government, and such was their religious conception of the state that they believed their alternative system could harness the spiritual force of the ancestors and the holy earth. The type of organization espoused by the insurgents in various areas is also interesting from an analytical point of view, since it shows how diverse were people's opinions of the national constitution.

In the north the rebel leaders succeeded in recruiting many local officials of the old administration. The chain of command imitated that of the Christian government. Each leader of standing had his own treasury and officials. The insurrection in the southern provinces of Ambodirano and Vakinisisaony was more disparate. Contingents were mostly led by the guardians of their own talismans, and relied for coordination far more heavily upon ties of kinship. The districts which had resisted central reforms and Christianity most successfully in the past committed themselves to the most archaic form of organization.

Perhaps until the *fandroana* of November 1895 there was little to distinguish the agitation in the south from that in the north. Both were a combination of banditry and the revival of ancestral religion. Thereafter, while Rabozaka was conspiring with other northern officials, the two movements assumed quite different identities. The southern insurrection was more fragmented. Such unity as it had in the beginning depended upon the great prestige of Kelimalaza, traditionally the paramount royal talisman. In January 1896 Rambinintsoa presided over meetings at which it was sworn 'to kill all Europeans who might appear among them.'[41] Undoubtedly one of his aims was to enlist in the rising the holy village of Ambohimanambola, Kelimalaza's resting-place for over a century, which had rejected the talisman twenty-six years before but where there was a strong faction urging his return. Rambinintsoa was seen there late in 1895 dressed in the traditional red robes and carrying the red parasol of the guardians of the talismans. People came to see him from all over the south. They presented allegiance to Rambinintsoa and in return received charms to protect them from bullets.[42]

The villages most often cited as the centres of the revival of Kelimalaza form two groups, connected by ties of blood. One lay around the old noble settlement at Anosibe, whose people were related to the fief-holders of Manarintsoa and Mangabe. The second group lay around Iheramalaza and Ankobakobaka. The people of these two districts met regularly at the market of Mananjara, which is precisely where Rambinintsoa had lived since 1869. These details come mostly from government intelligence reports and from later statements made by captured *menalamba*. The southern rebels were less literate than their northern counterparts and communicated with each other far more by word of mouth. There does survive, though, a letter written probably in March 1896 which instructs the village governor to whom it was addressed to organize a rising. The writer was clearly aware of preparations elsewhere in Imerina and he warned against the dangers of an isolated revolt like that which had been mounted by the Zanakantitra of Ambodirano in the previous November. It is interesting to observe the degree to which the insurgents were aware of taking part in a nationwide movement despite the lack of central direction:

> Observe carefully what the people are doing. If you see any large assembly, and if there is a command for an attack by all the provinces of Imerina and the coast, let us know. If the province of Vakinisisaony can follow these principles, it need not fear the same fate as Ambodirano.[43]

It is plain that by the beginning of March 1896 at the very latest the devotees of Kelimalaza in the south of Vakinisisaony had firm plans for a national rising. There was talk of marching on Antananarivo. In fact an insurrection was sparked off almost accidentally, rather as it had been at Amboanana in November 1895. Three French gold-prospectors passed through the village of Manarintsoa on about 23 March 1896. The governor warned them of the dangers of going further, but they ignored him. Six days later they ran into Rainibetsimisaraka's band. They were chased back to Manarintsoa. The governor and leading church officials tried to protect them, but fled to Antananarivo in the afternoon and left the three foreigners to be killed by the rebels.

It soon became apparent that the talk of leading an army to the capital was wildly exaggerated. As after the murder of the Johnsons at Amboanana, with which there are many other parallels, the insurgents did not head for Antananarivo but threatened to attack centres of government influence within their own province, in this case Tsiafahy, Andramasina and Ambohimanjaka. They were said to be over 1,000 in number but they were much worse armed than Rabozaka's men who were raising the Mandiavato at the same moment. A French detachment arrived at Manarintsoa on 3 April 1896 accompanied by Randriantavy, a relative of the queen and one of the court representatives of Vakinisisaony province. They burnt some of the rebel villages. Rainibetsimisaraka and Ratsizehena headed further south, but Rambinintsoa was tracked down at Mananjara and killed there on 22 April 1896.

Even at this early stage, it was plain that the rising in Vakinisisaony differed from the insurrection in the north. The patterns of collaboration and resistance were far more localized, for one thing, and far more dependant upon a single talisman. It was generally agreed that the insurgents were led by notables and fief-holders of the villages around Anosibe and Iheramalaza which had been at the heart of the revival of the talismans, while Randriantavy and Colonel Oudri received co-operation from some of the villages where the government had successfully installed its own nominees as fief-holders in recent decades. It was also widely agreed that very few village governors had joined the rising voluntarily, and certainly had not instigated it as they did in the north. A French officer made a full report on the participants in the rising. Interestingly, his description of the village leaders is reminiscent of a description made some years earlier of those who had suffered most from the centralizing policies of the royal government:

> Apart from a few people, who lived in Mananjara and who were guardians of talismans, the other leaders are prominent villagers, rich people, owners of houses, land, slaves. These men, who were more of a hindrance than a help to village governors and who were perhaps afraid that the new political order might be prejudicial to their interests, were disposed to extend a hand to agitators with a certain credibility, such as Rainibetsimisaraka, who represented strength, and Rambinintsoa, who had religious prestige . . . It is reasonable to suppose that in several places the village governors really did have their hands forced . . . [44]

After the death of Rambinintsoa the rising in the south lost some of its unity but none of its violence. New centres and patterns of revolt emerged as the fighting spread. Ratsizehena and Rainibetsimisaraka argued over what to do next. They split up, although they were to meet again in July 1896 for the funeral of Ratsizehena's father, who was also Rainibetsimisaraka's father-in-law. Rainbetsimisaraka returned to his old haunts on the borders of Voromahery, to make war on the regional government which had driven him and many of those who followed him into a life of banditry seven years before. The insurgents infested the countryside, burning the churches and driving off all who would not join them. Rainibetsimisaraka, informed that the Norwegian missionaries of Antsirabe were away at a conference, decided to attack the capital of eastern Vakinankaratra. On 24 May 1896 1,500 *menalamba* descended on the little town. They were poorly armed, but swollen with 'all the bad elements of the Loharano and Sirabe districts'.[45] The town was burned and the governor killed, and for fifty-three hours a party of Norwegian women and children and Malagasy troops under two French sergeants were besieged in the mission-station. Just when it seemed that all was lost, in the best wild west fashion Rainijaonary arrived with 1,000 loyal troops and drove off the rebels.

The story became very well known. It was a dramatic affair and seems to have struck a chord in the colonial siege mentality. Its real significance was appreciated only in the fullness of time. It was the first and last time that the *menalamba* attacked a considerable party of Europeans in the open and head on. It demonstrated that the loyalist general Rainijaonary was able to defend western Vakinankaratra almost single-handed, and indeed his sphere of influence was virtually the only part of Imerina barely touched by the *menalamba*. And, like many similar battles on a smaller scale, it was interpreted by many Malagasy as a test of the *menalambas'* religious power. The words of a Norwegian missionary, used to describe the siege, were equally true of the whole struggle between the insurgents and the Christians or the French:[46]

> From the beginning but especially in the later stages, the insurrection was a struggle against Christianity, a duel between two religions. The pagans observed with interest which would emerge victorious. It was in this frame of mind that an old pagan who was observing the siege of Antsirabe from a hill said: 'If the Europeans escape from Antsirabe, I will know that there is a Christian God.' The opinion was widespread among the pagans that, if the rebels were defeated at Antsirabe, it was because they had attacked the families of the missionaries who were *olona marina'* [right thinking people].

General Rainijaonary may have saved the Europeans at Antsirabe, but it rapidly became evident that there was a certain price to be paid for his collaboration. He continued to use the Lutheran Church as an instrument of government and a vehicle for his personal ambition. In the valley of the Manandona, for example, it was Rainibetsimisaraka's old enemy Pastor Robena who was given forty Snider rifles and ordered to restore the local government.[47] Furthermore, French support aided Rainijaonary's territorial ambitions. Each time that he was summoned to quell a rising outside his native province he used the occasion to instal his own clients and his own garrisons, so as to annex a new area for Vakinankaratra.

General Rainijaonary had long harboured the ambition of acquiring the autonomous province of the Voromahery, which had refused to surrender its weapons to him when the French ordered a general disarmament in 1895. Incorporation in Vakinankaratra for the Voromahery meant the end of their exemption from taxes, forced labour and military service.[48] Equally they had no love for the *menalamba*, who were the same people as had raided cattle from them in the past. They were willing to tolerate Rainibetsimisaraka's presence on their frontier, but when Ratsizehena tried to raise the province in the name of the queen they drove him off. Rainijaonary told the French that the Voromahery were in revolt, which was not true. Subsequently they were attacked by a French force, but the Voromahery remained adamant. 'They will never submit willingly', one of their chiefs said, 'as long as they are administered from Vakinankaratra.'[49] The French were not only misled by Rainijaonary, but believed that the resistance of the Voromahery was evidence of encouragement from Antananarivo, as Rasanjy among others had important assets in the province.

A French gold prospector who contended that 'our authorities have understood nothing of the affairs of this region' was proved right by subsequent events.[50] Every leader of consequence among the Voromahery, with one possible exception, was actively collaborating with the French by Christmas 1896, when a more sane policy prevailed.

As with the northern *menalamba*, there was a tendency for the southern insurgents to gain in strategic skill and to use Christian sectarian disputes to their advantage. Rainibetsimisaraka exploited the hegemony of the Lutheran Church in Vakinankaratra by continuing to burn Protestant temples while leaving Catholic churches unharmed. He was able to recruit a number of former Catholics into the *menalamba* in this way. The most interesting case was of a man called Leopold, who became Rainibetsimisaraka's secretary. He was a former Catholic schoolmaster, known and respected by the Jesuits, who had led a sectarian revolt against Pastor Robena and the Norwegian mission in 1888.[51] It is notable that whereas the northern *menalamba* came to see the Congregationalist churches of the LMS as an ally against the French, in Vakinankaratra it was the other way round: Catholics could be used to defeat the Lutheran hierarchy. It was a measure of the different concept of the state in the two areas, and also of the very different approaches by French administrators.

The private war between Rainibetsimisaraka and the Lutheran officials in Vakinankaratra shows how fragile was the unity of the southern *menalamba* once Rambinintsoa had been killed. Several new centres of agitation emerged, in places which had joined in the general revival of the talismans in late 1895 but had not joined the devotees of Kelimalaza. This was the case of Vakiniadiana, a division of Vakinisisaony which adjoined the province of Avaradrano, where there were a number of tensions arising from the rivalry between the two provinces. A missionary stationed at Soavina, the southernmost village of Avaradrano in this region, described how 'a spirit of disaffection had been smouldering' in Vakiniadiana all through the early part of 1896. It was based on the cult of a talisman at Ankadimaga, led by a guardian called Ihasina.[52] The people of Vakiniadiana did not take part in the risings of Alahamady, although they were not far from doing so. They threw off all allegiance to the fief-holders who had lived among them since their submission to Andrianampoinmerina, and obeyed only their traditional family chiefs and the guardians of their talismans.

The religious revival in Vakiniadiana did not turn into open revolt until the end of April 1896. By that time Rabozaka's men were spreading south to threaten Soavina and the strategically vital road to Tamatave. Ihasina was urging the devotees who came to visit him to revolt against the governor of Antanamalaza, Governor Rafaralahibadaoro. The latter responded by leading a party of soldiers to arrest Ihasina, and they took him to the citadel at Manjakandriana. There the royal soldiers were attacked by a mob of Ihasina's followers. On 30 April 1896 Rafaralahibadaoro and his men were burned to death in the citadel where they had been defending themselves. 'This rising in the East is important', a missionary rightly observed, 'as it supplies the link between the North and South.'[53] Rabozaka thought so too, for he soon sent a contingent to help the people of Vakiniadiana. Together they headed towards Soavina, burning all the churches which they found and proclaiming death to the French.

Meanwhile the territory south of the road to Tamatave, Vakinampasina, was also moving towards a rising. Some notables there had already been associated with the agitation at Ankadimanga in 1895, especially one Rafiringa, the hereditary fief-holder of Ambohipaniry. In the first week of June 1896 it was reported that the venerable noble populations of Ambohipaniry, Mantasoa and Lazaina had all joined the rising.

The insurrection in Vakinisisaony was never to lose its very localized character, but by July 1896 its progress in the east was assured by coalitions cut on traditional political lines. The people of Vakiniadiana were led by Ihasina's son Rasamba, who commanded perhaps 2,000 people and had acquired about 200 guns, most of them bought from Rabozaka. He had enlisted the former evangelist Randriamisaodray, who was important for his administrative ability, his high noble status and his intimate knowledge of national politics. They harried caravans from Tamatave very effectively, cutting off supplies of food to the capital to the extent that the price of rice there doubled in the last fortnight of July 1896. It was probably Randriamisaodray who cut the telegraph line on 22 June 1896 and left Antananarivo temporarily isolated from the outside world.

Further south, in Vakinampasina, the spiritual leaders of the *menalamba* were Rafiringa of Ambohipaniry and Ramanambololona, the guardian of a talisman. Neither appears to have actually led warriors into battle. There were several minor warlords, including Rafiringa's two sons, and Ramarokoto of Lazaina, who organized his followers into centuries. All of them recruited a few followers among the Bezanozano and Tanala of the forest, and received guns and supplies from Anosibe, the scene of the rising in March 1896. Their reverence for the talismans was probably greater than among any other group of *menalamba* after the death of Rambinintsoa. Certainly, traditional guardians of talismans were prominent among their leaders. Their attacks were most often directed against regional centres of government and collaboration such as Ambatomanga, Antanamalaza and Anerindrano, a village containing nobles of different origin.

It was Rafiringa who presided over an extraordinary gathering on the mountain of Andrarakasina on 12 September 1896. Ambassadors came from all over Vakinisisaony, from the forest people and from Rabozaka. A message was sent to Rainibetsimisaraka. Ratsizehena attended in person. And Rafiringa was proclaimed King of Madagascar.[54]

His nomination provides not only a fascinating insight into the traditions and aspirations of the southern *menalamba*, but also a measure of the fierce local independence of the southerners. It has already been noted that no northerner ever proclaimed himself king, and indeed that it was essential for the unity of the northern insurrection that the *menalamba* should appear loyal to the queen. The *menalamba* of Vakinisisaony, on the other hand, were much less concerned to claim leadership in the capital, either through the queen or through the imaginary courtiers Ratiatanindrazana and Ratsitiavola. Rafiringa was a relatively minor leader, probably unknown outside his native province.

There are several factors which assist interpretation of the nomination. It is possible – but no more than that – that Rafiringa had some family connection with the queen, as her family originated near Mantasoa. It is possible too that he was a direct descendant of one of the earliest kings of the region. Some of the most hallowed families of Mantasoa can still trace their ancestry to the very earliest sovereigns of the Merina. But the most important clue is the site, the holy mountain of Andrarakasina. It was a most sacred place for the people of Vakinisisaony, one to which they had often travelled to perform the ceremonies outlawed in 1869. The *menalamba* of Vakinisisaony renamed the hill Antananarivokely, 'little Antananarivo', in imitation of the holy Vazimba place of that name which had enjoyed real political power over two centuries before. By so doing they expressed their wish to reconstruct a government whose model lay far in the past, certainly before the days of King Andrianampoinimerina. It was an image of the constitution which represented the sovereign primarily as a ritual leader, associated with the talismans in the granting of virtue and bounty to the people. It should be recalled that Rainisingomby of Amboanana had also called himself a king, but prematurely, because his revolt was not supported by the nobles who could act as king makers and legitimize his claim. The southerner Ratsizehena too was eventually to demand 'to be hailed as a sovereign, and moreover that is the aim of his rebellion'.[55]

The only Merina who were hailed as kings by the *menalamba* came from demes which had once been subjects of the early kings in Vakinisisaony before the seventeenth century. These demes had a very different notion of the state and of the national constitution from that of the northern insurgents. Their ideal was in many respects archaic, reflecting an older time which for them had been a better time. The *menalamba* did much to probe the depths of Merina history and to explore the maladies which had given rise to their movement over a long period.

THE KEYS OF THE KINGDOM

A lawyer who was present at the interrogation of many *menalamba* noted how they had 'a certain idea of nationhood, a deep love of their country', and how, when questioned, they gave as the main reason for their rising, 'the rumour, which had been planted by the ruling class, that the French intended to take from them their ancestral land'.[56]

The idea of a Malagasy nation, and indeed the very name Madagascar, were originally European imports, just as much as were the guns with which the Merina kings subdued their neighbours. The nationalist ideal had spread rapidly wherever the Merina lived. The political rhetoric of the period reveals from its vocabulary in particular that the idea of nationalism had grown from the ancient beliefs that a freeman had an inalienable right to ownership of his ancestral land, and that the sacredness of the earth was linked to political power. Madagascar was for the Malagasy. It was not enough that there should be a government; the body politic had to be imbued with supernatural virtue, which the French protectorate was not. The *menalamba* wore small charms of earth taken from ancestral tombs as symbols of this power.

The dissidents of 1895 reasoned that their national ideal had been undermined mainly by the Christian conversion of the queen in 1869, which had destroyed the system which they thought necessary to ensure harmony. At the same time the *menalamba*, and their concept of Malagasy nationalism, owed much to Christianity. It was reflected in the names borrowed from *The Pilgrim's Progress*. It affected the forms of their rituals: tradition had no substitute for the weekly gathering at church, and so the *menalamba* in Antsihanaka invented a suitable ceremony to fill the gap. It was difficult to fight a national war while removing all trace of Christianity, and indeed in general the areas which restored the talismans most thoroughly were the least effective in fighting the French.

Some of the most advanced nationalists among the *menalamba*, generally to be found in the north, were former churchmen. Some even kept Christian literature in their houses. Occasionally there are traces of Christian imagery in their letters. But there is no suggestion that this was a syncretic movement. Not all the *menalamba* were equally affected by Christianity, and in fact it was really a point of distinction between the leaders and the rank-and-file. Some of the *menalamba* were people whose Christianity lapsed for a fairly short time, and was later resumed. According to a Norwegian missionary, there were others who remained Christian at heart, thinking that they could side with the pagan revivalists for national purposes and then resume their faith when the French were defeated.[57] The *menalamba* resented most the material and negative aspects of the Church, its use as the administrative arm of a thoroughly unpleasant government. They were against the state Church more often than they were against Christianity.

After the French invasion there was a widespread conviction that the establishment of the Church had been an elaborate and cynical trick. The Malagasy had wanted western technical knowledge, which they considered to include the Bible, but they felt that they had been deceived into accepting only an inferior ritual. 'It is rifles and cannon which are destroying us', Père Berthieu was told by his captors. 'Will you teach us about them? It is useless to teach us about God. Is there anyone who doesn't know God already?'[58] Another put it more colourfully:

> you are killing the people now because the first Europeans who came here brought the Bible, the Gospel, and hymns. The Malagasy consented to all this. In many places they took it to heart and found Christianity to be good. But now you are killing the Malagasy whom you sought to convert: you gave us the

Bible instead of cannon, the Gospel instead of Gardiner machine-guns, hymns instead of rifles. You ruined our way of life. You took away the will to resist.[59]

The *menalamba* attack on Christianity was only the central part of an assault on certain European values. One writer explained how the Malagasy ruling classes had become too clever by half, using the glittering foreign culture as a weapon against tradition, and then too late finding themselves trapped by the Europeans.[60] The Malagasy had lost their purity to false promises, like the heroine in a Victorian novel. The *menalamba* specifically rejected foreign culture and yet their leaders made use even of its vocabulary, referring to European ways as '*ny sivilizesona*' ('civilization'). Their titles were sometimes European. In the north they referred to meetings of insurrectionary leaders as a cabinet ('*kabinetra*') or a committee ('*komity*'). Again, with sufficient evidence it would probably be possible to distinguish between leaders and led among the *menalamba* on linguistic grounds.

The *menalamba* view, that the establishment of state Christianity in 1869 was a crucial event in the intrusion of imperialism, corresponds to an economic analysis. An earlier chapter has already defined the 1860s as a decade in which European economic penetration of inland markets began on a large scale, to the detriment of the Merina economy. The Merina did not need an economist to tell them that the failure to evolve a satisfactory money economy lay near the root of their problems. *Menalamba* proclamations often expressed hatred of the oligarchy in Antananarivo which had sold Madagascar, and of its excessive love of silver. Rainilaiarivony was a 'miser', 'the richest man amongst us, who preferred money to justice'.[61] The generals who failed woefully to defend the country in 1895 'for the love of silver . . . have betrayed the land of their birth.'[62] All who collaborated with the French were said to be people made rotten with money. Only those who scorned foreign silver could restore independence to Madagascar, the *menalamba* said. It does appear that even the richest of the *menalamba*, village notables and middle-ranking governors, had nothing compared to the vast wealth of the oligarchy.[63] The invention of 'Mr Does-not-love-money' reveals how deeply the *menalamba* longed for uncorrupt government.

The French could consider themselves unfortunate in reaping the discontent which had been sown by generations of Merina rulers. The nineteenth century had seen Merina society rent with disputes over status and territory which were a direct result of the type of government established by King Andrianampoinimerina before 1810 and subsequently developed by the Andafy-Avaratra prime ministers. In recent years the intrusion of officials into villages had turned even kinsmen one against another. This, said the *menalamba*, could be rectified only by restoring a harmonious society in which every group would have its proper territory and status. The message of the northern *menalamba* was that the golden age of the past had been during the reign of Andrianampoinimerina. The demes of Vakinisisaony looked even further back for their model of order.

When Rabozaka's followers spoke of restoring the standing-stones set up by Andrianampoinimerina and Radama I, as they often did, they were referring both to a metaphor and a fact. Many demes had suffered alterations in the territory and status which were marked by the standing-stones which defined the boundaries of deme lands. It was as though several decades of history had taken a wrong turning, and there must now be an investigation of that history to find the point at which the mistake had been made, and to relive what should have been.

The best of the *menalamba* leaders knew how to turn these metaphors to solid political advantage, which was the traditional skill required of Merina statesmen. The more enterprising played on the ambiguities of words like *tanindrazana* (literally, 'land of the ancestors') and addressed their followers in terms which could equally be applied to the individual deme, or to the people of Imerina, or to the people of all Madagascar. The reference to standing-stones could be used as an obvious symbol of national boundaries. They aimed to subsume all the pressures towards civil war into an anti-foreign movement, which later became an anti-French movement. But the nationalist leaders were never completely successful in this respect. They too were Malagasy, believing that the French could be defeated only by a united people who would have behind them the force of a supernatural power.

The strength of the rising was undoubtedly exaggerated by disagreements between Frenchmen, notably between Resident-General Laroche and General Voyron, and by French failure to form a militia by locating and arming potential collaborators among the Malagasy. Voyron thought that all who were not actively fighting with the French must be *menalamba*. In reality many villagers wanted peace above all else, or perhaps had local scores to settle but were not rabidly anti-French. Sometimes we hear of villagers driving off *menalamba* attacks armed only with sticks and stones. Others burned their local church but refused to take to the bush. For all their efforts, *menalamba* leaders could rarely assemble more than a few dozen men in one place. Each contingent was often more concerned to drive Christians from its own local homeland than to fight in a strategic war. It was this which obliged the *menalamba* to press-gang recruits; and this was the error of the French in burning deserted villages, for it forced refugees to join the true *menalamba* bands. 'Against this invasion *all* the people sympathize and wish success to the rebellion', wrote a missionary. But he added that eighty per cent of the population knew that the French would win in the end, and so supported the rising only half-heartedly.[64] Secretary-General Paul Bourde reckoned in June 1896 that 90,000 people were living in areas under *menalamba* control, and two months later he gave the figure as 300,000. British missionaries put the figure of 'hard-core' insurgents at between one-tenth and one-fifth of the population, depending on the area.[65]

Despite these impressive numbers the insurgents never inflicted anything like a heavy defeat on any French force. The bloodiest French reverse, in which they lost still only seven men, occurred as late as September 1898, although native loyalist troops suffered some very heavy defeats. It is true, of course, that the *menalamba* as a whole were hopelessly ill-equipped to defeat a European foe in the field. Nevertheless certain groups, like those northerners who had got their hands on government arsenals and who could obtain ammunition from Indian merchants, made no attempt to concentrate their fire-power on any crucial French target. It is worth examining the strategy and tactics of the *menalamba* to see why this was so.

Their structure of command and communications, impressive though it was, was primarily political. It existed to demonstrate the patriotic nature of the insurrection according to the premise that insurgents without a clear commitment to royal government were really only bandits. The overwhelming goal of the insurgents in every region, according to their different traditions and styles, was to establish a legitimate government. Hence the discrepancy between the rebels' considerable numbers and their disproportionately minor military effectiveness. For the southerners and the people of Ambodirano, heirs to a rather older tradition than most of their northern counterparts, this meant establishing small local kings, each with his talisman, each in contact with the paramount sovereign in Antananarivo. This was a reconstruction of what they considered the authentic, ancient constitution of the country. For the northerners, the assertion that they were a true government meant not only loyalty to the queen and her courtiers and the restoration of old rituals, but also the creation by each leader of his own secretariat, treasury and system of justice and taxation – in short, of a miniature government in imitation of the larger one in Antananarivo. In fact Rabozaka, rather like some of those who rose against the French in Madagascar in the major nationalist insurrection of 1947, seems to have been as concerned to administer justice and order in the proper way as to put the country on a war footing. Acting under alleged instruction from the queen (which he in fact invented himself but attributed to her for the sake of form), Rabozaka gave orders to individual villages, each represented by a body which he called a committee ('*komity*'). From the point of view of military effectiveness a very large amount of time was spent creating structures or debating topics of purely political intent, or of settling arguments with fellow Malagasy, and too little on beating the French. All this indicates how profound was the place of a properly constituted central government in Merina culture. In religious terms it was essential. The *menalamba* were willing to die for it. But they never succeeded in turning the patriotism of most Malagasy into a really effective military movement.

The more the *menalamba* held an old-fashioned view of the constitution, like the southerners, the more they regarded their prime duty as that of restoring the customs of the ancestors and of purging their own local territory of Christians. Only in the early months of the southern rising, from the time when Rambinintsoa was still alive and in league with the former outlaw Rainibestimisaraka until the siege of Antsirabe in May 1896, did their ambitions extend to full-scale military action. The northerners' war aims were conceived on a larger scale, which is not surprising given their more sophisticated organization. Up to the middle of 1896 the main target of Rabozaka's and Rabezavana's bands was the loyalist garrison at Ambatondrazaka, one of the most important military and administrative centres in all the north of Madagascar. There was certainly a deep personal animosity between Rabozaka and Rabeony, the governor of Ambatondrazaka. It was shared by many of the Marofotsy who followed Rabezavana. Rabeony had been their oppressor for many years. But an attack on Ambatondrazaka also made some strategic sense. As long as it remained in loyalist hands Rabozaka and Rabezavana could not advance on the capital without fear of a counter-attack from the rear, or without being cut off from the northern hinterland whence they drew their supplies. Rafanenitra in particular was always an advocate of the direct advance to Antananarivo, but then he did not have such a large or disparate band of followers as the other northern leaders. It was largely through Rafanenitra's efforts that Vonizongo was brought so swiftly into the revolt in June 1896. It was he who liaised with the western leaders Laimiza and Rajamaria to co-ordinate the encirclement of the capital. Not even Rafanenitra, though, appears to have advocated a direct assault on Antananarivo. Doubtless he and his colleagues were correct in calculating that a head-on attack even on a French column was sheer suicide.

The movement was most effective from June to August 1896 when Antananarivo was starved of supplies by the blockade and when large tracts of countryside were under *menalamba* control. When the French put some purpose into their strategy after October 1896 the insurgents' initiative was lost. Thereafter the northerners' main objective was to take the holy town of Ambohimanga and hold it throughout an auspicious period such as the feast of the bath on 22 November 1896 or the first day of Alahamady in 1897. They hoped that if they could do so, their claim to legitimacy would be greatly strengthened.

In a sense the war-aims of the *menalamba* only became realistic in military terms in proportion as their initiative was lost. They came to realize that they would never drive the French out of Madagascar, 'but they say they will carry on this guerrilla warfare and torment the French so, that they will bitterly regret the day they robbed them of their fatherland'.[66]

Apart from during the two big sieges, of Ambatondrazaka in the north and of Antsirabe in the south, the *menalamba* bands were small. The principal leaders had headquarters, normally based in a mountain or forest retreat, where they kept their records. From there they would co-ordinate the activity of local groups, sending out orders in the name of the queen, gathering intelligence, seeking new allies, administering government in the territory they controlled. All the leaders had their particular talismans. When a war-party was out on business, ambushing a supply-convoy or attacking a loyalist village or burning a church, the local leaders would often plan in advance. They would often burn churches during the night to soften up an area which was considered ripe for defection. When there was a head-on clash, the *menalamba* would usually be accompanied and even led into battle by the guardians of their talismans.

The key to understanding the *menalamba's* actions is to appreciate their determination to behave in the way expected of loyal citizens: to observe the customs of the ancestors, to reproduce exactly the government which they thought proper. For this, they had to believe that the queen was on their side. In some mysterious way she must be directing the rising despite the fact that she was a French prisoner.

5

The war of the sects (November 1896 to November 1897)

they shall lay their hands on you, and persecute you . . . And ye shall be betrayed both by parents, and brethren, and kinsfolks, and friends; and some of you shall they cause to be put to death.

Luke, XXI, xii, xvi

THE CREATION OF A CONSPIRACY

There never was a plot with the object of driving the French from Madagascar among any of the Malagasy politicians in Antananarivo. There were plenty of ill-informed people who thought that such a conspiracy existed, and some malicious ones who pretended that it did. Many French soldiers of low rank were disposed to believe that there was some sort of Protestant Anglo-Merina combination in support of the *menalamba*. The occasional evidence that there might be some truth in the allegation came either from forgeries made by interested parties, or from the fact that most of the *menalamba* were persuaded by their religious convictions to believe that the queen must in some sense be on their side.

The Merina politicians constantly manoeuvred to obtain the good graces of the French and to win sufficient friends to shield themselves against suspicion of treachery. During the last years of the old regime, the most prominent factions in the capital had centred either on the queen or on the prime minister's family. The most recent party, formed shortly before the French invasion, included the government secretary Rasanjy. He had been shrewd enough to realize well in advance that association with the Andafy-Avaratra would not do him any good under a French government and had put himself at the head of a pro-French party shortly before the fall of Antananarivo. He had found allies in Rainianjanoro, head of the native section of the intelligence service after October 1895, and Prince Ramahatra, a Catholic noble.

It is impossible to say which of the various factions forged the so-called Ambohimanga letter which was shown to Laroche in February 1896 and which convinced many Europeans that one party or another was in league with the *menalamba*. From then onwards every Merina politician strove to plant doubts about his rivals' loyalty to the French. Rasanjy was often said to be the real head of the *menalamba*, but it emerged that he had chosen his friends wisely. Prince Ramahatra in particular was generally absolved from suspicion because he had shown to the French a letter received from

Rabezavana and, probably on Rasanjy's suggestion, had told them that Rainandriamampandry too had received a letter from the *menalamba* but had treacherously said nothing about it, which was a complete fabrication.[1] Ramahatra had also won grudging respect from the French military for his part in assisting the repression of the rising in the north.

Laroche had the impossible task of enforcing an ill-conceived protectorate without control over military affairs. He soon contrived to lose the support of every influential member of the civil administration too. When in late May 1896 the military intelligence service uncovered evidence of a very dubious nature to support allegations of a conspiracy, Laroche was forced to act, especially since the *menalamba* were burning the suburban churches of the capital at that time. He ordered the execution or exile of a number of minor political figures, but not enough to stifle criticism of his lack of purpose. He did not believe in the rumours of a conspiracy and was too honest to feign such a belief.

Nearly all the French officials developed persecution mania. "Sometimes I think I am in a mad-house', Laroche wrote to the minister of colonies. 'I am surrounded by people who have lost all self-control.'[2] He was vilified in the French press, he said. Voyron was incompetent and the military were provoking revolt by their brutality. French settlers were against him. Secretary-General Bourde had designs on his job. The soldiers in turn widely believed Laroche to be a dupe of British missionaries and Merina politicians, and that he was prejudiced against the army. The junior officers who actually pursued the *menalamba* were often told by their prisoners that the leaders of the rising were in the capital. They can hardly be blamed for thinking that the political authorities were not supporting their campaign against the rebels.

It was evident that constitutional changes would have to be made in Madagascar. Already in January 1896 the French colonial ministry, which had taken charge of Malagasy affairs from the foreign ministry, had made Queen Ranavalona III sign a declaration which put Madagascar half-way between a colony and a protectorate. This was intended for domestic opinion in France, which had been disturbed by the failure to take a firm hold on the commerce of a country which had been conquered at great financial and human expense. It soon became obvious too that a protectorate was unworkable because of events in Madagascar. The massacre of Merina officials on the east coast seemed to indicate what many Frenchmen were inclined to believe, that the subject peoples of Madagascar would see France as a liberator and would demand to be freed from Merina tyranny. Official thinking was already groping towards full annexation and containment of the Merina role in administration, despite the opposition of the French foreign ministry, when the rising of the *menalamba* put the whole question beyond doubt. Madagascar was declared a French colony on 6 August 1896.

Annexation posed another problem. There was a lobby in France which called for the abolition of slavery in Madagascar and which had been kept at bay with vague promises as long as the island remained a protectorate. Once it had been declared a colony it was impossible to allow slavery to continue indefinitely. Immediately after the vote on annexation the Chamber of Deputies voted the 'immediate emancipation' of slaves in Madagascar. Colonial Minister Lebon was not altogether enthusiastic, and probably intended that Laroche's successor should enforce the decision only when he saw fit.

The first governor of the new colony of Madagascar would have to be in charge of both civil and military forces, and would therefore have to be a soldier himself. The choice fell on Colonel Joseph Gallieni, who had had a successful if somewhat unorthodox colonial career in the Soudan and Indo-China. In August 1896 he was promoted to the rank of general, briefed on his mission, and told to dismantle the protectorate by using Malagasy officials only in their areas of family or ethnic origin. This last was what Gallieni termed a '*politique des races*'. He probably had a hand in drawing up these instructions himself.

Gallieni was personally in favour of an immediate abolition of the Merina monarchy, but was dissuaded. He was one of the new generation of radicals in matters of colonial policy: highly intelligent, a freethinker in religion, an admirer of Herbert Spencer – very different from the conservatives of the quai d'Orsay. It is not recorded who in Paris briefed Gallieni on the political and military position in Madagascar – certainly Colonial Minister Lebon, and certainly officials at the ministry of war. He must have heard much which supported his personal convictions. Lebon had already received reports that some senior Merina officials might be involved in the leadership of the *menalamba*; so had the officials at the war ministry. General Oudri, who had personally led a column against the southern *menalamba* in April 1896, had himself read a letter which seemed to indicate that the rebels had high-level support, and he had returned to Paris and told the war minister that 'the insurrectionary movement was due to start on an order from the capital'. He considered that the most likely ringleaders were Rasanjy and Rainandriamampandry. He thought some British missionaries might also be party to the conspiracy.[3]

In Madagascar French people generally expected that Gallieni would take firm action against the alleged traitors in Antananarivo. When he arrived in September 1896, he had not yet decided on what he termed 'the choice of whom to put aside and to punish and whom . . . to employ in the service of our policy'.[4] For some days he worked in uneasy harness with Laroche, who by now bore a distinct grudge against the military, whom he thought to have let him down, and against history, which had unfairly condemned him. While he was still resident-general he was technically responsible for enacting the emancipation of slaves which had recently been ordered by the colonial ministry, although it was normal practice to leave such a major and complicated piece of legislation to his successor. But Laroche had long found it repugnant to preside over a society in which slavery was legal. He could not resist the temptation to put his name in the history books as the author of a humanitarian measure worthy of the name of France. He probably had the malicious intention of snubbing Gallieni by announcing a law which he, Laroche, would not have to implement. On 26 September 1896, slavery was abolished.

Gallieni was understandably furious. Apart from anything else the emancipation law was badly drafted and open to a variety of interpretations. Three days after its promulgation he issued a countermanding order, informing all native officials that the law was a 'simple form of words in use among Europeans, and having no application in Madagascar'.[5] But the damage was done. The news spread very quickly.

Personal animosities produced a very bitter atmosphere in the European community. When Laroche left the capital for the last time on 10 October 1896 the sharper wits among the French said that his heavy escort was mainly intended to prevent Laroche from fraternizing with the *menalamba*. Within twenty-four hours Gallieni had arrested Rainandriamampandry, who had been on good terms with Laroche, and Prince Ratsimamanga, the queen's uncle. After a mockery of a trial they were convicted of treason largely on Rasanjy's testimony and shot in public on 15 October 1896.

Perhaps at this time Gallieni honestly believed that someone in the capital was in league with the *menalamba*, although he probably did not think that either of the two men executed was really guilty. More than anything he wanted to win the support of the army and to show that his administration would stand for no nonsense. He therefore decided to make an example of two leading politicians, one from the court party, a noble, and one from the old government party, preferably a commoner. The leading commoner politicians were Rasanjy and Rainandriamampandry, both highly capable administrators. It was Emil Gautier, the government's Madagascar specialist, who cynically advised the choice of Rainandriamampandry for the firing-squad, although he had for some months worked in an office adjoining that of the minister of the interior. Gautier reasoned that Rainandriamampandry was dispensable because he had few political friends. He advised that Rasanjy had better be preserved as he had a considerable hold on the native administration and had earned the respect of Paul Bourde, who himself had friends in high places in Paris.[6]

Bourde in fact was the only French administrator to give serious thought to the causes of the *menalamba* rising before Gallieni's arrival. He noticed the prominent role of some groups of nobles, and therefore deduced that the rising represented a movement on the part of the nobility, standing for all that was reactionary in Imerina. Merina nobles were to be equated with the old European aristocracy. This bare summary does not do justice to Bourde's subtlety. But like most Europeans of his day, and quite a few since, he was so well versed in the history of Europe that he pushed too far the analogy between aristocrats and *andriana*. The latter, it should be repeated, is only translated as 'noble' for want of a better word. Bourde assumed that Imerina was playing out a change of phase universal in history, from the feudal to the modern. Many French officials eventually made broadly similar deductions. These easily became simplified into the mistaken belief that the *menalamba*, led by the nobles and with the secret support of the monarchy, could be classed as aristocratic and feudal. Gallieni certainly felt, on both emotional and intellectual grounds, that France's role should be to side with the third estate, as it were, and so to defeat the rising and hasten the country's progress into glorious republican liberty.

The execution of Ratsimamanga and Rainandriamampandry was equivalent to an official statement on the existence of a conspiracy. Gallieni was subsequently to use this, even though he knew it to be a lie, as the main justification for the destruction of any Merina faction or institution which did not fit in with his plans. The government enacted a series of draconian land and labour laws, designed to punish the Merina, to create a mobile labour force and to attract French settlers. In February 1897 Gallieni ordered the abolition of the monarchy. The queen was exiled, together with several of the royal family and some Protestant magnates, on the pretext that they had attended meetings of an 'insurrectional committee' during 1896. Rainandriamampandry was said to have been the person behind the pseudonym of Ratiatanindrazana, although in fact the *menalamba* continued to issue orders in the name of the queen and Ratiatanindrazana until well into 1897. In April 1897 the institution of fief-holders and all the legal privileges of noble status were swept away.

Gallieni's firmness was applauded by French people in Paris and Madagascar. The substantial number of civilian administrators who lamented the destruction of the protectorate could not answer the charge that it had been found wanting and that they had been deceived by the alleged treachery of the Merina élite. Priority lay in restoring peace to Madagascar, and in this Gallieni was much more effective than his predecessors. Rather than trying to seek and destroy the enemy, like Voyron, he established a network of small garrisons. He had the confidence to form a native militia, so that for the first time loyalists had a means of resisting *menalamba* attacks.

The execution of Rainandriamampandry and Ratsimamanga inspired other reactions which Gallieni had not foreseen. The anarchy of 1896 was sometimes translated into disputes between Catholics and Protestants, Protestantism being considered British and Catholicism French. Such strife was really inevitable in a state where citizens were accustomed to regard every type of government as having a ritual form of its own.

During 1896 some Merina Catholic politicians tried to curry favour with the French by encouraging rumours that the alleged conspiracy in Antananarivo was Protestant-dominated. Rainandriamampandry in particular was widely known as a leading Protestant and anglophile. His son had received a doctor's degree from Edinburgh University and was the only

105

Malagasy member of the Antananarivo Lawn Tennis Club. Rainandriamampandry's execution, in itself a great talking-point, provoked further controversy when a Jesuit priest tried to convert him in his death-cell. His execution frightened the Protestant population of Antananarivo, and he became a martyr in the eyes of that influential Protestant faction which Gallieni wished to dismiss from national politics.

The *menalamba*, who had no love for the Protestant magnates, greeted the news of Rainandriamampandry's death with contempt. But the execution reinforced certain ideas which were already circulating in the northern camps. One aspect of the Merina passion for western learning had been a lively interest in foreign affairs. In the 1870s, for example, the Franco-Prussian war had been quite extensively discussed by Malagasy interested to learn that France was not invulnerable. The name Bismarck entered the Malagasy language as *bizy*, meaning 'cunning'.[7] Similarly in 1895 Protestants who felt trapped between French and *menalamba* had found comfort in the thought that Britain would come and help them. On the whole, though, the *menalamba* in the early months had shown little mercy to either British or Malagasy Protestants.

A change in the attitude of the northerners can be detected from about July 1896 onwards. It became increasingly common to hear of former churchmen joining *menalamba* bands. Partly this was because the pagan revival was running out of steam, partly because the *menalamba* leaders were taking a more sophisticated view of the strategies available to them in combating the French. In August 1896 a British trader was spared because of his nationality. In the same month an anonymous *menalamba* wrote to the northern leaders in the name of a leading magnate in Antananarivo, as was customary when an important strategic measure was being discussed. He borrowed the name of Randriantavy, who had in reality given considerable help to the French, and was a friend of Prince Ramahatra. The anonymous author wrote:

> You should not kill or persecute Evangelists and pastors . . . We should not fight two nations at once, so be careful not to harm British subjects or their property . . . You should send out circular letters about the property of British citizens . . . on these lines: 'We are at war with France. Put up a sign which will allow us to recognize houses occupied by British subjects so that we can distinguish them from other Europeans. You British have never done us any harm. All you have done is to teach us your civilization.'[8]

The false Randriantavy said that the queen had given him these instructions to transmit. A similar letter purported to come from Peill and Matthews, two missionaries well known in northern Imerina. The author, calling himself 'Mr Pillin', said he considered himself a Malagasy. He encouraged the *menalamba* by saying, 'You should read the history of Germany when they [*sic*] defended their homeland', a clear reference to the Franco-Prussian war.[9] It was in the same month of August 1896 that Rabezavana's twelve-year old son was captured by the French. He was kept for a time near Ambohimanga, where the Reverend Jeremiah Peill and his wife Anna were stationed. Anna Peill heard that the French were going to shoot the boy, who may once have been a pupil at the Peills' school, and she successfully appealed for mercy. When he escaped shortly afterwards, he told his father about the incident. Rabezavana claimed that the boy had been saved by magic, but at the same time he seems to have been genuinely grateful to the Peills.[10]

In retrospect it appears that much of the *menalamba* propaganda in favour of the British was preparation for an attack on Ambohimanga, which turned out to be the last major *menalamba* offensive. As King Andria-nampoinimerina's first capital, Ambohimanga enjoyed an unrivalled prestige, especially among the northern demes. It would have greatly enhanced the *menalamba* claim to be endowed with supernatural power if they had been able to capture the village and perform their rituals there on an auspicious day. It was held only by a force of militia, and it was known that there was a considerable anti-French faction among the inhabitants. One of Rabezavana's principal lieutenants, Ramazana, came from the same hamlet near Ambohimanga where the Peills lived, and it may well have been he who forged letters purporting to come from the missionaries. From August 1896 onwards there were numerous letters in circulation reporting that the British would help the *menalamba* to take Ambohimanga. These rumours seemed infinitely more plausible after the execution of Rainandriamampandry. The propaganda campaign culminated in an attack on Ambohimanga on 18 November 1896 by Rabezavana, timed so as to hold the village during the feast of the bath, four days later. In fact the *menalamba* occupied it only for a few hours, and although one war-party was overheard discussing an attack on the Peills' house, they left it alone. The attack coincided with the posting of *menalamba* proclamations in various regions, all claiming 'that the English are a strong and well-meaning people, but that the French are weak and lack perseverance'.[11]

The incidents involving Rainandriamampandry and the Peills gave great impetus to the belief in forthcoming British intervention. Although Gallieni seems to have seen the position in its true light, he was willing to use the rumours for his own purposes. Ironically, it was in the wake of these events that the queen's pastor Andrianaivoravelona was said to have written to the *menalamba* chief and former evangelist Randriamisaodray, who was of the same noble deme as he. For once, the rumour could conceivably have been true, although that is highly debatable. If so, it was a case of reality corresponding to the fiction which Gallieni had done so much to create. The story of a Protestant, pro-British intrigue held a grain of truth only in the aftermath of Rainandriamampandry's death.

CATHOLICS AND PROTESTANTS

The churches in Madagascar had often shown signs of fierce local conflicts. These were thrown into sharp, even violent, relief by the rising in Imerina. It was generally assumed that the French would treat all Catholics favourably, a belief which strengthened the hand of the Catholic faction in national politics, largely composed of nobles from Ambodirano and Vakinisisaony, as well as Catholic congregations in the provinces.

Among the Betsileo, as far north as Ambositra, the rumour in late 1895 was that Protestants would be killed or enslaved, while Catholics would be exempt from forced labour as officials of the state Church had formerly been. During this period, political power still lay with the Merina officials who remained from pre-war days. February 1896 saw the return to Betsileo-land of Dr Louis Besson, who had acted as French vice-resident at Fianarantsoa since 1886 and was notable among French officials for his deep knowledge of Madagascar. He decided that if he were to keep the peace in Betsileo-land he would have to act on his own initiative. Potential trouble lay on several fronts. The beginning of the dry season, in March, was usually the signal for raids by the Bara and Sakalava. Moreover, it was possible that Merina settlers in the province might be affected by the same national feeling as their fellow countrymen. There was a further danger that the Betsileo might rise against their Merina oppressors as the Bestimisaraka had done.

'During the early weeks of the year', a British missionary wrote in reference to the first part of 1896, 'the small band of LMS missionaries in Betsileo were the objects of a most virulent and unjustifiable attack from the French Resident, Dr Besson, immediately after his return to take up his official position in Fianarantsoa.'[12] The Jesuits interpreted the Catholic enthusiasm of the Betsileo rather differently. 'It is obvious', Archbishop Cazet wrote, 'that the Betsileo are coming over to us *en masse*, but that the English and especially the Norwegians are doing everything in their power to stop this tendency.'[13] He held the latter responsible for rumours that Britain would attack France and for physical attacks on Catholic school-pupils.

Care must be taken in allowing for the tendency of Catholic and Protestant missionaries to think the worst of one another. But Besson himself, who had previously enjoyed good relations with Protestant missionaries, cheerfully admitted that 'he cared nothing for religion personally, but he found the Jesuits the best weapon to annoy the LMS with, and injure their work'.[14] He was aware that the Protestant churches had been the main arm of the old royal government in Betsileo-land, and that in early 1896 they represented multiple dangers. Merina preachers were inciting anti-French feeling by taking as their texts the resurrection of Lazarus and the return from captivity in Babylon, the symbolism of which was obvious. At the same time LMS Church officials were still trying to use the old methods, by forcing all and sundry to attend school and chapel, which threatened to inflame the Betsileo.

Besson, acting on his own initiative, decided to act against the Protestant churches. He announced that all *corvées* were abolished except for work on existing roads, that people could attend any school they wished, and that government officials would no longer be allowed to preach. One LMS evangelist, a Merina, was imprisoned after a French priest had accused him of forcing children to attend an LMS school. Another was fined for allegedly striking a priest. Such punishments encouraged the Catholics to believe that France was indeed on their side. But Besson was careful not to go too far in allowing the Jesuits to establish what he called 'a miniature Malagasy theocracy', as the Protestant missionaries had unwittingly done in earlier years.[15]

Whether there was a real threat of a Merina rising in Betsileo-land is unclear. In March and April 1896 there were reports that a particularly unpopular Merina governor had disarmed his Betsileo subjects and was hoarding weapons, allegedly to attack the French. Besson had him arrested. There may have been some truth in this but it is more likely that it was just a part of Besson's campaign to check some of the abuses of the old government. He had to resort to such subterfuge as fabricating charges of subversion because he was not officially permitted to tamper with the existing administration, since the protectorate was then in force. Besson evidently did not believe that a general rising of the Merina colonists in Betsileo-land was imminent. Every other principal Merina governor in the province was left in place and allowed to keep his weapons, thanks to the possibility of bandit attacks. A new Merina governor-general of Betsileo-land had already been appointed on Besson's advice in December 1895, and Besson continued to use Merina officials as advisers. Without any French troops at his disposal he was remarkably successful in preventing a rising in Betsileo-land and stopping conflict from spilling outside the churches. By July 1896 it was said that he was becoming much more favourably disposed towards the LMS, presumably because he thought that its power had now been curbed by the encouragement given to the Catholic congregations.

In Vakinankaratra, immediately to the north of Betsileo-land, French policy responded differently to very similar problems. Alby, the French resident there, was new to Madagascar but had worked closely with Protestant missionaries during his career in Tahiti. Towards the end of 1895, before Alby's arrival, there were already cases of arson and reports of violent disputes over the enrolment of school-pupils. The main trouble-spots were around Ambositra and Betafo, where communities of Betsileo or indigenous Vakinankaratra lived alongside Merina immigrants. Gautier was sent to Vakinankaratra to investigate complaints in March 1896, but his visit had little effect. In eastern Vakinankaratra there was also, of course, a considerable revival of ancestral religion associated with Rainibetsimisaraka.

Matters were further complicated in Vakinankaratra after the *menalamba* attack on Antsirabe in May 1896 by the arrival of French troops, a problem which Besson did not have to face. It was widely said that many French officers were pro-Catholic. Archbishop Cazet himself explained why when he described how 'A police inspector came to tell me that he and his superintendent are convinced that the risings are at least in part encouraged by the Protestants; and that . . . the Resident-General [Laroche] . . . will not believe them.'[16] When this was written in April 1896 there was really no substance to such a charge. It is true that more Protestants than Catholics had abandoned their faith for the *menalamba*, but then Protestants were far more numerous. What really spread such beliefs was the rumour circulating in Malagasy Protestant circles that Britain would help Madagascar. A detachment which came to Antsirabe was led by Captain Lamy, himself a fervent Catholic and a cousin of the Jesuit missionary at Ambositra. He was impressed by the help given to him by the leader of the Catholic faction at Antsirabe, and wanted to promote the man in government service. Alby thought the man untrustworthy and unpopular, saying that his appointment would upset the existing system of government in Vakinankaratra.[17]

This was the sort of case which aligned not only Catholic against Protestant missionaries, but military against civilian administrators. Alby, when he first arrived in Vakinankaratra, may not have realized the extent to which the government there depended on the Lutheran Church. But he consistently supported the existing administration to the extent of underwriting General Rainijaonary's territorial ambitions. Alby had a difficult choice, for any weakening of Rainijaonary's power would have left Rainibetsimisaraka's *menalamba* free rein. It required considerable nerve to allow Rainijaonary such freedom as Alby gave him, as there were many rumours that he would join the *menalamba*. Even some of the Norwegian missionaries finished by half-believing these rumours. The drawback in Alby's commitment to indirect rule in Vakinankaratra was that France was seen to be doing nothing to remove the abuses of the state Church in the province, which in the end drove some Catholics into Rainibetsimisaraka's camp.

The belief that Britain stood for Protestantism and France for Catholicism began to have a notable effect even in areas where Catholic missionary work had previously made little impact. Père Labaste in Marovatana described how a village governor who had briefly fought for the *menalamba* came to beg for atonement. Labaste had him released from custody, and the man became a Catholic. 'A good number of others have behaved in the same way', the priest remarked. 'How many villages I could name where twenty-five or thirty families have left the Protestants to come over to us!'[18] The aftermath or threat of a *menalamba* raid could in itself provoke a crisis of conscience, if that is the phrase to describe such a manifestly political conversion.

This trend was also in evidence in Vakinisisaony, which was both a place with a history of sectarian dispute and the area where, of all Imerina, fighting with the *menalamba* most closely resembled a civil war. 'Note', a French Protestant missionary wrote, '. . . that this is the region which, in the opinion of all, has most suffered from the revolt.'[19] Many people observed that there were two areas of Vakinisisaony which staunchly refused to join the *menalamba* and formed little oases of collaboration. One was the area west of Tsiafahy running into the province of Ambodirano, the territory of the Maroandriana. The other lay in the region bounded by Antanamalaza, Ambohimalaza, and Ambatomanga.

The sharp distinction between collaborators and resisters in Vakinisisaony province ran along lines which had been drawn in earlier years and which reflected old family feuds. In December 1895 a part of the congregation at Antanamalaza asked for the church to be transferred to the Catholics. There had previously been a minority Catholic cult there, persecuted by the Protestant village governor. Throughout the early months of 1896 the dispute between the governor and the Catholics continued. By September 1896 it was complicated by the fact that the village was under constant *menalamba* threat and was packed with refugees from further south.

At Ambohimanambola the problem was even more acute, for this was the former home of the paramount talisman Kelimalaza, from which Rambinintsoa had fled in 1869 and which he revisited in 1895. There was a considerable faction in Ambohimanambola and its outlying villages which supported Rambinintsoa and might have assisted a *menalamba* attack. The governor, Ravalomanda, had to guard against such a possibility, but was himself on bad terms with the Protestant evangelist and schoolmaster because he had recently been divorced. In early April 1896, while Rambinintsoa was still at large in the south, Governor Ravalomanda complained to the government about the evangelist and schoolteacher and tried to have them dismissed. The missionary in charge of the district advised against it, giving the opinion that the governor was probably trying to placate the anti-Christian faction in the village.[20] By the end of the same month, after the death of Rambinintsoa, Governor Ravalomanda changed his tack. He asked the French to establish a garrison in the village, which was done, and then for a Catholic church to be established. He had good contacts in the capital and realized which way the wind was blowing. By October 1896 this manoeuvring had had the effect of drawing the Protestant and pagan factions in Ambohimanambola closer together, so that the Protestants were seriously considering freeing four devotees of Kelimalaza from prison and murdering Ravalomanda.[21]

Ambohimalaza, the site of the only Catholic school in the area before 1896, was also under threat from the *menalamba*. Early in 1896 the French appointed as governor one Razafindrainibe, a member of the leading noble family which had first established the Catholic church at Ambohimalaza. Born in 1862, he had been brought up in the faith and was an ardent Catholic. He had attended a Jesuit school in Antananarivo where he learned to speak and write French. By 1894 he had become the leader of the congregation at Ambohimalaza and head of a union of all the fifteen Catholic congregations in Vakinampasina district. French administrators were satisfied with his ability and his loyalty. But the more powerful he became, the more pressure he put on the people of Ambohimalaza to become Catholics. In the first three weeks of September 1895 the LMS temple was almost completely abandoned, and the Catholics won over 1,000 converts.[22]

In every major case of dispute within a deme or neighbourhood there is a direct continuity in political stances hidden in a succession of different guises, including those of collaboration and resistance and Catholics versus Protestants. That is, feuds which dated back even as far as the eighteenth century had caused certain areas to adopt attitudes directly opposed to their local rivals. The basic dispute might concern people of Avaradrano opposed to people of Vakinisisaony, or quarrels between rival families on other grounds. The French invasion, by destroying the state Church, automatically gave the upper hand in a hundred local disputes to whichever faction belonged to the Catholic Church.

ATTACK ON THE PROTESTANTS

The hostile factions in various parts of Imerina and Betsileo-land which took the Catholic or Protestant labels were driven to violence by the deliberate exploitation of certain myths. Rabezavana was making propaganda for his own insurrectionary purposes which seemed to confirm the suspicion that the *menalamba* had Protestant and British support. The greatest incentive to violence, on the other hand, came from changes in French policy.

A dismantling of the old Merina state, such as Gallieni intended, inevitably involved an assault on the temporal power of the Protestant churches. The *politique des races* could be enforced only by removing powerful Merina churchmen to their place of origin. Gallieni hoped to slacken religious tensions by declaring churches to be the property of the village commune. And, although this was effective in breaking the Protestant hierarchy, it proved to be a signal for anarchy in the guise of Church independence. The LMS had anticipated moves of this kind by inviting representatives of the French Société des Missions Evangéliques (SME) to inspect their work with a view to taking over certain districts. A delegation from the French mission was present in Imerina during 1896, but it was only in May 1897 that the SME began to take over the administration of specific districts.

Gallieni almost certainly underestimated the effect of his policy of attack against the LMS and, to a lesser extent, the Lutherans. He was aware that British missionaries were not personally responsible for the wild rumours spreading through their congregations, and he had no special love for the Jesuits. If his policy were interpreted as pro-Catholic, then that was the price which had to be paid. Sure enough, within a fortnight of Rainandriamampandry's execution a Jesuit wrote that 'General Gallieni is very well disposed towards us.'[23] A French Protestant missionary described how 'an official who is very well-informed about the situation' told him that 'today there has been declared a "war to the knife"', meaning that the government was to launch an attack on the Protestant churches.[24] From October 1896 onwards there was a sharp increase in incidents of sectarian violence, mostly in areas where the Catholics were already established. The virulence of the government's religious policy was reinforced by a number of factors. Local governors now had weapons and could quickly summon the help of French troops. Rainandriamampandry's execution seemed to signify that the attack on the Protestant churches was to be a murderous one. Native officials believed that they had been given a mandate to destroy Protestant influence by firing-squad if necessary.

Moreover Gallieni had ordered the establishment of military administration and direct rule in areas affected by the rising. Under Laroche's protectorate most local officials had been left in place to manage as best they could without the means of coercion. Governors who had survived *menalamba* attacks only by compromising with the rebels were now held to be tainted with treachery. When a French officer came to consider the appointment of trustworthy collaborators he would often distrust the existing governor and seek a local replacement. In any area with a history of sectarian conflict, this local alternative was often a Catholic, because political dissidents had so often used the Catholic Church as a means of expressing opposition. Some officers, puzzled by the complexity of village politics and ignorant of the Malagasy language, would consult a Jesuit missionary, who would naturally recommend a man he trusted, almost invariably a Catholic. Since direct rule meant the installation of French administrators on a large scale, French-speaking interpreters and secretaries were needed. These posts could be filled only by graduates of the Jesuit schools, who were the only Malagasy literate in French. 'Wherever possible, even at the royal palace', a Protestant missionary wrote, 'catholic interpreters are being appointed who are devoted to the priests. As a result the Protestants, misinterpreted by these people, cannot address their complaints to the officers in command.'[25] At the higher levels of the native administration there were many capable Protestant administrators who had collaborated loyally with the French. Official policy was to transfer them to new posts, in order to establish the circulation of personnel on the French model and to break the personal power of those who had been accustomed to rule as laws unto themselves, like Rainijaonary in Vakinankaratra or Rabeony in Antsihanaka.

There was another factor too which added to the tendency to sectarian violence. The emancipation of slaves had created perhaps 300,000 new citizens in Imerina alone who had not been to school, attendance being regarded as a form of forced labour owed by freemen only. The competition to enrol their children on the school-registers greatly intensified local rivalries between the religious confessions.

Among the Betsileo, Gallieni had given orders to Dr Besson as early as 30 September 1896 that the *politique des races* should be implemented and that people of different ethnic or social groups should be made to live in their place of origin. He wrote:

> Overall, I would like to achieve the following position . . . The Betsileo, discreetly encouraged by yourself, are to get rid of their Merina governors and leaders and they are to request you . . . to establish an administration independent of all Merina influence . . . I would like to be able to say to the queen, 'You see, I regret that much as I would like to conserve Your Majesty's authority over the Betsileo, they have thrown out their Merina governors.'[26]

Since many Merina governors in Betsileo-land doubled as evangelists, or at least worked closely with them, this was a clear instruction to Besson to proceed against the Protestant churches in the same way as he had tentatively done already on his own initiative.

Gallieni's arrival had in any case released a new spate of rumours, Protestants claiming that Britain was shortly to intervene, Catholics that Protestantism was now a forbidden religion whose adherents would be made to suffer. At the village level disputes were usually spontaneous and devolved upon the question of schools, so intimately connected with the recruitment of forced labour. From October 1896 Besson was again openly encouraging the movement towards Catholicism, on the grounds that Merina influence must be eradicated. By December 1896 he had declared that Merina Church officials would be repatriated to Imerina. Many thereupon became Catholics. In the south of Betsileo-land, where Merina settlers were least numerous, over twenty LMS churches had been claimed for Catholicism by their congregations, and had been closed pending an official enquiry. According to a Norwegian, Besson told all native officials that in order to retain his confidence they should become Catholic. When the Merina governor-general of the province protested, he was replaced by a Betsileo Catholic, who was also a paramount king in his own right.[27]

By the end of 1896 attacks by Catholics upon LMS school-pupils, and occasional Protestant counter-attacks, were reported from all over the province. The process of repatriation had begun too. Over the next six months about fifty leading Merina churchmen were officially expelled to war-torn Imerina. According to a contemporary estimate that figure could be multiplied by about thirty to allow for their dependants who accompanied them. That does not include those who left under unofficial pressure.[28] Besson generally accepted Malagasy of the Lutheran persuasion as officials, although there were certainly incidents of Lutherans and Catholics fighting one another. The persecutions never totally escaped French control as they were to do in Imerina. Thus Merina officials could remain in favour by becoming Catholic.

114

The lower levels of government in Betsileo-land had always been staffed by native Betsileo rather than Merina, which made Besson's task rather easier. In many places, 'these little lords in their own districts are almost invariably Catholics', a British Protestant said.[29] Having taken control of a local church from the LMS they would then claim exemption from labour dues, which was the traditional right of the leaders of a Protestant congregation. This was in theory forbidden by new labour laws but a sympathetic priest could usually have his leading parishioners nominally registered as working for a French settler so as to secure exemption. The pattern in most country districts was for a predominantly Betsileo congregation, led by its traditional chiefs, to convert to Catholicism and to claim the village church as its own. A Catholic priest would then come to inspect his new flock. LMS missionaries observed the pressure put on these congregations by local officials, and suspected it of being the result of Jesuit intrigue. It was said that Jesuit priests were taking the names of Protestants and telling them that they would not only go to Hell, but that they would have to suffer heavy forced labour in the present life first.

Protestant missionaries generally refused to believe that the Betsileo, who were still on the whole pro-French in 1896–7, might sincerely wish to convert to Catholicism. When the Reverend George Peake saw one of his former temples with a cross on the roof he climbed up and kicked it off, and was duly brought before a tribunal of the native administration which was composed of Catholics. Other missionaries claimed that the Jesuits were encouraging conversions by packing village assemblies with their own followers from outside, or threatening dire consequences if the people remained Protestant. No doubt there were cases where a priest warned Protestants of the danger of eternal damnation, and the congregation interpreted his words in a more worldly sense. Doubtless too priests warned that Protestants would suffer heavier labour dues, which was a fact of life given that local administration was now firmly in the hands of Catholic officials. But in at least one case an LMS missionary was able to produce documentary evidence of intimidation sufficient to convince Gallieni that the Jesuits had gone too far.[30]

The height of the movement in Betsileo-land was in the first half of 1897, when over seventy LMS churches were closed because they were claimed by Catholic congregations. By 1898, when the troubles had died down, the French Protestant missionary society reckoned that the LMS had lost between one-half and two-thirds of its adherents in the province. But at least the movement never degenerated into systematic bloodshed. The arrival of French Protestant missionaries in late 1897 helped to damp rumours that all Protestants were pro-British, while by September 1897 Gallieni had become so disturbed at the excesses of warring factions that he made a tour of Betsileo-land to pronounce on religious liberty. He released some Protestant churchmen from prison. This had some of the desired effect. By the end of the year Besson was allowing Merina Church officials to return, although there were still to be some further expulsions. He announced that any village with fifteen or more Protestant school-pupils could reclaim its temple and school-room. There was something of a return to Protestantism.[31] A factor of at least equal importance was that the French were starting to press the Betsileo hard for forced labour, and this was disproving the belief that Betsileo Catholics would be exempt from labour dues.

Alby, the resident in Vakinankaratra, took a very different line from Besson by supporting the existing administration, and it was largely thanks to this that western Vakinankaratra was hardly touched by the *menalamba*. Strictly speaking Rainijaonary's position as native governor-general of Vakinankaratra province was quite compatible with the *politique des races* since his family came from the province. But Gallieni's policy could not tolerate a magnate of such independent power. In any case Alby's support for Rainijaonary had begun to have considerable disadvantages once the immediate threat of the *menalamba* had receded.

In November 1896 Gallieni posted Alby to the coast, which was part of a wider campaign to purge the administration in Imerina of Laroche's former associates. Alby had become so closely identified with his Malagasy collaborators in Vakinankaratra that the rumour at once spread in the area that he had been sent back to France for execution. It was clear that the Lutheran theocracy was on the wane. Bands of Catholics up to fifty strong were roaming the countryside, chasing Protestant churchmen from their homes and enrolling children by force in Catholic schools. 'They claim quite openly', a Norwegian wrote to Gallieni, 'that if the General wants to impose a policy which they do not themselves desire, he will soon suffer the same fate as Mr Laroche, whom they boast of having chased out.'[32] And it was no use quoting at them Gallieni's pronouncements on religious tolerance, for the Catholic partisans reigned supreme in the villages. As in Betsileo-land, many village notables had long been inclined to regard Catholicism as less oppressive than the Protestant churches. The army officer who succeeded Alby as administrator at Betafo intended to employ such notables as junior officials, in order to break 'the power of the pastors . . . previously the sole intermediary between the authorities and the people'.[33] By March 1897 Rainijaonary and his brother had been transferred to other posts, and some districts where Betsileo communities were numerous had been transferred to the administration of Betsileo province. Again, the movement towards Catholicism was undoubtedly popular in areas settled by Betsileo or by indigenous Vakinankaratra opposed to the old regime of Rainijaonary.

Catholicism seemed to many Malagasy in these areas to hold out the best hope of establishing local autonomy under a loose French hegemony. It was minor village chiefs who led attacks on Protestant churchmen and set up crucifixes on Lutheran temples. There is a curious and illuminating similarity between these types of attacks and *menalamba* assaults on churches and churchmen. In each case the desire to expel agents of the central government was of prime importance.

Ambositra was one of the Betsileo districts worst affected. It had also been the most liable to sectarian violence before 1895, which is evidence that these disputes were not merely the result of Jesuit perfidy as Protestants often claimed. By October 1897 the LMS mission there, now transferred to the French Protestant society, had had eleven of its sixty-two churches destroyed. Forty more had been taken by the Catholics, although more than half of these had not contained a single Catholic before 1895. Four evangelists had converted to Catholicism.[34] At one stage in mid-1897 the movement became completely out of control, as the Lutherans counter-attacked by burning Catholic churches. Even allowing for the bias in missionary sources, it is apparent that in many cases the most ardent 'Catholics' turned out to be from villages which in the past had been most opposed to any form of government control whatsoever. 'Rogues and bandits of every sort', one Protestant called them.[35] This is not the first time that we have observed how the *menalamba* and the Catholic enthusiasts arose from the same quarters in Vakinankaratra, indeed were sometimes the very same people. There was a danger that in destroying the Lutheran apparatus the French might destroy the goodwill of the most prosperous and law-abiding part of the population. By the end of 1897 there was a distinct revival of Protestantism in Vakinankaratra. Still, the commandant of Betafo wrote, 'the religious truce is only superficial, and religious conflicts can break out at any time at all on any pretext'.[36]

Sectarian disputes in central Imerina were far more localized than in Vakinankaratra or Betsileo-land despite the fact that the Jesuits sought converts wherever they could. In one or two districts recently occupied by the *menalamba* LMS evangelists returned to find that although congregations had naturally fallen now that it was no longer compulsory to attend church, they were nevertheless rather more numerous than had been feared. If anything, the rumour that the Protestants were anti-French assisted the LMS in attracting congregations in the north, for everywhere in those regions people were sullenly opposed to the French. There are several known instances of former *menalamba* becoming staunch churchmen in their later years. It seems that many in the north now saw the Protestant Church as the refuge of national pride.

Quarrels between churches were most lethal in those parts of Ambodirano and Vakinisisaony which had previously been worked by Catholic missionaries and where religion was the outward sign of old family feuds. Catholicism was especially associated with noble élites which had been engaged in a long struggle for national power and now saw a chance of reasserting themselves. As in Betsileo-land, from October 1896 onwards there was a spectacular increase in cases of congregations converting to Catholicism *en masse* and claiming the village church for their new faith. Many villages in the north of Vakinisisaony had been attacked or infiltrated by the *menalamba*. It soon emerged that the deadliest weapon in local politics was to accuse an opponent of complicity with the rebels. It was a

117

technique which could be used to full effect only by Catholics, since many French people were by now convinced of the fiction that all Protestants had been more or less sympathetic to the rebels. Thus when the Protestants of Ambohimanambola, now allied to the pagan faction in the village, accused their Catholic governor of being a *menalamba*, the officer in charge asked the opinion of a Jesuit priest. The latter correctly said that the charge was baseless, and the governor was released to take his revenge on his accusers.[37]

The charge carried much more weight when levelled against a leading Protestant. At Fenoarivo there was a long-standing quarrel between Catholics and Protestants, the former being represented largely by an important family of fief-holders. The village was also the station of the governor-general of Ambodirano, a former LMS evangelist who had recently converted to Catholicism when he saw where power now lay. Two evangelists in the district were accused of spreading rumours that Britain was to return in strength to Madagascar, their accusers being men 'who had formerly been put out of Church because of their evil deeds'.[38] The evangelists were beaten and imprisoned, the local French commandant maintaining that they had previously directed the *menalamba* of the area in secret, just as Rainandriamampandry was said to have done on a national scale. From Fenoarivo the Catholics spread out to try and intimidate Protestant congregations in surrounding villages.

In this and many other cases one may observe the lines of local politics being redrawn in just a few short weeks. In the northern part of Vakinisisaony, which had so stoutly resisted *menalamba* attacks, no one emerged stronger after October 1896 than Razafindrainibe. By November 1896 he had at his disposal a force of armed militia to back up his authority as governor of Ambohimalaza. He was related to many of those Malagasy who were now being appointed to the highest administrative posts by the French in recognition of their loyalty.

The troubles of the following months in Vakinisisaony were quite narrowly limited to the territory of the Maroandriana, from Tsiafahy westwards, and to the north of Vakinisisaony, precisely the two areas which had co-operated most fully with the French in the previous year. One after another village churches in these regions were claimed by Catholics. At Antanamalaza the Catholics accused the Protestant governor of rebellion and he was sentenced to chains for life, although he had given military help to the French.[39] At Tsiafahy all the leading Malagasy officers became Catholic almost overnight. The LMS could count only forty to sixty supporters there by the end of October 1896, where previously there had not been a single Catholic. At Ambohimanambola, Governor Ravalomanda was released from prison and set out to regain control of the village from the Protestants. The village contained two churches, one Catholic and one Protestant. Ravalomanda could now command the help of Razafindrainibe, and he used it to put pressure on the Protestants of his village. On Sunday 20 December 1896 Governor Ravalomanda ordered the entire population of

Ambohimanambola to attend the Catholic church. Some refused, so he told the bishop of Antananarivo that his people all wished to become Catholic, and therefore had the right to claim the Protestant church as their own, but were being prevented by a few Protestant leaders. Next Sunday, 27 December, Bishop Cazet appeared at the Protestant temple during a service, apparently in all good faith, 'and after stopping the singing, he walked to the pulpit and informed the congregation that he had come to conduct a Catholic service in that building'. The evangelist stood and argued with him in front of the congregation. Governor Ravalomanda was summoned and he ruled that the majority of the congregation wished to become Catholic, publicly stating that 'Protestants are the *fahavalo* [enemies] of France, which, as we are now under martial law, means that, if formally accused, they may be seized and shot as rebels.'[40] Bishop Cazet also reported the event to the commandant of the military district in which Ambohimanambola lay. The commandant declared the temple now to be Catholic, and he had his soldiers fix a notice to the door to that effect. Within three months Governor Ravalomanda, having regained control of the two churches in his village, had accused the evangelist of rebellion. This man was sentenced to death but later released after an appeal.[41]

Protestant missionaries were convinced that in many similar cases mass conversions were carried out only under intimidation. British missionaries were always inclined to think the worst of their Jesuit counterparts and of the French in general, but there is abundant evidence that the accusation was justified. Jesuit sources themselves sometimes rejoice in the fact that French soldiers were prepared to encourage the intimidation of Protestants.[42] Indeed Gallieni issued a rebuke to the colonel commanding the military district of Ambatomanga, which included Ambohimanambola and the rest of northern Vakinisisaony, and he ordered his transfer in March 1897. For the priests the serious business of saving souls was of paramount importance. The soldiers were more than ever convinced that all Protestants were suspect.

But the partiality of some officers, and the over-enthusiasm of some priests, were not the main factors in the incidence of sectarian quarrels. North Vakinisisaony had a history of such disputes. The role of Razafindrainibe is of special interest because he was a member of a family which had been prominent in sectarian disputes for over twenty years. By the beginning of 1897 he was acting as the principal Malagasy official in the large military district of Ambatomanga and he was confirmed as native governor-general of the district in March 1897. It is no coincidence that the sectarian quarrels degenerated into wholesale executions from this time onwards. Apart from his extensive family connections among the nobles of northern Vakinisisaony, Razafindrainibe had contacts with the Catholic party in the capital which was supreme once Rainandriamampandry had been killed. There is every reason to believe a Protestant description of Razafindrainibe's 'personal system of conversion'. 'It consists', he wrote, 'in

119

obliging Protestant village governors to change their religion; if they refuse, he replaces them with Catholics . . . Since these village governors are miniature dictators, who can impose crippling forced labour on anyone whom they have reason to dislike, and since they can even accuse people of rebellion, the villagers tremble at their very word.'[43]

Prince Ramahatra, one of the chiefs of the Catholic party in national politics, had much influence in nominating native officials in Vakinisisaony. He generally used it to recommend members or clients of the Catholic families at court which had established themselves as the leading French collaborators. Thus after October 1896 many of the old noble fief-holders and representatives of Vakinisisaony reappeared in a new guise as officials of the French administration. Many of them were doubly useful in that their long association with the Catholic Church had taught them some French. When Razafindrainibe made a recommendation or an accusation he could rely on support at the highest level. When he claimed that Betafo and some other villages in his military district should be incorporated in the territory of Ambohimalaza, Ramahatra and Rasanjy supported him. The pastors of Betafo and Ambohimahatsinjo, who complained that they belonged to the province of Avaradrano and did not wish to pass under the administrative control of Ambohimalaza, were accused of rebellion and shot, 'consequent upon information gathered by Mr Rasanjy and upon his orders'.[44]

After Razafindrainibe's appointment as governor-general of Ambatomanga military district no Protestant official in that area could feel safe, since he had the backing of everyone who mattered. In at least eight villages under his authority Protestant governors or pastors were shot on trumped-up charges of rebellion. At Anjeva no fewer than thirty-seven people were shot in one day after a denunciation by the governor, a former Protestant who had become Razafindrainibe's man. 'It became a common saying among the people that: "Formerly they had but one sovereign . . . but now they had one in every village."'[45]

Ramahatra, who had the whole of Vakinisisaony under his authority, saw the religious controversy both as a means of putting his clients in charge of every village through intermediaries like Razafindrainibe, and as a means of stamping out the last traces of rebellion. One of the many anti-French rumours circulating in Malagasy Protestant circles was that Britain and France were at war, and that a British fleet was coming to save Madagascar. It was to dispel such doubts about French permanence that the Reverend W. J. Edmonds was accused of spreading anti-French propaganda in Vakinisisaony and was put on trial. It emerged that the accusation was false, and had probably been initiated by Ramahatra.[46]

The Edmonds affair in particular convinced Gallieni that things had gone too far, and indeed questions were now being asked in the Chamber of Deputies in Paris. The removal of the pro-Catholic Colonel Borbal-Combret as commandant of Ambatomanga military district did some good, but false denunciations still occurred because French officers were reliant on Malagasy Catholic interpreters. Rasanjy, Ramahatra and their party could not be dismissed from their control of the native administration without sparking off a Protestant counter-attack and completely undoing the work of pacification. The execution of Rainandriamampandry and the abolition of the monarchy had left them unassailable as France's leading collaborators. Even more embarrassing was the murder of two French Protestant missionaries, Escande and Minault, by the remnants of a *menalamba* band which had been joined by fugitives from forced labour. This occurred in May 1897 at a time when Gallieni was making premature claims that the work of pacification was all but complete. Relations between Protestant and Catholic missionaries were so bad that many Protestants both European and Malagasy seriously considered the murder to have been the work of the Jesuits. Gallieni began to regret having ordered the sacrifice of Rainandriamampandry, especially as it had earned him a reprimand from his superiors in Paris. By the end of 1897, though, the general had succeeded in persuading his officers in Vakinisisaony not to heed every accusation emanating from native officials and to take action against false witnesses. The transfer of some mission districts to the French Protestant missionaries from May 1897 also provided some relief. The pendulum had swung so far that one of the main problems now was how to remove the privileges of Catholic communities, because the Jesuits were claiming that their leading parishioners should be exempt from forced labour. A temporary compromise was found by proclaiming that Protestant schoolteachers too should be exempt, which further helped to defuse the religious problem. But even as late as 1899, the governor of Manarintsoa was denounced and sentenced to chains for life for his alleged part in the murder of three Frenchmen in 1896.

There was certainly a close connection between control of churches and schools and the recruitment of forced labourers. There was a marked release of tension when it was established that Catholics and Protestants would receive equal treatment in respect of labour dues. In the north of Vakinisisaony, an area of mixed settlement, this was linked to other disputes. When the pastor of Betafo complained that he wished to remain in the administrative orbit of Ilafy, it was partly because the Catholics at Ambohimalaza, being rivals of long standing, would surely use their power to heap the heaviest labour on the Tsimiamboholahy of Betafo, who were intruders on their territory.[47] The false accusation against Protestants was also a means by which old enemies settled personal scores, or debtors got rid of their creditors.

The disputes were most bitter in Vakinisisaony, where there was a high concentration of demes of great antiquity and prestige bidding for a share in whatever structure of power would emerge from the French invasion. The exceptional savagery of the war in this area, and of the ensuing religious disputes, arose from the fact that both collaborators and resisters were often descended from the same source, that is from the kings who had reigned in the first cradle of the Merina monarchy. Some of the demes of the north and west of the province had become split from their erstwhile allies at some time in the eighteenth century. Since then, only those who had co-operated with Andrianampoinimerina and his successors had been associated either with government posts or with trade privileges.

Both Razafindrainibe, the leader of the pro-French faction at Ambohimalaza, and Rafiringa, whom the southern *menalamba* elected king of Madagascar, were heirs to the same tradition. Rafiringa saw himself as the head of a loose federation of demes owing allegiance to no outside group, whether of Avaradrano or of France. The Catholics of Ambohimalaza also wished to control their own affairs and return to their rightful place in the national constitution, as they saw it. The Catholic Church, not the *menalamba* rising, was to be the instrument of their restoration. There was a belief that a republican constitution, often misleadingly translated into Malagasy as *menabe*,[48] meaning an area of self-governing demes, would allow a greater degree of autonomy than the constitutional monarchy of Queen Ranavalona III and the Andafy-Avaratra had permitted. The leading Andriantompokoindrindra of Ambohimalaza and their allies, who collaborated with the French throughout 1896, had been close enough to the centre of the old royal government to realize that Europeans were a permanent feature of the political landscape. They had also accepted, by and large, the destruction of the talismans, in sharp contrast to the people of southern and eastern Vakinisisaony who sheltered Kelimalaza after 1869 and supported its restoration by the *menalamba*. When Rambinintsoa brought the talisman back into the open in 1895, the quarrel which was provoked in Vakinisisaony was very like a family dispute.

Within eighteen months of his arrival in Madagascar Gallieni had succeeded in dismantling the Protestant churches as an organ of government. He did this at considerable political cost. He earned the hatred of a number of wealthy and powerful Protestant families who made life difficult for the colonial government over the next few years by employing French lawyers to claim French citizenship on their behalf and to argue against the legality of certain requisitions of property. This same Protestant faction was to be at the heart of the first major nationalist movement of the twentieth century. Later Gallieni was to pay considerable amounts of money from government funds to Rainandriamampandry's widow and to other families that he had harmed, in an effort to buy their goodwill.[49]

In ousting the Protestant magnates from the government Gallieni had tipped the balance of power in favour of the rival Catholic faction led by Rasanjy and Ramahatra. The former was to live up to his merited reputation as a political in-fighter on numerous occasions in extending his control over the native administration. Ramahatra, although apparently rather less mercenary than Rasanjy, used his power to place the province of Vakinisisaony in the hands of his noble Catholic associates and kinsmen. It is ironic that Gallieni, who thought he had come to Madagascar to destroy feudalism, should unwittingly have been the means of restoring the nobility of Imerina's oldest province to a position of real political power. Similarly, in many circles the Protestant Church gained a reputation for representing a pure strain of Malagasy nationalism which few would have accorded it before 1896.

RELIGION, RESISTANCE AND COLLABORATION

Analysis of the religious disputes of 1896–7 throws into relief the position of those Malagasy who actively collaborated with the French. When the invaders took Antananarivo in October 1895 virtually the only Merina who saw any merit in the new regime were the wealthier members of the Catholic élite, like Ramahatra, or like Paul Rafiringa whose diaries have been the subject of an exhaustive study.[50] Most Catholic courtiers were nobles from the south of Imerina who had been bitter enemies of the northern Andafy-Avaratra for decades. Once Gallieni had declared war on the Protestant churches, as he did in effect by having Rainandriamampandry and Ratsimamanga executed in October 1896, the Catholic faction in national politics had an ideal opportunity to extend its provincial power-base by purging Protestant officials. This they did wherever the Catholics had an existing foothold, particularly in northern Vakinisisaony.

The Protestant élite which had run the state before 1895 was put in a very different position. The majority of Protestant officials were sincere patriots, even nationalists. But they were too closely associated with the old regime to join a provincial and anti-Christian movement such as that of the *menalamba*. Protestant magnates in fact proved themselves useful allies of France in those cases where they were allowed to show their worth, as Governor Rainijaonary was able to do in Vakinankaratra. The problem was that the French did not want them as collaborators.

Ranchot and Duchesne, respectively the civil and military chiefs of the French administration from October 1895 to January 1896, had a clear brief from their foreign ministry to protect the existing Merina government of Madagascar while at the same time preventing any counter-attack. They failed utterly to appreciate the gravity of Imerina's internal crisis or the strength of anti-government and anti-French feeling in the country at large. Rather than disarm loyalist Protestant officials, as they did, Ranchot and Duchesne would have done better to put extra troops at the disposal of the native administration, although that would have required unusual courage or recklessness in such a newly conquered territory. In the crucial early months of the French conquest there were very few French officials who had sufficient knowledge of Madagascar to distinguish potential collaborators. The few who did, like Dr Besson, were to prove their worth in the months ahead.

The official policy of the protectorate was further hampered by the anti-Merina sentiments of French soldiers and settlers. There was, after all, a long French tradition of supporting the non-Merina peoples of Madagascar against the government in Antananarivo. The French liked to think that they would be welcomed in much of Madagascar as liberators from the tyranny of Merina over-rule. And sure enough there was evidence from the first that the Antankarana, the Betsimisaraka and the Betsileo saw them in that light. If France were to have supported the protectorate to the hilt, it would have involved helping Protestant and allegedly anglophile Merina officials to repress separatist movements among the Betsimisaraka and others who had greeted the French invasion favourably. This was distasteful, although it was nevertheless done in some places. Since Imerina was a theocracy, a strict protectorate would also have implied aiding the British-influenced state Church to curtail the activities of French Jesuits, which was clearly absurd. In fact until Gallieni's arrival the French compromised by leaving Merina Protestant officials in place but leaving them unarmed and largely unaided against the forces of discontent that stalked the country.

Merina Protestant officials, even if they were inclined reluctantly to work with the French, were placed in an impossible position for much of 1896. They were distrusted by their French masters and persecuted by the *menalamba*. Some of the insurgents saw the situation clearly and realized that these Protestant officials were potentially valuable allies or even leaders. When the government persecution of Protestants began in earnest in October 1896 the Protestants came to look increasingly like true Malagasy patriots: the French disliked them, therefore they must be on the side of the *menalamba*. Ever since that time there has existed an important tradition of Protestant anti-colonialism in Imerina. However, that Protestant tradition is not the same as the less articulate and less well documented mass nationalism which is descended from the *menalamba*.

The position of the French administration in 1895–6 was almost untenable, which reflects the fact that the invaders had opened a Pandora's box by invading Madagascar. French policy during 1896–9 then tried to change from backing a Merina-dominated protectorate, half-heartedly espoused, to one of divide and rule. The latter was euphemistically known as the *politique des races*. But who could administer the colony of Madagascar for France if not the Merina? What other people had experience of administration on a national scale? And if Merina Protestants were unacceptable, then the collaborators would have to be Merina Catholics. For several years the French achieved the notable feat of alienating almost every group in Madagascar with the exception of the Betsileo and the Merina Catholics, led by the nobles of Vakinisisaony who returned triumphant to reclaim some of the power taken from them by Andrianampoinimerina a century before.

Too late, the subject peoples of Madagascar saw their error in welcoming the French, who had no intention of giving them their freedom. As the *menalamba* died, other movements of resistance were born.

6

The spread of resistance (1897 to 1899)

People of Madagascar, unite . . . The strength of Madagascar and of its defenders will soon be clear.

Letter from Rabezavana, written in his base called 'the Camp of Misery', 27 February 1897

THE LAST OF THE *MENALAMBA*

One of the most curious features of the rising was the way in which reality fed on myth to an unusual degree. This is most obvious in the northerners' adoption of a pro-British and pro-Protestant attitude which had been created largely by French belief. In the same way, the rising had begun amidst rumours of French atrocities and of imminent changes in old customs which were baseless, but which had a firm foundation in fact by the end of 1896. French massacres and burnings drove people into the rebel camps and convinced the veterans that they were fighting a war to the death. Similarly the French had respected tombs until the start of the rising, but thereafter sometimes defiled them as a means of spreading terror. The abolition of slavery and noble privileges, and the imposition of harsh land and labour laws, also fulfilled earlier predictions. By May 1897 it was impossible to distinguish between veteran resisters and fugitives from colonial laws in the band which killed Escande and Minault. The rising changed markedly in character even while it was in progress.

The *menalamba* were at the height of their power between June and August 1896, but even then some people were deserting to sow their rice. The scorched earth policy was beginning to bring forth its results. By the end of the year people were surrendering in large numbers to avoid famine. The only people not threatened with starvation were the Europeans, since after September 1896 they were able to secure enough imported supplies. Still, the effect of the *menalamba* blockade should not be underestimated. It cost a lot of money, while one French soldier at least did not get his first pair of boots or full rations until March 1897.[1]

As the rebels grew thinner, their attacks grew weaker. The siege of Ambatondrazaka was finally raised in October 1896. A month later occurred the last big *menalamba* attack, on Amobhimanga. The rebels' proclamations began to carry the ring of despair. In November 1896 Rabezavana was still telling the French that they should fear 'never to see the fine city of Paris again'. They were, he said, like rats who try to chew a

125

piece of iron.[2] But three months later he had renamed his base 'the Camp of Misery', and was making a last desperate appeal to all Malagasy to join him, even those who had previously collaborated with the invaders.[3]

The first of Gallieni's new measures to come into effect was the abolition of slavery. Although the timing of emancipation was not of his choosing there is no doubt that he had intended to enact the measure very soon in any case. Some people thought that the *menalamba* at first included a relatively small proportion of slaves. Gallieni hoped that emancipation would win all slaves to the French cause and encourage desertions from the *menalamba*. Once feudal privileges had been abolished this would, he thought, create a large and mobile labour force 'to the benefit of the lower classes and the freed slaves'.[4] Freemen, no longer obliged to work for their feudal masters, would have to do forced labour for the state and to pay taxes which would encourage them to find wage employment. The new labour-dues were in theory lighter than had been customary under the old regime, but they were often abused. Many people were obliged to do two or three times their legal quota. It was quite common for subsistence farmers to be declared vagrants, which then made them subject to imprisonment and penal labour. Gallieni intended that the labour force should serve to encourage French settlers and above all to carry out his ambitious programme of public works.

In the past Merina slaves had often been distinctly unwilling to receive manumission. Freedom brought a desirable increase in social status, but it also carried very heavy labour-dues and military service. It was not surprising therefore that the former slaves regarded their freedom in 1896 with very mixed feelings. In central Imerina, where there were as many as two slaves to one freeman, the news of emancipation brought widespread jubilation. There were reports of freed slaves giving to French administrators the symbols of allegiance traditionally given by freemen to their lord. It was in the same spirit that so many former slaves were to join the Catholic Church. Quite a few stayed with their former masters as though nothing had changed and worked as share-croppers. The thing which most surprised the old Madagascar hands was the considerable number of freed slaves who left central Imerina to seek new lands or to return to the distant parts of the island from which their forefathers had been taken as captives. Even in heavily populated central Imerina the overall effect was to reduce the economies of scale which could increase agricultural production.[5]

It was in the more thinly populated border-lands that emancipation brought real hardship to former slaves. It almost led to a revolt in parts of Vakinankaratra because the owners had lost a capital investment and the former slaves were without means of subsistence. Again, this led to the break-up of some of the larger agricultural units.[6] Around Lake Itasy there was a noticeable movement of ex-slaves towards the *menalamba* camps. A banker with long experience of Madagascar recalled how emancipation in general led to 'a distinct increase of frustration'. He continued:[7] 'Recall the events of October and November 1896 and the bitterness with which the tribes on the edge of the forest fought . . . Above all it should be noted how, in these forest retreats, masters and emancipated slaves combined in a common hatred of ourselves.'

Only among the Betsileo were conditions such that emancipation was an unqualified success. None but the richest Betsileo had owned slaves, but they drew some benefit from the return of those of their compatriots who had for generations been slaves in Imerina. In most other territories outside Imerina proper, emancipation played an important part in spreading the rising of the *menalamba*.

Within a few months of the emancipation decree French troops were pushing the *menalamba* further afield, occupying their base camps and their precious rice-fields. The southern bands were shrinking daily from disease and desertion. They took refuge in the traditional sanctuary, the forest, and there dissidents of every origin gathered. Rainibetsimisaraka resumed relations with some of the independent Malagasy groups which had bought plunder from him in the old days of banditry. He was in close touch with groups of Tanala and Bezanozano, and had ambassadors with King Toera of Menabe, hundreds of miles away on the west coast.[8]

Those who suffered the worst were probably Rabozaka's followers, who likewise took to the forest but had fewer resources to fall back on. They were already dying of starvation by the beginning of 1897. Rabezavana was more fortunate in having behind him a hinterland rich with cattle, where the French had not yet penetrated. It was here that there rose to prominence the last of the main *menalamba* leaders, a man called Rainitavy. He was a Merina from just outside Antananarivo who had fought against the French in the war of 1883–5. Later he was sent to be governor of Mampikomy in the far north-west of Madagascar. The population of this area was very mixed, but was mainly Sakalava with a fair number of Merina troops and settlers.

Like Rabezavana, whom he probably knew before 1895, Rainitavy was responsible for governing a region noted for banditry. He survived and prospered, despite the weakness of the forces at his disposal, by successful use of local politics. He joined the *menalamba* in June 1896, but his name was rarely heard in the days when the French were confined in Antananarivo. He recruited Merina troops, Sakalava herdsmen, and fugitives from the Suberbie gold-fields. With them he attacked loyalist garrisons from the province of Boina almost as far as the north-east coast, and sent contingents to fight in the siege of Ambatondrazaka. But his main function at this stage was to buy guns from the Indian and creole traders of the coast and send them to Rabozaka.[9] It was only in December 1896 that France first penetrated the hinterland north of Ambatondrazaka in the person of the civilian administrator Pradon, at the head of a company of Betsimisaraka troops. He arrived at the garrison town of Mandritsara to find that Rainitavy's men had already killed the Merina governor. In any case the *politique des races* required Pradon to adopt as collaborators local Tsimihety, Sakalava and Betsimisaraka notables. His main choice at Mandritsara was a Tsimihety chief who had already clashed with the Merina administration in 1895. He appointed as a junior governor a Sakalava who had only recently returned from fighting against France at the siege of Ambatondrazaka. It may have been official policy to pretend that the Merina were anti-French and the other peoples pro-French, but administrators on the spot knew otherwise.[10]

Pradon noted that many of the richest people in the far north, Merina or not, were with the *menalamba*, while those who had lost cattle to the bandits in recent years were generally inclined to favour the French.[11] This was the only *menalamba* movement in which control of commerce was instrumental in determining patterns of collaboration and resistance. Many of the Merina in the area, military and civilian alike, had in the past worked as commercial agents for the European, creole and Indian traders who had recently begun to penetrate inland markets. The Sakalava herdsmen were often engaged in cattle- and slave-raiding, which was a booming business. It is safe to say that any Merina governor who managed to remain powerful in the far north did so only by turning a blind eye to such activities. Indeed, there is a report that Rainitavy actually led a bandit raid in 1895.[12] Henceforth he enlisted some of these colleagues into the *menalamba*, but always under the name of 'the patriots'. One of their favourite targets was the Indian and European stores which were a feature of the larger northern villages. Indian and creole traders on the coast, many of them British subjects, found the *menalamba* rather more useful, since there was money to be made selling them guns in exchange for their captured cattle and slaves. Gallieni was informed of this by his agents on the coast, and the need to strengthen his hand against these troublesome traders may well have been one of the reasons for his encouragement of the rumours of British intervention in the rising of the *menalamba*.

The news of the abolition of slavery united still further the disparate elements who followed Rainitavy, because so many of them had vested interests in the slave trade. When the French arrived in the north-west in force, in May 1897, they found him to have perhaps 1,000 Merina troops and as many Sakalava herdsmen and refugees of other origin. He commanded them in the same way as the other northern *menalamba*, writing to his lieutenants in the name of the homeland, issuing proclamations, threatening to burn Majunga and throw the French into the sea.[13]

The history of Rainitavy is a demonstration of how the *menalamba* leaders adapted their appeal to take account of rapidly changing conditions. By the time Rainitavy became a force to be reckoned with, the earliest *menalamba* were ceasing to be an organized movement. They had been dealt two blows from which they could not recover. The first, in February 1897, was the abolition of the Merina monarchy.

The second blow, two weeks after the abolition of the monarchy, was the greatest desecration which could be imagined, and it destroyed the Merina kingdom for ever. Gallieni had realized that the *menalamba* could only achieve a real success, once they had lost the military initiative, by taking the holy town of Ambohimanga on an auspicious day as they had tried to do for the feast of *fandroana* in November 1896. He therefore ordered that the remains of the kings at Ambohimanga should be exhumed and transferred to Antananarivo.

The tombs were opened on Sunday 14 March 1897, exactly one year after the northern rising had erupted. Great care was taken to observe the due rituals of royal burial. Only a privileged group of nobles was permitted to handle the silver coffin which was found inside Andrianampoinimerina's tomb. Among the large crowd which gathered to witness the exhumation there was a moment of consternation when they realized that the royal coffin had inadvertently been placed with its head facing south, which was the direction associated with sorcery. The coffin was duly loaded onto a cart. Preceded by torch-bearers who illuminated the night sky, the procession of porters, military escort and mourners set off on the twelve-mile journey to Antananarivo. It took nine and a half hours, retracing the same route which Andrianampoinimerina had himself taken when he left Ambohimanga to conquer the citadel of Antananarivo a century before. Up to 30,000 people followed his coffin, in silence except for the sound of 'strange music, of an infinite sweetness and incomparable sadness'.[14]

At Antananarivo the coffins of Andrianampoinimerina and his royal forebears were opened. The objects inside them were put in the palace of the queen who had so recently been exiled, which henceforth served as a museum. The bodies were put in new tombs in the citadel of the capital where they lie to this day. And there, as Hubert Deschamps observed, Andrianampoinimerina's tomb continues to dominate the plain of Antananarivo as his life had dominated its history.

By March 1897 French military superiority was so overwhelming that Gallieni could be confident of eventually starving the *menalamba* into submission. But that would take time, and the remaining *menalamba* leaders were having a disturbing effect on the non-Merina peoples whom the French hoped to enlist as collaborators. It was important to restore peace to Imerina, which was now in a dreadful state. The rising and the famine which lasted into 1898 cost a total of between 50,000 and 100,000 Malagasy lives.[15] French casualties were not negligible either: 62 soldiers died from enemy action and 314 from disease in the year from 1 July 1896.[16] This does not include the handful of European civilians killed by the *menalamba*, nor the casualties received in the early part of 1896. More importantly, it disguises the number of troops of the old royal army who stayed loyal to the French and died in their service.

The first suggestion that France should negotiate peace with the *menalamba* seems to have come from Prince Ramahatra. Just four days after Rainandriamampandry's death he suggested using the story of a high-level conspiracy as a basis for discussions with Rabezavana.[17] In March 1897 the idea was revived. Emissaries were carefully chosen from among those royal officials who had collaborated with the French and who had had personal contact with the *menalamba* leaders before the war. Thus negotiations with Rainibetsimisaraka were entrusted first to a former governor of Antsirabe and then to his old enemy Pastor Robena. Rabezavana was to be sought by Rainianjanoro, who had done business with the governors of the north in the days of recruitment for the gold-workings. The negotiators were sent out with instructions to win the confidence of the *menalamba* chiefs and persuade them to treat with French officers in person. Behind the scenes there was a great deal of intrigue. Rasanjy, the undisputed master of manoeuvre since he had seen his rivals destroyed, was giving secret orders of his own to his friend Rainianjanoro. He wanted to extend his system of private patronage to the far north. More immediately he advanced the money for Rainianjanoro to buy cattle cheap from the *menalamba* and to sell them for a handsome profit at Antananarivo.[18] Rasanjy's power was now such that Gallieni was unable to prevent his omnipresent influence, despite complaints from senior officers and even from the colonial minister in Paris.[19]

Gallieni had intrigues of his own. The officer who was to supervise the surrender of Rabezavana was Hubert Lyautey, whom Gallieni liked and trusted. The general gave him secret instructions to give Rabezavana a guarantee of liberty in return for providing faked evidence that Rainandriamampandry had directed the original rising of the *menalamba*. Government emissaries demanded the same conditions of Rainibetsimisaraka. Both men surrendered in June 1897, providing false letters said to have come from Rainandriamampandry in January and February 1896. They then went to the capital and made formal acts of surrender, declaring, in speeches written for them by one of Gallieni's aides, that they had been mere tools of the Merina oligarchy and of Rainandriamampandry in particular. Gallieni then sent this retrospective 'evidence' to Paris, as proof that he had not been mistaken. This became the accepted version of events in history books. Once more one may see myth and reality intruding upon one another.[20]

The negotiations enabled Gallieni to use Rabezavana's insurrectionary organization in the interests of pacification. Within a few weeks of his first meeting with Lyautey on 31 May 1897, the former governor of Antsatrana had persuaded several of his allies to surrender on the understanding that they would be spared. Rafanenitra too submitted and saved his life by giving information about an alleged British connection. Before long even minor chiefs in the north were making the wildest allegations about British agents as a prerequisite to their surrender. Poor Reverend Jeremiah Peill was frequently accused of having encouraged the *menalamba*, the consequence of his name having been used as propaganda some months earlier.[21] Gallieni was now seeking the same sort of forged documents against the LMS as he had already obtained against Rainandriamampandry. It would help him to justify his assault upon the Protestant churches. Lyautey responded by ordering one of his officers to find a letter from Peill to the *menalamba*. 'I guarantee that I will support any promise which you may make, financial or otherwise', he wrote to one of his junior officers. '*No such letter can ever be too expensive for us.*'[22] It is no wonder that the belief in British intervention proved so durable when the French authorities were willing to pay for forged evidence of its existence.

Rainitavy surrendered in November 1897. Of the main northern leaders only Rabozaka was left hiding in the forest until February 1898, when he too surrendered and went through the charade of providing the text of a letter from Rainandriamampandry and declaring in public that his revolt had been ordered by a higher authority. Now that the *menalamba* chiefs had fulfilled the role which Gallieni required of them they were dispensable. Rabozaka and Rafanenitra were sent into exile. Rainitavy was shot, despite the promise of clemency which he had received. Rabezavana feared the same fate and took to the hills to rejoin the remnants of his band.

There followed a war of nerves in which the prize was control of local government in the north. The royal administration in and around Maro-fotsy-land had joined the rising so completely that it was not easy to find useful collaborators other than former *menalamba*. Furthermore some of the minor northern leaders, including Rabezavana's secretary, continued to roam the hills with a few followers, raiding cattle, enlisting fugitive labourers and army deserters. The latter were especially dangerous because they were armed and trained by the French. Rabezavana played on this fear by letting it be known that he would rejoin the last *menalamba* for good if he or his people were pressed too far. It was in September 1898, shortly after his brief return to active resistance, that the French suffered their heaviest single loss of the entire campaign. A group of Merina militia deserters, armed with the latest Lebel rifles and in touch with the *menalamba* groups, ambushed a French patrol and killed seven men.[23]

The remaining *menalamba* could still muster a band up to 230 strong on occasion – hence the danger if they were to obtain guns either from deserters or from British traders. Lyautey thought that they might even spark off a new wave of revolt if the government persisted in using Merina troops in the north, and if the labour burdens on the settled part of the population were not eased. The financial and human resources of Imerina were stretched near to breaking point.[24]

Lyautey was not far wrong. When news arrived of the famous Anglo-French clash of 1898 at Fashoda in the Sudan there was a return of seditious rumours all over Imerina, and indeed in some other parts of Madagascar. Among the Mandiavato, Rabozaka's people, there was trouble. Protestant pastors, schoolteachers and an evangelist were inciting people to revolt over taxes and 'especially in protest over the numerous labour-dues to which the Malagasy are subjected'. They were said to be in league with one of Rabozaka's former lieutenants who was still at large. The Zafimamy seemed on the verge of joining them.[25] There was a marked increase in activity by the northern bands led by some of Rabezavana's old friends, who were rumoured to have contacts in the capital. There was a danger that they might raise the province of Vonizongo.[26] To maintain order there was no choice but to treat with respect those ex-*menalamba* who were prepared to collaborate, and to bring Rabezavana back from exile despite the fact that he had reneged on his submission.

The same insurrectionary revival was in evidence in south Imerina. There was a series of arrests of conspirators in the villages around Ambohimalaza and Antanamalaza, accused of planning a rising for 17 March 1899. Their object, the suspects said, was to drive the French out of Antananarivo 'and to restore to the Malagasy their former rights'. The leading conspirators were said to be former *menalamba* who gained a hearing because of the misery in the countryside. They claimed to have secret sympathizers among the leading Protestants in the capital, just as the *menalamba* had done three years before.[27] This is further proof that the allegations of a conspiracy among the urban élite in 1896 were unfounded, but that they corresponded to a very basic political structure of Merina society. It is interesting that these reports from Vakinisisaony in 1899 came from two villages which had been centres of collaboration in 1896. It seems most likely that the agitation stemmed from some of the Protestants who had been so ruthlessly persecuted by Governor Razafindrainibe of Ambohimalaza and who continued to live under his administration. The areas named were close to the route to Tamatave where people were obliged to work on the new road which was under construction.

In other parts of Imerina, and even in Betsileo-land, the discontent was more muted, but always it had the same causes: heavy taxes and labour-dues, and the rumour that Britain and France were at war. At Anosibe, the pagan centre from which the *menalamba* in Vakinisisaony had arisen in 1896, there was a movement towards the Protestant Church, now administered by the Société des Missions Evangéliques.[28] It was a far cry from the burning of churches and the killing of churchmen in 1895–6. The religious persecutions also encouraged a millenarian element which had previously been immersed in orthodox belief. Some natural disasters in 1897 were popularly attributed to the wrath of God. Several millenarian movements arose in Betsileo-land during the next ten years.

The most remarkable case of millenarian belief arose in 1899. It was sparked off by a scientific article in one of the reviews which the British missionary societies published in the Malagasy language. The article was apparently written in a rather apocalyptic tone. It probably discussed shifts in world climate or calculated the likelihood of a major flood or some similar natural catastrophe. It was not by all accounts intended to have a political effect, but the ideas fell on ground which had already been made fertile for millenarian beliefs. Many Malagasy readers interpreted the article to mean that the world would come to an end on 13 November 1899. This rumour was so widely believed in all the highlands, including among the Betsileo, that many who heard it travelled to their ancestral tombs to be sure of eternal rest among their families when the end came. An administrator wrote:[29]

> This reaction has been so widespread that the inhabitants of this area, and probably those of the whole island, have been living for several days in the grip of real terror. All work has been neglected and my officials add that many people have left their homes *to go and die near their family tombs*!

But there was no risk of the French being seriously threatened by this unrest unless the predictions of British intervention were fulfilled. The metropolitan government in fact took such a possibility so seriously that it moved the deposed Queen Ranavalona III from her place of exile in Réunion to Algiers, where she was out of harm's way. For the colonial administration in Madagascar the agitation served as a warning that the Merina could not be pressured to provide forced labour indefinitely. It was now all too obvious that the net result of Gallieni's policy of pacification, and especially of the story of an Anglo-Protestant plot, had been to confirm the Protestant Church as a hotbed of nationalism.

Those ex-*menalamba* who were appointed to official posts in the north proved valuable collaborators, but they were never slow to complain if they thought that the government was exacting too much from their areas. There is an interesting continuity in the history of the northern part of Imerina. It was here that the *menalamba* had been most effective, in the opinion of Gallieni and of most observers. It was here that their leaders surrendered on the most advantageous terms and eventually secured more lenient conditions for their people than was the case elsewhere. It has not been possible to find reliable data showing the incidence of forced labour in the various regions of Imerina, but from fragmentary statistics and administrative correspondence it would appear that labour-dues were heaviest in western and southern Vakinankaratra and parts of Ambodirano. These were precisely the areas which in general had given least support to the *menalamba*. The implication that the French made the heaviest demands upon those who were passive in 1895–6 is also supported by evidence of rice prices. They fell quite sharply after 1897 in war-ravaged districts when farmers began planting again. But in the Ambositra region which had been little troubled by the *menalamba* the price fell much more slowly and the area under cultivation actually diminished, probably because heavy labour-dues prevented planting.[30]

The agitation of 1899 was still recognizably similar to that of the *menalamba* and was sometimes encouraged by veterans of the earlier movement. Strange to say, one of the last of the northern leaders was Ramahafinaritra of Analaroa, the same man whose arrest in 1895 had done much to provoke the rising of the north.[31] Stripped of his wealth, he got out of prison and fled to join the *menalamba*. He was captured and executed in July 1899. It is possible to trace the activities of the remnants of the northern bands until the 1900s, but there the trail goes cold. The few who had once fought with the famous Rabezavana became no more than bandits now that their leaders and their dream of an independent Madagascar were gone.

During the first eighteen months of French occupation there was virtually no penetration of those parts of Madagascar which had been independent of the Merina kingdom. French penetration had to await the pacification of Imerina. There were exceptions to this only at coastal enclaves like Diego-Suarez and Fort Dauphin, which contained French administrators from the beginning.

To continue the geometric analogy, each of the three circles of government radiating from Antananarivo responded in a distinct way to the French invasion. The *menalamba* were essentially a product of the first circle, of Imerina proper. In general the peoples of the second circle were best disposed towards the French during the early months of conquest. The Tsimihety, the Betsileo and the east coast peoples all showed themselves more or less content to see French over-rule substituted for that of the Merina, but not for long. By mid-1896 there were already signs that the Betsimisaraka were no fonder of the French than of their earlier masters. Among the Betsileo the honeymoon lasted longer, thanks largely to the individual approach and the pragmatism of Dr Besson. Ordered to implement the *politique des races*, he aimed not to destroy existing units of power in the interests of direct rule, but to build a series of protectorates based on the traditional paramount kings of the Betsileo. Besson later described how he used to ignore official orders from the capital, but governed according to his own experience of the Betsileo and what he understood to be the tenets of the colonial theorist Chailley-Bert.[32] Gallieni himself was a severe critic of 'the rigidity and the uniformity . . . of our French colonial system'.[33] He realized that Besson was a man of independent spirit and was prepared to tolerate him as long as he could keep the peace in Betsileo-land and fill his quota of forced labour. But even the Betsileo, the great success of French policy in those days, were to express their dissatisfaction through millenarian movements and by peddling rumours of British intervention.

The outstanding cause of disenchantment in all these cases was the back-breaking labour-dues which the French demanded. A missionary in Imerina reported that 'the people say they did not know what the *corvée* meant in old times, and they are only now learning what a terrible burden it is'.[34] The same was heard of any region where French power was implanted. The harsh tax and labour laws originally intended as punitive measures for the *menalamba* became normal everywhere. The army needed supplies; the Malagasy must carry them. Gallieni wanted roads from Antananarivo to

Majunga and Tamatave; the Malagasy must build them. French settlers were to be encouraged; the Malagasy must cultivate their crops. Direct rule was expensive; the Malagasy must pay for it. The *menalamba* who survived the insurrection sometimes continued to protest, even to threaten. And so the people who had to carry, build, plant or pay the most were those who had proved passive hitherto. Such was the reward of fidelity to France.

The prevailing French belief that the non-Merina peoples would see the colonial government as a liberator was not without foundation in the early stages. But Frenchmen continued to reason thus long after it had ceased to be true. It went on to become one of the basic tenets of colonial faith in Madagascar, together with the belief in an unending Anglo-Merina–Protestant conspiracy.

Those Malagasy who were independent of Antananarivo and who watched the risings of 1895–6 from the sidelines heard increasingly unfavourable reports of French actions. By late 1896 most of the island was being visited by refugees or travellers with first-hand news of events in Imerina. The surviving *menalamba* leaders were soon seeking support from independent groups and were inciting magnates like King Toera of Menabe to join them. These veterans were reinforced by non-Merina who may once have looked with tolerance upon the new regime but had now fled from its oppression, and had nothing good to say of it. Former slaves, newly emigrated from Imerina, wandered in search of a home. They may sometimes have owed a personal debt of gratitude to France, but they spread the news of emancipation among peoples who had profited from the slave trade.

Malagasy who observed the rising in Imerina with detachment were mostly subjects of the independent kings of the south and west who had posed the principal military threat to the Merina kingdom before 1895. The first known instance of one of these groups being directly affected by Merina attitudes to colonization occurred among the Bara. Successive Merina commanders at Ihosy, the largest garrison in Bara-land, had done their best to influence local politics by supporting the oldest-established Bara kings against the younger upstarts and breakaway groups which were a menace both to Imerina and the Bara paramount kings. King Ramieba of the Bara-be had the greatest reputation as a Merina collaborator.[35] In November 1896 some of the Merina officials at Ihosy wrote to Ramieba and tried to enlist him in opposition to the French by telling him of the emancipation of slaves, warning that the French would disarm the Bara as soon as they had penetrated the south.[36] The letter had the desired effect. When the first French force arrived at Ihosy in January 1897 it found the foremost king of the Bara-be already organizing opposition in his own kingdom and among his Zafimanely cousins. The French deposed Ramieba and tried to find a suitable replacement, but without much success. Moreover they immediately demanded very heavy taxes. Ramieba himself described the plan which had been elaborated to resist the French:[37]

> The Bara-be, rising as a group, were to go to Ihosy and kill those Merina officers who were known to be pro-French . . . At Ihosy, the Merina community would then join the Bara-be. Together they would take all the guns and ammunition and attack the French resident . . . in order to proceed to Imerina and reinforce the Merina insurgents against the French.

Despite Ramieba's imprisonment a rising broke out among the Bara-be in June 1897. It was led by some of his relatives among the Zafimanely line. Ramieba escaped from prison to join them and the confederation was reinforced by a number of Merina who came from Fianarantsoa for the purpose.[38] This was the first of several Bara insurrections which were not finally stopped until the general southern rising of 1904–5.

The resistance offered by the Bara, like that of all the independent peoples, does not fall into the scope of this book. What is of interest for present purposes is the way in which resistance at Ihosy was fomented by Merina acting on their assessment of the rising of the *menalamba*. The Merina element in Bara resistance disappeared after the repression of the initial rising in 1897, but for the French this was the worst possible start to their penetration of the south. They gained the reputation of being opposed to the powerful Zafimanely dynasty, a reputation which took years to overcome. Only when Lyautey took overall command of the south in 1900 did official policy turn to backing the paramount kings to the hilt as a means of creating interior protectorates.

In Tanala-land, as at Ihosy, the French found that their penetration was preceded by agitators spreading the *menalamba* manifesto. Most of the groups of Tanala-land had supported the banditry and the anti-Merina rising which had taken place on the east coast at the end of 1895. There were certainly many people there who had no cause to lament the passing of the Merina kingdom. At Sahavato, an important trade centre for the collection of rubber and other products of the forest, the northern Tanala groups were reported early in 1896 as working in conjunction with French creoles to attack Merina garrisons.[39] The politics of the forest region were too anarchic to be easily summarized, but it is fair to say that at the beginning of 1896 the Tanala were not ill-disposed towards the French. There was a rapid change during the year as the forest filled with refugees from areas under French rule. In March 1896 King Revanarivo of Ambohimanga-Atsimo reported that his brother was preaching resistance to the French. He was said to have enlisted several Tanala notables and to be in contact with some Merina at Fianarantsoa. Revanarivo himself gave some help to the French government, and was assured that his little state would remain independent under the eye of the French resident of Mananjary.[40]

A dramatic change in Tanala attitudes to France occurred in the last quarter of 1896. In November 1896 a man called Rainimanganoro, probably a Tanala, wrote to leaders of the northern Tanala groups. His letters are typical of the style used by the *menalamba*. He claimed to have received orders from Queen Ranavalona III and from Prince Ramahatra telling him to organize the Tanala and the Betsimisaraka to drive out the French. He cited the emancipation of slaves as an example of the sort of unpopular measures which the French were enforcing.[41] It is inconceivable that he had really received such orders as Ramahatra was a leading French collaborator. Probably he had got the idea from a *menalamba* chief.

In January 1897 Rainimanganoro led an attack on creole plantations and trading-houses at Sahavato, and then retreated deeper into the forest to join the *menalamba* leader Rainibetsimisaraka. Both men then got in touch with King Revanarivo, whose earlier pro-French sympathies had evaporated.[42] When the French arrived at Ambohimanga-Atsimo in April 1897 they were attacked by King Revanarivo, who had made peace with his brother. The French were taken aback by this sudden switch of allegiance on Revanarivo's part. Although all of his 2,000 followers were Tanala, Gallieni and his staff were convinced that this hostility had been provoked by Merina dissidents, not just Rainibetsimisaraka's men but perhaps the contingent of Church officials at Ambohimanga-Atsimo and King Revanarivo's Merina secretary. They also thought that Malagasy agents of the British businesses on the coast, who were suffering from new economic measures designed to protect French trade, might have contributed to the unrest. King Revanarivo and his brother Ramonja issued written orders to their followers telling them to cut communications with the coast, to attack the French but not the British, with whom they claimed to be 'on good terms', and to punish fugitive slaves.[43]

What is interesting is not the fact that the Tanala resisted, but the speed with which they did so, sometimes in the name of the queen of Madagascar. Until 1896 her representatives in the region had been very unpopular. Resistance to France was then stiffened by the infiltration of Merina dissidents who persuaded the Tanala that the best means of resisting foreign domination was to support the national rising. It is also interesting to note the role played by Malagasy traders threatened by the advantages now enjoyed by French citizens. Compare the two attacks on Sahavato. The first, early in 1896, had as its target the Merina traders who had been favoured by the old regime. Eight months later, the object was chiefly to plunder creole plantations.

King Revanarivo, who had been prepared to collaborate with the French as late as September 1896, had become alarmed by the emancipation of slaves and the realization that the French would not leave him to govern with the freedom to which he was accustomed. When the French arrived at his capital it became known that they would demand far heavier taxes than had previously been usual. *Menalamba* propaganda and French intransigence combined to unite the Tanala in opposition to France. As with the Bara, they were not to be pacified finally until into the twentieth century.

Still, Gallieni could afford to be fairly optimistic. The pacification of Imerina was well advanced. Work had started on the road to Tamatave which, he hoped, was to be the road to a golden future. Plans for a railway from the east coast to Antananarivo were pushing ahead. He would have liked more time to consolidate his plans before embarking on new conquests, but it is in the nature of power to abhor a vacuum. Everywhere the *menalamba* were falling back but were inciting opposition even in areas which had not been sorry to see Imerina humbled.

Once the *menalamba* leaders had been beaten, which they had been in most cases by July 1897, arguably the most powerful Malagasy warlord was Toera, king of Menabe, the main Sakalava kingdom of the west coast. To his north lay the minor Sakalava kingdoms of Ambongo, ruled by Toera's distant cousins. Of all the Sakalava states it was those of Ambongo which had had the closest relations with the *menalamba*. Some groups had joined their kinsmen the Mamindra in the bands led by Rajamaria and Laimiza. Others had fought with Rabezavana and still wandered with his remaining lieutenants in the far north. When the Mamindra retreated into the wilderness which lay between Imerina and Sakalava-land they resumed relations with the kings of Ambongo who had given them shelter in 1863 and with whom they had often traded for slaves and cattle.[44]

King Toera himself had to tread very carefully. He was well informed about French military strength, having received missionaries at his court in the past. He was on good terms with a French trader called Samat, one of a family which had been installed on the west coast for fifty years. Besides, Toera was challenged by a claimant to the throne in the person of his brother, and so he would have to handle carefully such an important issue as the attitude to adopt towards the French if he were to stay in power.

King Toera seems to have tried hard to restrain those of his vassals who were in favour of an aggressive policy. He even made friendly overtures to the French in Vakinankaratra. But there were many pressures urging him to fight. When news came of the emancipation of slaves, those of Toera's subjects who had traded in slaves, backed by the Indian traders on the coast, called for resistance.[45] Now Toera received ambassadors from the *menalamba* chief Rainibetsimisaraka. He came under pressure from those of his vassals who were fugitives from Imerina, some of whom were deserters from the ramshackle army which had dissolved before the French in 1895, others of whom had already fought with the *menalamba*.

Gallieni meanwhile had learned, from the Tanala and Bara risings and from the resistance of Rainitavy, of the danger of allowing opposition to form before the French had been able to enter a new territory. All the signs were that he could expect some sort of resistance in the west. It was therefore imperative to reach an understanding with the ruler of Menabe before the remaining western *menalamba* rallied round the coalition which King Toera had formed. A column was fitted out under the command of one of Gallieni's most trusted officers, his chief of staff Commandant Gérard. Gallieni's precise orders to Gérard have not survived, but the general appears to have envisaged replacing King Toera, if necessary, with a puppet chosen by the French.

138

Gérard's column marched west and established contact with Samat, who was to act as an intermediary with Toera. What happened next is a subject of disagreement. According to some reports Gérard made friendly overtures to Toera through Samat, but then tricked him by attacking his camp, killing the king and several hundred of his followers. This is the most plausible version. Others said that Toera was planning to attack the French, and that the massacre was what would nowadays be called a pre-emptive strike. Gérard himself thought that killing Toera and dividing his domains among a number of minor chiefs was the best way of destroying potential Sakalava resistance.[46] Whatever the morality of the attack on 30 August 1897, all agreed, including Gallieni, that it was a political mistake. Gérard was severely reprimanded. Within six weeks all of Menabe had risen in arms. The French were to spend the next seven years trying to establish a ruler strong enough to command all the people of Menabe. How much easier it would have been if Toera had stayed alive.

Ambongo too resisted early French incursions, as was to be expected from its importance in the slave trade and from the number of *menalamba* who had sought refuge there, remaining in contact with their kinsmen in Imerina. But Lyautey, who was in charge of the conquest of Ambongo, proved far more effective than Gérard in the policy of the soft approach, negotiating, threatening, playing one king against another.

It was in the far north-west that the French had the highest hopes of being well received by the Sakalava and their northern neighbours because of the long pro-French tradition there. True to expectations, the Antankarana and northern Sakalava kings collaborated with France in the war of 1895, as they had done in 1883–5. And although Rainitavy recruited some Sakalava in the north-west in the name of the *menalamba*, the paramount kings of the Antankarana and northern Sakalava refused to join him. They expected to be rewarded for their loyalty by the grant of substantial power. Instead they found that they were expected to enforce the decisions of French administrators. They were the victims of a political shift which had not been thought through by French policy-makers. The belief that the Antankarana were pro-French had been based on a definite policy of alliance. Once the French had taken over control of the centre of Madagascar, in 1895, there was no longer any logic in supporting the periphery against the capital. As early as 1897 one administrator in the north-west warned that the *politique des races* was resulting in the appointment of unsuitable candidates as village chiefs. Another officer later had to remind his subordinates that the wearing of European dress was not in itself a sufficient criterion for choosing native officials.[47] The Sakalava King Tsiarasso and his sister both spent periods in prison for minor infringements.

A general feeling of dissatisfaction in the north-west was partly due to a long-term shift in trade patterns. The traditional trade of the area lay in transporting slaves and cattle from the hinterland to the minor ports of the coast, where they were bought by Indian, Zanzibari and creole traders.

Even before 1895 the creoles in particular had begun moving inland in search of produce, a grievance which had been exploited by Rainitavy's *menalamba*. The establishment of French administration in the area further encouraged economic penetration. Creoles from Réunion settled on the fertile coastal plain which had been singled out by the government as a zone for plantation agriculture. They were the subject of frequent complaint. One administrator described how they 'announced that fields, villages and rivers belonged to them and that they alone would trade and would throw out the Indian traders'.[48] They also abused their workers. Gallieni himself noted, in a letter to the deputy for Réunion, how 'they confiscated arable and grazing land, stole the cattle which were traditionally allowed by their owners to graze on unfenced land and neglected, very often, to pay the workers whom they employed'.[49] The Réunionnais creoles were especially troublesome because they were French citizens and benefited from the drive to monopolize the commerce of Madagascar which was a feature of Gallieni's economic policy. One of the most damaging rumours circulating in 1898 was the news that the colonists of the Sambirano region were to be joined by the concessionary company run by Monsieur Locamus of Diego-Suarez, who had an unsavoury reputation.

The colonists frequently worked hand-in-glove with junior administrators to recruit labourers by force illegally. Other forced labourers had to travel far from home to work on the road from Antananarivo to Majunga. The Sakalava and Antankarana found that their loyalty to France had earned them the dubious distinction of being reputed one of the martial races of Madagascar, a distinction that made them more liable to conscription in the militia than any other Malagasy people. By 1898 this had already resulted in a number of cases of wholesale flight from villages at the approach of a recruiting-sergeant.

In retrospect the signs of an insurrection were clear. In 1898 the mountains behind Sambirano became the refuge of *menalamba* who were held responsible for sowing anti-French ideas in the minds of the settled villagers. In September 1898 a rich Tsimihety who faced ruin from the competition of the creoles wrote to a contact asking for guns and men for a rising.[50] It was noted that some of the Malagasy and foreign Moslem cattle-traders 'have not hesitated to spend a great deal of money to organize a rising'.[51] King Tsiarasso's imprisonment was the last straw. 'We were wrong', some minor kings were reported as saying, 'not to help the Merina during the invasion of Madagascar.'[52]

Throughout the latter half of 1898 rumblings of discontent gave way to active conspiracy. Those who took the lead in stirring up unrest were the petty kings of the main groups and Moslem cattle-traders. Some of them were on good terms with Merina settlers or refugees, and one administrator went as far as to suggest that the rising was chiefly due to incitement by former *menalamba*.[53] It is not clear whether there was any prearranged signal for a rising, but it erupted on 26 October 1898, when a band attacked a

French post at Marotoalana and killed its administrator, who had become very unpopular for his brutal methods of recruitment. The attack coincided with news of the Anglo-French clash at Fashoda. Given that some of the leading cattle-traders were British Indians, it is a real possibility that the incident on the Nile was taken as a sign to act. This led some administrators to hint darkly that the rising was planned by 'secret agents of a rival power'.[54] As usual, the French were eager to accept the theory of foreign involvement because they thought the Malagasy incapable of organizing themselves. The rising showed evidence of 'a superior intelligence which gave to the insurgents a guarantee of external support'.[55]

The insurgents began a general attack on white colonists. The rising swiftly spread to Queen Binao's Sakalava, and to wherever it had been discussed in advance. In several places the local militia joined the rebels, who thus included people who had fought as French auxiliaries in 1895 and against the *menalamba*. Each band followed its own king or leader and obeyed its traditional religious customs. Some carried the white flag of Queen Ranavalona III. One Tsimihety governor was told to display a Union Jack if he wished to be immune from attack. But in general the rebels' targets were extremely precise. They were Europeans or creoles and their farms, administrative centres, and officials who had been particularly harsh in recruiting for forced labour or the militia. The object, said one leader, was to fight 'until there are no more Europeans in the land of the Sakalavas'.[56] It was generally agreed that the paramount kings, Tsiarasso especially, had had foreknowledge of the rising and may actually have encouraged it, but that none of the paramount sovereigns took arms in person. Leadership of the armed bands generally fell to the minor kings, to members of Tsiarasso's family, and to traders. A well-informed opinion was that the rising 'found its main support in isolated commercial centres', where the Indians and Zanzibaris 'by their trade and by their system of buying rice at source have acquired a considerable influence over the people'.[57]

Gallieni at first thought the rising to be more serious than was in fact the case, and that it threatened to spread as far as the province of Ambatondrazaka and to inflame all the north. He was criticized in Paris for overreacting. In fact the rising in Sambirano resulted in the deaths of nine European civilians and one sergeant. But when it is recalled that the rising coincided with news of Fashoda, and with a revival of discontent in Imerina, it is easy to understand Gallieni's fears.

The rising was certainly encouraged by remaining *menalamba* but not to the extent that some embarrassed administrators found it convenient to believe. The region south of Sambirano where the *menalamba* bands hid responded to the call to revolt only after the Antankarana had taken the lead. The Sambirano rising in fact was hardly a war of resistance, but the first anti-colonial protest on a large scale. Unlike the *menalamba*, the insurgents did not aim to unite the whole of Madagascar and to restore its independence but had the far more limited aim of freeing the north-west

141

from the abuses to which it was subject. It bore little structural resemblance to the *menalamba* movement. Still, Hubert Deschamps was right to call it the last of the *menalamba* movements.[58] It was the last significant rising in which the *menalamba* and their propaganda can be shown to have played a considerable part. The many risings and resistance movements which occurred elsewhere in Madagascar up to 1905 bear very little relation to the *menalamba* either in terms of the people who participated or by analogy. The most that can be said is that they all occurred in the same island, which later became a nation-state, and during the administration of the same governor-general.

GALLIENI IN MADAGASCAR

Gallieni's report to the minister of colonies on the Sambirano rising was not altogether frank. It was caused by the paramount kings' loss of power, he said, and by the abuses of some settlers. He stressed the role of the Indian traders, setting great store by the fact that some of them were British subjects.[59] It is true that they had played a leading role, but one has the impression that the general was glad to find a good reason for excluding British subjects from a land now reserved for French trade. He expressly denied that the rising had been caused by heavy labour-dues. Gallieni had something to hide.

The administrator of Nossi-be, who had watched the rising from close range, perceived accurately the policy which was the essence of Gallieni's plans, together with its main flaw: 'I think that the *hurry-up-and-let's-finish-by-tomorrow* method is not the best when we lack the necessary armed force . . .'[60] It had often been observed that Gallieni had made a bold gamble in sacrificing everything to the creation of modern economic and political structures in Madagascar. No Europeans at that time had much doubt that with sufficient injection of European capital and expertise Madagascar would be developed to the general good and gratitude of its people. Certainly Gallieni thought this both possible and desirable. It was the foundation of his colonial philosophy. His only doubts lay in whether the government in Paris would keep faith long enough for him to fulfil this ambition, and to what extent the Malagasy would resist. The Sambirano rising was evidence of the strain which breakneck development was putting on the bonds of collaboration. This was what Gallieni sought to conceal from the colonial ministry. He could ill afford violent protests in areas which had supposedly been pacified while there were still large numbers of French troops committed in Menabe and Bara-land. The Sambirano rising so stretched French military resources that Gallieni was obliged to ask the minister for reinforcements.[61]

The high hopes of two years previously had disappeared. Gallieni had succeeded in his first task of defeating the *menalamba* and had been applauded for it. But for him, radical that he was, this was only part of a wider plan to build a new society. The rising had given him an excuse to make fundamental changes which would otherwise have seemed too daring, and it was for this reason that he had encouraged a distorted version of the rising of the *menalamba*. Already by 1898 he was privately expressing his disappointment. The most frustrating thing was not the resistance of the Sakalava and Bara, which had been expected, but the continuing sullen hostility of the Merina, and the failure of the former slaves and the peoples of the east coast to respond to colonial rule with a burst of creative energy.[62] Other Frenchmen who believed in their civilizing mission were similarly puzzled. A Jesuit priest wondered why, after eighteen months of French rule, 'the flag of France remains an object of hatred for some people and, for the majority, an object of defiance'.[63]

Gallieni soon found that Paris was not interested in social engineering. The colonial lobby had been willing enough to pay for the expedition of 1895, but not for years of military rule. In 1897 Gallieni overspent on his allocation from the metropolitan budget by over 16 million francs, which was excused only because of the expense of pacification. He raised the income from Malagasy contributions to the local budget from 5,500,000 francs in 1896 to 13,772,000 francs in 1899. By 1904 it went as high as 24,651,000 francs, which represented an enormous effort on the part of Malagasy tax-payers. The colony continued to cost an alarming amount of French money too, generally between 25 and 30 million francs for the maintenance of up to 16,000 troops. This excludes the militia which was paid for from the local budget.[64] When Gallieni's proposal for the 1898 budget was trimmed, it became clear that the building of a new Madagascar would have to be financed by the Malagasy. Gallieni nevertheless remained determined to press ahead with his programme of road-building, the construction of a railway, and the encouragement of European immigration. His theory was that if the Malagasy could withstand a few years of hardship the new economic infrastructure would bring down prices and increase the prosperity of all.

The pressure on the Malagasy grew. The more courageous French officers, Lyautey in particular, warned of the dangers. It was not only resulting in hardship, but was threatening to undermine the loyalty of those Merina who had collaborated in 1895–6 and had been entrusted with weapons. Forced labour could occupy over 200 days in a year. Work on the main roads was especially hated because it involved considerable travel and lodging in camps where the workers were subject to flogging and other ill-treatment. One French visitor reckoned that up to twenty per cent of those employed on the road to Tamatave died as a result. A modern estimate speaks of seventy per cent mortality on some sites.[65]

Until the end of 1897 it was the Merina and Betsileo who bore the brunt of this. They alone had the institutions, surviving from the old regime, through which labourers could be recruited in large numbers. In other conquered areas administrators reported that the application of the *politique des races*

143

made large-scale recruitment impossible. Among the Betsimisaraka, French officials found it almost impossible to find competent, literate officials. Military penetration of Menabe too was made more difficult because the Merina who inhabited the supply route were returning to their homeland. The government went as far as importing Chinese and even Sicilian labourers to work on the Tamatave road, but without success. The only solution was to improve the system of recruitment in the east, and by the middle of 1898 Gallieni was instructing his officials to encourage Merina to return to the east as a means of promoting its commerce. An Anglican missionary described this reversal of policy with a certain malicious pleasure:[66]

> Prices have gone up by leaps and bounds and something closely resembling ruin obtains owing to the dearth of native labour [next word illegible]. Driven to their wits' end by the state of affairs, the result of their own incapacity, the French are clamouring for the 'collaboration précieuse' of those very Hova [Merina] whom rather more than three years ago they execrated and expelled . . . The Hovas, past-masters in the art of setting their fellows to work, are to be called in to the assistance of their embarrassed rulers; in fact most advantageous offers are being held out to induce them to settle on the coast as of old.

The reports of visitors to Madagascar in the last years of the century make depressing reading. Gallieni was himself disappointed by the failure of French commerce to take advantage of its opportunities. Most of the settlers who came had little capital and were inclined to set up as middlemen rather than producers, which had been precisely one of the weaknesses of the economy before 1895. The colonists' frequent brutality made them more of a liability than an asset, while they constantly criticized the colonial government for its failure to give them greater support. According to a British diplomat, the average Malagasy labourer on the east coast earned about six pounds sterling per year, of which no less than two-thirds went in taxes.[67] Small wonder that many fled to the forest as of old, and that wherever a programme of public works was begun people migrated to a region where forced labour was less onerous. Gallieni continued to present a rosy picture of Madagascar's economic progress, but no amount of juggling with figures could hide the fact that the colony was importing far more than it exported and that the budget was balanced only by the pressure put on the Malagasy. If one consults the description of the pre-colonial economy above, all this sounds strangely familiar.

Those who had criticized Imerina in the past for failing to abolish forced labour and increase production were finding how difficult such a feat was. The *politique des races* looked increasingly like a form of words and nothing more. Merina traders were encouraged to spread outside their homeland and French officials became more willing to learn from their Merina predecessors in the strategy to adopt in penetrating the south. One of the most useful Merina traditions, Gallieni learned, was the habit of forced labour. Some of his successors wished he had left a little more of the old structure too.[68]

But Gallieni refused to compromise on his basic determination to modernize the economy as fast as possible. And more than ever, as his political initiatives were blunted, this came to mean building the road and railway to Tamatave. Gallieni decided some time in 1899 that he would have to go to Paris in person to secure finance for these projects. There were other reasons for returning too: the budget commission of the Chamber of Deputies had thrown out Gallieni's proposals for 1899, and had recommended suspending military activity in Madagascar. The minister for colonies telegraphed this news to Gallieni at the beginning of 1899. The governor-general replied, rightly enough, that not only would such a suspension be a blow to French prestige, but that it would be impossible to prevent armed raids from the independent regions of Madagascar unless a line of forts was built, which would hardly cost less than continuing the process of conquest.[69] Gallieni had also come under attack in the Chamber of Deputies and by humanitarian lobbies for his use of forced labour. As soon as the agitation of 1899 had died down in Madagascar, he took a steamship for France.

He left the colony under the temporary administration of General Pennequin, who had ideas of his own. Pennequin soon implemented some of the reforms towards which Gallieni had been feeling his way in 1898. After an initial tour of Imerina and Betsileo-land Pennequin recommended an easing of forced labour and full encouragement to the Merina to settle outside their homeland, where their habits of employment and tax-paying would serve as a good example. The *politique des races* was to be abandoned. 'The Merina have no affection for us and . . . our rule is still based on force', he observed. 'We still have to undertake the moral conquest of the country.'[70] And just as the Merina were to be allowed to resume the economic dominance which Gallieni had originally tried to forbid, the French commander in Sakalava-land was ordered to 'win over to our cause the hereditary chiefs', even if this involved promising the Sakalava exemption from taxes.[71]

Gallieni returned from France in July 1900 with a promise of 60 million francs for his railway, but with a clearer indication than ever that the colony must pay its own way. He found that Pennequin had gone a long way to resurrecting the external policies of the last Merina sovereigns, and on balance Gallieni supported his innovations. He ordered a complete suspension of military activities in the far south and south-west. 'I would not wish under any circumstances to see a repetition of the situation created among the Sakalava by the operations of 1897', he wrote, referring to Gérard's heavy-handedness.[72] Where the French had already penetrated but not conquered, settlements were to be made as quickly as possible by seeking out paramount kings and building protectorates around them. Within Imerina the government successfully legislated on the traditional village councils, making them an integral part of the colonial administrative system. Again, this was a measure designed to stabilize local government by leaving it in the hands of traditional chiefs and notables.

Now all this represented, if not a defeat for Gallieni, at least a recognition that he could not rebuild the country as radically as he hoped. Henceforth the Merina were no longer officially regarded as an oppressive yoke from which the coastal peoples were to be freed, but as 'a salutary example for the more lethargic and primitive tribes'. 'From the point of view of the island's economic development', Gallieni wrote to his officials, '. . . we have the clearest interest in encouraging the emigration towards the fertile lands of the coast of the active and industrious populations of Imerina and Betsileoland.'[73] There followed laws permitting the highland peoples to travel where they wished and abolishing forced labour in principle.

The relaxation came none too soon. The death rate in Imerina was appallingly high, while plague and famine threatened on the construction sites. But Gallieni persisted in his ambitious programme of public works, and on this he was willing to stake his reputation. The east coast peoples, especially the Betsimisaraka and the Antemoro, bore a heavier share of labour on the roads and the railway, but still the manpower of Imerina was stretched to the utmost. A young French soldier newly arrived in Antananarivo one market day in 1902 was horrified by the number of victims of an epidemic which had broken out in the labour-gangs working in the forest and by the sight of carts moving among the market-crowds to pick up bodies.[74] A government mission of inspection, one of the few controls which a governor-general had to fear, had the same impression:[75] 'Our new subjects say nothing, but they are suffering nonetheless . . . crushed by taxes, weighed down by labour-dues, passing from the building-sites of the Public Works Department into the prisons and from the prisons to the building-sites . . . Misery, according to the majority of administrators, has overtaken the country.'

The burden of supporting this structure was at least shared among a greater number of people, but it acted to the detriment of trade. In mid-1902 there was a notable number of business failures attributed to fierce competition between middlemen and lack of consumption by the Malagasy, quite similar in fact to the collapse ten years earlier which had precipitated the downfall of the kingdom of Madagascar.[76]

The administration in Antanarivo looked increasingly to the non-Merina to pay for their government and to work on the roads. This was an important factor in causing the southern rising of 1904–5. That insurrection was much more than an anti-colonial protest, though. In some areas it was the continuation of earlier resistance to French penetration, in others a restructuring of old hierarchies and patterns of government quite as profound as that which took place in Imerina in 1895–7. The rising of the south was to lead to severe criticism of Gallieni's administration and of his forward policy. Eventually it brought about his resignation. He was reprimanded by colonial minister Clémentel. A second mission of inspection put the blame quite squarely on his policy of development at all costs.[77] This ushered in a period when governors-general no longer had ambitions beyond governing as quietly and as smoothly as possible.

7

Conclusion

The shades of Rabezavana and Rabozaka are looking down upon us.
Proclamation by the nationalist secret society PANAMA, 1947

THE NATURE AND CAUSES OF THE *MENALAMBA* MOVEMENT

In this book the terms 'rebel' and 'rebellion' have been used to describe the *menalamba* movement. The rising was directed against a government which the insurgents held to be illegitimate in every respect except that of the queen's right to reign. She was on the side of the French. The *menalamba* therefore took great pains to excuse their revolt by claiming that Queen Ranavalona III and her leading counsellors were on their side. They even went as far to say that it was those who served the queen's real government, and thereby the French, who were rebels. The *menalamba* considered themselves to be the guarantors of the true royal heritage, and those who served France to represent a corrupt form of it. The kingdom was split into two camps, each claiming, with considerable support, to be the sole legitimate government of the state. This is one definition of a civil war.

It was a war in which society was split less vertically than horizontally. That is, it did not divide the state into two geographical units, although it is possible to distinguish certain regions as particularly ardent for or against the *menalamba*. The crucial division was between the top and the bottom of the scale of power measured by the standard which had been in force since 1869. Almost everyone possessing a certain wealth, or above a certain grade in the hierarchy of the royal government, and almost all orthodox Christians, were on the side which supported the French. The collaborators were therefore those Malagasy who continued to serve or to obey the rump of the old royal government after 1895, and the colonial government after the abolition of the monarchy in 1897. The resisters were those who subscribed to the *menalamba* programme, who swore the oaths of loyalty to the old kings, revered the talismans, or took up weapons against the French and the royal government. It was simultaneously a rebellion and a war of national resistance.

It was also a war of religion. Imerina had become accustomed to the conduct of politics through religious channels and the Christian government had thus assumed an important function of the sovereign, which was to

148

ensure the harmony of society, nature and the cosmic order. People attributed any disaster on a large scale to a failure in royal power. When the government became unable to ensure stability, which was so in the later nineteenth century, and when it could not guard the nation's independence, which was the case in 1895, then it followed that the system of government must be to blame. The worse conditions of life became, the more the Merina suspected a massive disruption of the social order to be traced back to the queen's conversion to Christianity. They turned to the outlawed cults of the talismans, which formed an organized opposition, prevented from expression until 1895 by the Church persecution and by the guilty knowledge that the queen had herself rejected the cult. The forces which caused the failure of the Christian government lie deep in Merina history. It was never considered wholly legitimate because of the upstart origin of its Andafy-Avaratra prime ministers, because of the foreign influence represented by its Christian rituals, and because it presided over an economy hampered by adverse conditions of trade.

The revolution in government and economy in the early nineteenth century had produced a dynamic which sent Merina settlers as far afield as Betsileo-land and the east coast at the same time as wealth and labour were sucked towards the capital. The process by which Antananarivo exploited the provinces had already produced clear patterns in the earlier nineteenth century. Each centre of provincial power had essentially reached its own collaborative bargains with the central government at the time of Andrianampoinimerina's political settlement or in subsequent reigns. The reactions encountered by the French were dictated largely by these earlier bargains.

The first distinction among these reactions is to be found in the aims of the revolts of 1895–9. Whether discontent took the form of an anti-Merina movement, as among the Betsimisaraka, or whether the response was a call to re-establish an acceptable Merina government, as in the case of the *menalamba*, depended on the degree to which the population in question had accepted the idea that it formed part of the kingdom of Madagascar. All *menalamba*, Merina or not, considered themselves subjects of the kingdom of Imerina, alias the kingdom of Madagascar; they form the centrepiece of this book. They came from the margins of the Christian kingdom, in every sense. Inside these margins there were striking differences in the type and intensity of response to French invasion, which depended upon the tacit political bargains already existing between Antananarivo and its provinces.

The variety of relations between Antananarivo and its periphery meant that it was possible to detect the same category of official or the same social group playing an opposite role in different provinces. One may take the example of the great marcher-lords, men who had acquired private armies and the command of large districts during the campaigns against outlaws before 1895. They existed only in areas too remote from the capital to have been utterly drained of resources in earlier times. Rainijaonary, the military commander of Vakinankaratra, was a most valuable ally of the French. His family had governed the province for generations, an instance of a provincial élite which had reached an understanding with the magnates of Antananarivo and enjoyed a local power-base. His ancestors had helped to repress the popular insurrection of 1863–4. Rabezavana, on the other hand, the leading warlord of Marofotsy-land, was perhaps the most powerful of the *menalamba*. He had risen to power in his home country mostly by his own efforts. He was often reprimanded for his disregard of orders from the central government.[1] Rabezavana, whose authority derived from his ability to rule where centrally appointed officials had failed, fought with the *menalamba*. Rainijaonary, whose status depended upon working with the government in Antananarivo, sided with the French.

The same almost perverse opposites of response occur in many ways. In Vakinankaratra, the *menalamba* finished by recruiting Catholics to attack the Lutheran Church. In the north it was the other way round: the *menalamba* moved closer to the Protestants. Once more the explanation is concerned with views of central government. In the south the Catholics often represented freedom from the tyranny of the state as it was seen in the Lutheran Church. In the north the Protestant Church, for all its past faults, was seen as an institution both more authentically Malagasy and less oppressive than the colonial government.

The same sort of approach is useful in discussing the opinion frequently given by French observers that the rising was some sort of feudal reaction. The view is a valid one only if the analogy with Europe is not pressed too far, as it invariably was by French officials. Imerina had indeed been subjected for several decades to an assault on local structures of power of the sort which occurred in France in the seventeenth and eighteenth centuries. In some parts of Imerina hereditary fief-holders or other notables had managed to retain their privileges and power by reaching an understanding with the central government. In Voromahery, local notables had been left in place because of the physical distance of their province from Antananarivo. Prime Minister Rainilaiarivony found them useful as allies in a province which he could not otherwise grasp. The leaders of the Voromahery turned out to be French collaborators as soon as the French understood the autonomous constitution of the province. In parts of Vakinisisaony close to the capital many fief-holders had successfully defended their position by alliance with the noble faction at court. They were able to do this because their power to recognize the government's legitimacy was essential to the prime minister. They used French influence after 1896 with great success, aided by the fact that their patron Prince Ramahatra was one of Gallieni's closest collaborators. However, in Vonizongo, where local power structures had suffered longer and more effective persecution at the hands of the old government, traditional fief-holders formed the backbone of the *menalamba*. It may be said that where fief-holders had been degraded by the old government they were often prominent among the *menalamba*. Where they had successfully resisted or compromised with the government, they frequently worked with the French.

The issue was further complicated because one of the most common mistakes of administrators arriving from France was to assume that nobles and fief-holders were one and the same thing, and that they were the natural enemies of republican France. They could point to the fact that certain noble groups were especially important among the *menalamba*, notably the Zanadralambo and the Zafimamy (if the latter are to be considered noble, which is not always the case). It is worth repeating that the nobles of Imerina were different from those of medieval France. They formed perhaps a quarter of the free population.[2] A few were fief-holders. Fewer still had great power. The majority were peasants who lived exactly like their neighbours, and might have a lower standard of living than many slaves. There was absolutely 'no cohesion among the *andrianas* as a body', one missionary wrote, of the sort which bound European aristocrats in the face of a rising bourgeoisie.[3] Just as much or as little as the commoner demes, some noble groups had prospered by association with the government of the Andafy-Avaratra while others had not.

The noble groups which supported the *menalamba* most fully were those which had declined in ritual status since their foundation. In the case of the Zafimamy they had declined so far that some said they were not noble at all. Those which collaborated with the French, like the Andriantompokoindrin-dra of Ambohimalaza, were those which had shared to a larger extent in the spoils of Rainilaiarivony's government. Thus the same criterion broadly applies to nobles as to fief-holders. The more closely a group was identified with the old government, the more it had succeeded in maintaining its status, the less likely it was to join the *menalamba*.

It is also possible to speculate that the distribution of the *menalamba* bore some relation to the patterns of earlier administrative changes. On the largest scale this is certainly untrue. That is to say there was no correlation between the degree to which a province participated in the rising and the extent to which it had been penetrated by centrally appointed officials. One has only to look at the very different histories of Avaradrano and eastern Vakinankaratra, which both played a conspicuous part in the *menalamba* movement. The main effect of administrative reforms of the Christian era was simply to shape the resistance which emerged. The *menalamba* in each province were cast in the mould of the government they knew best. The most modern provinces produced the most modern rebels.

To judge from the evidence on fief-holders, it seems that the response to administrative reforms of an earlier period determined the reactions of certain types of office-holders, but rarely entire provinces. The same may be said of the incidence of forced labour, which had fallen unevenly on various sections of the community. There is no evidence that it was decisive in turning regions for or against the *menalamba*. Western Vakinankaratra for example, which suffered from heavy labour-dues under both the old regime and under the French, was quiet throughout. This was perhaps because under its military commandant Rainijaonary it was ruled by a strong indigenous élite which had itself been strengthened, not weakened, by the techniques of modern government. The political status of western Vakinankaratra had apparently prevented it from being bled by the capital to the same extent as other provinces.

It may well be that such analyses of the impact of administrative reforms or of forced labour would be most useful in the detailed study of a small area. The implication of case-studies in earlier chapters is that pastors and governors appointed from outside a given village tended to collaborate with the French, at least in the sense that they urged people to remain calm. Officials who served in their native village tended to side with the *menalamba* or to look on helplessly, unless they were very unpopular for some reason. These suggestions could be tested only by further research. In any case the *menalamba* were a product of anarchy, and the first rule of anarchy is that there are no rules. It is possible to find many examples which do not conform to the general pattern because of local conditions. It is also important to note that the appeal of nationalism was strong enough to combine Malagasy of every conceivable origin in a common cause, in defiance of any sociological scheme.

In what ways can one describe the *menalamba* other than as insurgents and patriots? It is fair to say that they sprang from the periphery of Imerina and that, in the early days at least, they were staunchly anti-Christian and anti-foreign. The French usually saw them in terms of economic and political classes, the British missionaries in terms of religion. These two points of view are not irreconcilable. Many provinces had been so drained of their wealth by the government in Antananarivo as to have become almost a waste land; hence the extraordinary bitterness with which the *menalamba* spoke of the corrupting influence of money. The provinces contained refugees and malcontents of every sort, who had consistently rejected Christianity as the tool of a government of usurpers. Impoverished groups were equally likely to be nobles or commoners, for neither category suggested a certain level of wealth. They were less likely to include household slaves, because these had generally benefited from economic changes of the previous quarter century. This economic analysis is unsatisfactory in the sense that there were many groups of Malagasy who had suffered from economic changes but who neither joined the *menalamba* nor resisted the French. Conversely in the far north Rainitavy tended to recruit for the *menalamba* among the richer part of the population.

Slaves, in fact, are worthy of further discussion. The *menalamba* were strangely reticent on the subject of slavery which is interesting in itself since it was both a respectable Malagasy institution and one which was economically viable in the fringes of Imerina from where most of the *menalamba* sprang. One would therefore expect them to have had clear views on slaves and slavery. One prominent rebel leader, Rainijirika, was himself a slave.

Gallieni thought the slaves among the insurgents sufficiently numerous as to be worth splitting from the freemen and wooing to the French cause. But there is some evidence that the *menalamba* drew a disproportionately large amount of support from the free castes and from the slave-demes, who were not slaves in any economic sense.[4] It was only after the emancipation decree of September 1896 that slaves joined the *menalamba* on a large scale in some regions, in order to escape total destitution.

If relatively few slaves joined the insurrection until late 1896, then one may seek an explanation in the extent to which slaves had maintained or even increased their living standards in the late nineteenth century compared with freemen. The available statistics suggest that freemen decreased as a proportion of the total population during the nineteenth century. Their numbers may even have declined in absolute terms at certain periods.[5] The fall in the numbers of freemen relative to the population as a whole is so striking that it cannot simply be explained by the fact that slaves were imported in large numbers or by speculation that slaves had a higher birth-rate. It was freemen who bore the brunt of government oppression under Queen Ranavalona I and in later years for reasons which are very complex. Free demes have been very resistant to many aspects of central control throughout Merina history. They have stubbornly guarded their solidarity, their group identity and their ancestral land in the face of often heavy odds. The Andafy-Avaratra disliked that independence and coveted the ancestral land. The rising of the *menalamba* was an expression of the despair of the freemen, and in that sense a study of its origins involves contemplation of the relationship between autonomous demes and ambitious sovereigns or prime ministers through a long period.

The Merina define freemen and demes by reference to ancestral tombs. All fugitives, all who had left their tombs and their homelands, were held to have declined in status. The *menalamba* were created when fugitives of all types sought ritual leadership, which their outlaw-chiefs were unqualified to give them. They found this spiritual reassurance in the cults of the talismans, openly displayed once more in 1895. Thus the outlaws of yesteryear became patriots again. The talismans permitted them to return within the pale of respectable society according to the customs of the ancestors. Hence the leaders of the religious revival were generally old, settled demes which had been excluded from the Christian hierarchy for one reason or another and had clung to their talismans as reminders of better days. The Zanadralambo and Zafimamy again are good examples. The resulting union of bandits and deprived demes was cemented by nationalism, which was enunciated notably by those lapsed Christians who were such prominent leaders.[6]

This does not mean that the *menalamba* came from the lowliest or poorest class of society, only that they all were convinced that they had been cheated of their birthright. In the case of the fugitives the reasons for this are obvious. In some of the settled groups and adherents of the revival of the talismans the reasons are more complex. They might be families or demes who had lost status and political power in the face of recent political reforms; or individual pastors who had been deprived of their office by a rival, perhaps for adultery or rum-drinking. They might equally be demes which had suffered from the political settlement made in the days of King Andrianampoinimerina, who died in 1810. Ritual leadership of the *menalamba* bands tended to go to those who had fallen from the highest point. The more recently a group had joined the opposition to the central government, the more it would seek reassurance from a group of great antiquity or of high or once-high status. Some of the most distinguished of the ritual leaders were groups of fallen nobility, who formed a ready-made alternative to the existing government. *Menalamba* alliances therefore often worked in pairs, a group of relatively low status seeking one of higher status to which it had traditional affiliations. Examples can be found in the combinations of Manendy and Zanadralambo; of Mandiavato and Zafimamy; of Marofotsy and Tsimahafotsy. This is probably not an innovation of the *menalamba* but represents a revival of a traditional concept of ritual rank which had been neglected by recent governments.

The search for status was also a search for greater wealth and power. But the *menalamba* did not call for a redistribution of wealth. They prided themselves on their scorn of money and hated the plutocrats because their money had corrupted the constitution. The *menalamba* wanted to throw out the foreigners and to restore their own rightful place in the affairs of their homeland or province. To some extent this involved a rejection of the degree to which government had become centralized, but above all it was a rejection of the people who had carried out this policy, the Andafy-Avaratra and their allies.

The *menalamba*, then, included those whose golden age had been centuries before, and those who considered it to have passed only recently. The more distant the ideal, the more archaic were the forms of ritual and organization adopted by the *menalamba* contingent in question. The Mandiavato looked no further back than the early nineteenth century, for that was when they enjoyed the position to which Andrianampoinimerina had raised them. The followers of Rafiringa in Vakinisisaony referred to a much older time and a more antique concept of society, for their great days had gone even before Andrianampoinimerina. All were bound by the appeal to the sacred earth and homeland of Madagascar, ancient concepts influenced by a new, imported nationalism.

In this context it is useful to observe what some authors have discerned in protest movements which aspire to restore old orders. Millenarian activity is said to be characteristic of deprived groups, that is of those whose expectations have been most bitterly disappointed.[7] Insurrections whose programme consists of comprehensive and backward-looking demands are said to be associated with social groups which have been disappointed by the rise of new classes.[8] Further clues to the nature of the *menalamba* may be found in the instances of fanatical bravery on the part of insurgents who thought that garments blessed by a talisman would protect them against bullets, which is a belief recorded in many other revolts in Africa and elsewhere.[9] It is sometimes, but not always, a symptom of a millenarian movement. Other features commonly found in millenarian ideologies have interesting parallels in the *menalamba*,[10] but it is impossible to escape the impression that this was not a typical or fully fledged millenarian movement. Its leaders were somehow too calculating and had too firm a grasp of political reality to be placed in the same bracket as the millenarian leaders of other places and times.

The reports of religious ecstasy among the *menalamba*, or of fanatical charges in the face of bullets, were often exaggerated by Europeans who saw in the rising an irrational manifestation of the dark and diabolic. Furthermore the instances occurred mainly in the earliest or most isolated movements, especially the rising at Amboanana in 1895. The *menalamba* never believed that they were destined to build a paradise on earth, which is the principle of any millenarian movement. But syncretic or millenarian ideas were circulating before and after 1895 in Betsileo-land, which was hardly touched by the insurrection, and in Imerina during and after 1899.

The *menalamba* did not believe in a messiah. To some extent they believed in a messianic agency, in the sense that the northerners in particular thought that they might acquire the power of the old kings if they could capture the holy town of Ambohimanga. They made the greatest effort to do so only towards the end of the rising, in November 1896. Another element which might be considered evidence of millenarian belief was the curious assertion that the real leaders of the rising were not in the *menalamba* camps, but somewhere in Antananarivo. In the same way the belief in forthcoming British intervention took real hold only when the monarchy was abolished, and reached its height at the time of the Fashoda crisis in 1898. It may originally have been based on a shrewd political calculation, but it came to assume the proportions of a *deus ex machina*.

All this suggests that millenarianism was not far below the surface in the Malagasy response to invasion in areas like Imerina and Betsileo-land which had been heavily evangelized. It further suggests that this aspect of the movement was most in evidence when the insurgents lacked sophisticated leaders of the sort which they had in 1896. Hence the evidence of a millenarian movement is fairly persuasive in the Amboanana rising of 1895, and overwhelming only in the agitation of 1899. The fact that the leaders of the *menalamba* were of a very different type from their followers has already been mentioned in various contexts. On the whole they were more likely to be literate, to have travelled, to have been churchmen, and to have been employed in government service. In a word they were more like Europeans. These leaders knew that Ratsitiavola and Ratiatanindrazana, Mr Does-not-love-money and Mr Patriot, were fictitious characters. Whether they thought there was a real chance of British intervention is less clear. They exploited both myths for their own purposes, just as Gallieni did for his.

It is often suggested that millenarian movements occur at a specific point in the introduction of western and Christian ideas into a foreign country, the stage at which an attempt is made to adapt old ideologies to the needs of the modern world.[11] Imerina had seen this sort of response on an ideological level in the earlier nineteenth century. This had certainly been the case in the syncretic movement of 1834, and probably in the cult surrounding King Radama II.[12] Both movements were forward-looking. The *menalamba*, on the other hand, were comparatively unconcerned to blend old with new in the world of abstract ideas. They had no Christian eschatology. It would seem that popular culture had already decided, before 1895, which aspects of Christianity to assimilate, and which to reject. The *menalamba* represented a rather more advanced stage in coming to terms with the European world. For twenty-five years Imerina had been ruled by a westernized government which bullied its citizens to give, to pay, to buy, to sell, as a part of this new regime. The *menalamba* put to the test the acceptability of European and Christian organs of government and all that they implied in economics. In so doing they came to accept many imported institutions as authentically Malagasy.

Imerina after 1869 closely resembled a colonial society. It was ruled by an indigenous élite, but one so far distant from its citizens in taste, means of subsistence, and religion, as to be quite foreign. It was committed to encouraging the economic development of its subjects and to improving their morals, both attitudes being more usually associated with colonial governments. The *menalamba* movement was in many respects a revolt against this colonization from within. It therefore displayed features more often associated with modern nationalist movements than with the sort of campaigns of primary resistance analysed by Terence Ranger.[13]

This leads to consideration of a point made by Georges Balandier in writing about the anti-colonial or nationalist risings of the Mau Mau and of the Malagasy of 1947. He has tried to explain why both these risings were seen by their protagonists almost as dramas acted in the realm of myth.[14] The reason, he writes, is that the effective banning of indigenous politics in a colonial state frustrated normal expressions of discontent and the process by which fact is turned into myth or history. Grievances were instead translated into spiritual or ritual areas of thought and behaviour. This is true of Imerina after 1869. The Christian government did far more than outlaw the old talismans; it silenced the political and religious expression of a large part of society, the part which was most conservative in morals and politics and which was employed in the most backward sectors of the economy.

Traditional religion was a part of the mechanism by which recent events are explained, remembered and take their place in history. The great oral histories, the highest form of art developed in old Imerina, were charged with political significance. A whole generation after 1869 was afraid even to recite its histories,[15] because their local traditions disagreed with the official versions and could be interpreted as subversive. The traditional feasts at which they were recited had in some cases been forbidden. Little which occurred in the world could be incorporated into the historical and political schema by non-Christians. For twenty-five years all innovation was relegated to the domain of the anti-social and of the sorcerer. This is what Balandier wrote of the Mau Mau:[16]

> This insurrection failed not only because of its material weakness, but also because it was not conceived in terms of modern political subversion. It remained a force directed towards an idealized past, that of the pre-colonial period, more than a force directed towards a precisely defined future. In a manner of speaking – and here one may see the reasons for its failure – this revolt . . . was rooted in a mythological time-scale and was not situated in the context of a historical period which had been consciously studied and assimilated.

This is applicable to the *menalamba*. They believed certain things of the French and of their rulers which were obviously untrue. Even in 1895 there were rumours that the French were going to massacre or enslave all the Malagasy, whereas at this stage the invading army had behaved very correctly. Most Merina believed quite firmly that the queen was on the side of the *menalamba*, despite everything she said and did to the contrary, and that Great Britain was too. In many respects the *menalamba* were re-enacting a whole period of history which had not been allowed to take its place in the popular ideology. They sometimes appeared to be more concerned with probing old internal wounds and investigating Imerina's past than with fighting the French. Gallieni, not known as a whimsical man, grasped this very quickly. He realized that it was more effective and less expensive to open the royal tombs at Ambohimanga than to try and destroy the enemy in a pitched battle, as his predecessors had done. It is not of purely intellectual interest to comment on the *menalamba* obsession with history. Tradition, for the Merina, was the point of reference for all social organization and the legitimization of rule. The oligarchy of the nineteenth century had sought to confirm its power by a distortion of tradition, or so its opponents felt, and the *menalamba* sought to remake this history as it should have been. This helps to explain why the *menalamba*, in common with some other insurgents produced by basically oral cultures, were so concerned with rhetoric, myths, and constructs of the imagination.

The movement was most effective in terms of modern political subversion when it had strong Europeanized leaders who had assimilated ideas of European origin. A minority of *menalamba*, many of them lapsed Christians, used the rhetoric of nationalism and their familiarity with European techniques of warfare and organization as a way of uniting diverse grievances in one movement. They were leaders, and might be called nationalists according to almost any definition of that word. So the movement was notably most modern and most efficient in opposing the French in the north, where Christianity had taken the deepest root.

As is so often the case, it was not those who had suffered the most who

157

rebelled the most. The peoples who had been most vilely oppressed by the old Merina government were probably the Betsileo and Betsimisaraka, neither of whom joined the *menalamba* or resisted the French in significant numbers. If the same question is put to the history of Imerina, the question of the relation between hardship and revolt, the reply is similar. Probably the most bloody government known to old Imerina was that exercised in the middle years of Ranavalona I, say from 1836 to 1857. But the kingdom came closest to civil war slightly before and after these dates, in 1828–32 and 1863–4. In each case the main cause of unrest was a reshuffling of factions at court, and a rupture in the system of religion by which local government was conducted, order upheld and witchcraft averted. These conditions applied once more in 1895.

THE LEGACY OF THE *MENALAMBA*

During colonial times people who wrote about the African past – Europeans especially – tended to assume that anyone who had resisted the imposition of colonial rule was by definition a reactionary. It seemed self-evident that the true progressives, those Africans who were most in harmony with the spirit of the age, were the ones who collaborated with colonial governments and who served a colonial apprenticeship in the techniques of running a nation-state. Generally speaking it was the collaborators in Africa who formed new élites, or breathed new life into old ones, and who inherited the apparatus of the state when independence came to Africa. Since about 1963, by which time much of Africa had achieved political independence, a school of historiography has begun to question these assumptions in trying to define more thoughtfully the traditions established by the resisters of colonial rule and in estimating their contribution to modern African nationalism.[17]

Madagascar's experience was an unusual one. It has already been noted that the Merina kingdom after about 1810 was imposing a new national identity on most of Madagascar, and that after 1869 it bore a close structural resemblance to a colonial state. A form of Malagasy nationalism was already established when central Madagascar was plunged into civil war in 1895, dividing the population roughly into supporters and resisters of colonial rule. The *menalamba* leaders may have had a clearer and more sophisticated concept of that ideal than the majority of their followers, but the fact that the appeal to nationalism was the most powerful unifying force known to them says a great deal for its popularity. The collaborators in 1895–9, for obvious reasons, were not able to play the nationalist card. It was only after the defeat of the *menalamba* that those who had collaborated with the French took up the argument that they were working for the national unity of Madagascar by helping to submit the whole island to a central government committed to modernization. Indeed, Gallieni himself sometimes claimed to be one in a line of unifiers of the island starting with Andria-nampoinimerina.[18]

The principal method by which historians have sought to understand better the significance and effects of collaboration and resistance to European conquest in Africa has been by examining the relation, in sociological or structural terms, between the primary resisters and later generations of nationalists. They have for example studied whether groups which were militarily defeated by European invaders nevertheless succeeded in creating institutions or symbols which were to be at the heart of later nationalist movements. It has been demonstrated that in some parts of the African continent the resisters had a modernizing effect in surmounting former tribal units, in producing leaders of a new kind, in inventing or popularizing proto-nationalist ideas, or in negotiating special terms with the colonial power which, in its anxiety to make peace, may have granted concessions to former resisters.[19]

One of the main problems in following such an approach in the case of Madagascar has been the reluctance of historians and politicians of every type to contemplate the legacy of the *menalamba* until very recent times. Gallieni tried deliberately to falsify the history of the *menalamba*, and his fiction was reproduced by almost all the French officials who were his contemporaries and who had the wherewithal to have written a more penetrating analysis of the rising.[20] No other European has written at length on the subject since that generation wrote its memoirs. As for the Malagasy, they have been extremely reticent about the *menalamba*. Many Malagasy historians have been members of the Protestant Church, itself a later vehicle for nationalism, and quite a few have been direct descendants of the Merina churchmen who occupied a no man's land in 1896. And yet of the Malagasy Protestant authors with access to both oral and written sources only Maurice Rasamuel tried to answer the question of the *menalamba* directly.[21] The silence of other Protestants is partly because the *menalamba* have posed a dilemma for them, one very similar to that faced by thousands of Christians in 1895–6: if the *menalamba* were really patriots, as they claimed, then why did they burn churches? Similarly the oral traditions which have been collected in Imerina since 1896 rarely mention the *menalamba*, despite the fact – or more likely because of the fact – that the movement was so crucial in the destruction of those good old days of which the traditions are so fond. The secrecy surrounding the *menalamba* for most of the twentieth century has been so complete that many Malagasy came to understand the word *menalamba* as a general term meaning 'bandit'.[22] Even after the creation of an independent Malagasy state in 1960 no one at first wished to claim the inheritance of the *menalamba*. It would have called into question too sharply the nature of the state at that time and its continuing dependence upon collaboration with France. The nationalist rising of 1947 was still too recent and too painful to mention such a subject. The nationalism of the *menalamba* made the government uneasy. Only with the installation of a government proclaiming itself revolutionary after 1972 were the *menalamba* hailed as the direct ancestors of a modern radical nationalism.

The only visible exception to this general neglect occurred during the nationalist insurrection of 1947. The insurgents of that year sometimes referred to *menalamba* leaders by name in their proclamations. Like the *menalamba* they claimed to have central leaders who were in fact fulfilling an imaginary role assigned to them by the insurgents but who were vital to the cohesion of the movement. The rising was likewise aimed at a restoration of traditional values in an independent Madagascar. In 1947 as in 1896 the main weapon employed by the insurgents was the conviction that a united people would possess supernatural power. Again, this belief was associated with the expectation of help from a foreign ally whose role was quasi-mystical. In 1896 that help was supposed to come from Britain, in 1947 from the United States of America or the United Nations. There can be no doubt that the 1947 rising was in many ways consciously modelled on that of the *menalamba* and that in other respects it was inadvertently so. But whether the resisters of 1947 were direct descendants of the *menalamba* in a literal sense is a question which cannot yet be answered for lack of research. Despite Jacques Tronchon's major study,[23] we still do not know exactly who they were. Suffice it to say that the insurrection was strongest on the east coast. One of the major groups of insurgents of 1947, the Vorimo, were quite well disposed towards the French in 1895 but may have fought against them in the Tanala risings of 1897. Others, like the Zafimamy of Imerina, were insurgents in both risings.

Nowadays there are many different components to Malagasy nationalism. Not all of them fall within the scope of this study, which examines only the *menalamba*. Of those elements which were tempered in the crucible of 1895–9, the easiest to trace is that associated with the Protestant Church. Even during the year of 1896 *menalamba* ideas about the Church, and churchmen's feelings about the *menalamba*, changed dramatically. In some cases the Protestant Church ceased to be popularly regarded as an alien institution, to become one which could be used to oppose the French and to uphold true Malagasy values. Protestantism came to be accepted because it had formed part of the old monarchy and because it was known to be sponsored by Britain, an enemy of France. These notions were reinforced by the execution of Rainandriamampandry and the persecution of Protestants in 1896–7. The former LMS churches in particular came to be regarded as both genuinely Malagasy and yet a part of the twentieth century. The same cannot be said of the old talismans, which never recovered their popular appeal after 1896.

The modern Protestant Church is still closely associated with the bourgeoisie of Antananarivo whose ancestors controlled it before the French conquest. Many Protestant leaders of this century in fact could trace their ancestry directly to magnates of the old government. In shooting Rainandriamampandry and rejecting the Protestant élite which he represented, the French alienated a network of influential families allied by marriage and tradition. They were the core of the nationalist secret society known as the Vy, Vato, Sakelika (VVS) – Iron, Stone, Branch – [24] which is generally considered the first nationalist movement after the conquest. The VVS was suppressed in 1915. The tradition of Protestant nationalism was represented during the 1930s by leading city pastors like Rabary and Ravelojaona, who were also historians. It passed to the leaders of the Mouvement démo-cratique de la rénovation malgache (MDRM), such as Albert Rakoto-Ratsimamanga and Joseph Ravoahangy, who were respectively the grand-son of the Prince Ratsimamanga executed with Rainandriamampandry and the nephew of the last queen of Madagascar. These and others of their background sustained the nationalist agitation of 1947 but, like many leading Protestants before and since, they were at heart partisans of peaceful change. Here we encounter another reason for long Protestant silence concerning the *menalamba*: a real popular insurrection threatened the status of Merina Protestants within Madagascar. This was true in 1896, in 1947, and in more recent times.

Independence has not greatly changed the nature of Protestant national-ism. It still produces leaders from the same tradition, like Richard Andria-manjato – a biographer of Rainandriamampandry – or Roland Rabetafika, a great-grandson of the queen's pastor exiled in 1897. Moreover the rift caused in Antananarivo's oligarchy by the French conquest and by the feuding between prominent families which resulted in Rainandriamamp-andry's death has long since been resolved. For a generation or more the descendants of collaborators like Rasanjy, Ramahatra or Rainianjanoro were the bitterest enemies of the descendants of the Protestant magnates. Now they mix easily, their fundamental community of interest being greater than the fading memory of old divisions.

The legacy of the true *menalamba*, of those who lived in the rebel camps and occupied the countryside, is less easy to trace or to define. It is rarely seen in the politics of modern Antananarivo. It is largely a tradition of rural resistance to central government, of tax revolts, of a return to an idealized past. The *menalamba* were not the first to launch a peasant rising in Imerina. There are records of similar risings in earlier times, notably in western Imerina in 1863–4. Modern accounts of rural banditry have a distinct resemblance to those written over a century ago. Banditry still occurs in the very same margins where outlaws habitually gathered under the royal government and whence the *menalamba* drew some of their support, like the remote areas around Anjozorobe. But the *menalamba* were far more than rural malcontents, since they aimed not at the removal of specific grievances but at the reordering of society. They intended a social revolution of a type unrecorded in previous Merina history except perhaps in the distant times when the *hova* replaced the Vazimba as the rulers of Imerina. The means which they developed to express their aspirations have become part of an insurrectionary tradition most fully felt in 1947 and which again surfaced in 1972–5. One modern politician, Richard Ratsimandrava, attempted to harness his government to that tradition with a programme of radical rural reform. There are apparently some people who believe that Ratsimandrava was not really assassinated in 1975.[25] This is surely another echo of the rural dissident tradition by which fictitious or resurrected leaders are created in the popular imagination.

The *menalamba* made Malagasy nationalism into a creed so popular that it may be used by the people against the central government on occasion. Almost every Malagasy knows that there existed before the French conquest a state which claimed to be the sole government of Madagascar and whose capital was at Antananarivo. Before 1895 there had been many who resisted this claim and others, even Merina, who admitted it but detested its spokesmen. With the abolition of the monarchy much of the former unpopularity of this government faded, and left only the vague memory of a time when Madagascar belonged to the Malagasy. Regional jealousies continued to exist and were exploited by the French. But as early as 1896 there were former opponents of Merina hegemony who were willing to fight in the name of the queen and of the royal government because this was the factor most likely to unite all Malagasy against the French invaders. The *menalamba* were instrumental in putting the Merina royal tradition at the service of the whole people. When General de Gaulle came to Antananarivo in 1958 and made a famous speech promising independence, he was able to use the queen's palace as a symbol of Malagasy independence.[26] Similarly the protesters of 1972 in Antananarivo used the old royal colours of red and white as an emblem, while General Ramanantsoa, who restored peace after the troubles of that year, derived much of his authority from the fact that he was a descendant of Madagascar's last queen.[27] These symbols may have been appreciated by the Merina of Antananarivo more than by the other peoples of the island, but they show how an old royal tradition has been incorporated into modern, island-wide nationalism.

The memory of the *menalamba* is here to stay. In the past decade it has been popularized through newspapers and the radio as a means of restoring to the Malagasy that proper pride in their own past which the colonialists tried to remove. But in many respects the exact legacy of the *menalamba* is one of permanent opposition. The *menalamba* indeed reinforced and spread the nationalist idea but they did so in the context of creating or strengthening channels of resistance which still form a potential threat to a government of any ideological colour. Malagasy nationalism is sufficiently rich and diverse for both government and popular opposition to claim to incarnate older traditions. But the claim of governments since 1972 that they represent the radical tradition of the *menalamba* looks suspiciously like a revival of the old practice of manipulating genealogies to enhance current claims for power.

CAPITALISM AND RESISTANCE

One of the most striking claims made by the *menalamba* was that their rulers had been seduced by foreign silver. It was true in a metaphorical sense. Although few of Imerina's ruling class actively desired colonization they had been prepared for it economically and culturally by several decades of European influence. To put it crudely, they knew that they could flourish in the French colony of Madagascar more easily than they could have done in the sort of kingdom which the *menalamba* aimed to establish.

This raises the question of the extent to which the *menalamba* were protesting against the intrusion of certain forms of capitalist relations rather than against the imposition of foreign rule in itself.[28] That is not to deny that patriotism was crucial to the articulation of the *menalamba* movement. But close examination of the rising shows the importance of their revolt against what they felt to be an improper use of, and demand for, money. Many leaders of the rising came not from that section of the community which lived as far as possible from farming but from the ranks of small traders. We know that Rainijirika and Rafanenitra for example were former traders. Rabozaka and Randriamisaodray, to judge from their administrative grades, probably had some commercial interests too. Rainitavy actually acquired most of his followers from among traders who felt threatened by the influx of European, Indian and creole merchants into inland markets. A disproportionately large number of minor leaders came from the class of itinerant petty traders and rum-sellers, some of whom were also Christian lay-preachers, who had abandoned the life of sedentary agriculture without ever moving into the big league of wholesale merchants, urban landlords and money-lenders. All of these small traders felt their livelihood to be threatened by Europeans or by those Malagasy traders and capitalists who enjoyed political power.

Moreover although the rank-and-file of the *menalamba* were usually farmers rather than traders, they too were in revolt against an unacceptable economic order. The taxes which they were obliged to pay were levied by rulers who could no longer raise sufficient cash from customs receipts or from trade. When the magnates required them to do forced labour for blatantly private and commercial uses rather than for the public good, it was partly because forced labour gave Merina grandees a competitive edge over Europeans. The island's richest people were not themselves adversely affected either by the creeping colonization of European traders and creditors who intruded into inland markets from the 1860s, or by formal colonial rule. Many of the Merina magnates ceased to compete directly against Europeans in the last quarter of the nineteenth century, preferring to invest their money in property or in money-lending. In the long run they were not damaged even by the emancipation of slaves, either because they had had sufficient foresight to draw their investment out of slaves in time, or because they could continue to exploit freed slaves in new ways.[29]

By the late nineteenth century Imerina's rulers were caught between European demands – backed by force after 1883 – and popular intransigence. It is possible to identify three principal elements in the series of political equations which characterized the age of imperialism.[30] The imperial power had to have a working relationship with the indigenous élite, which in turn needed the acquiescence of the people whom it ruled. Every time that the imperial power made a heavier demand upon the indigenous élite of an African or Asian state, the local rulers had either to refuse the demand, which provoked the wrath of the imperial power, or to impose the demand on their subjects and constituents by force if necessary. European economic penetration after the mid-nineteenth century changed the balance of power between Europeans and various groups of Malagasy to the extent that some of the equations which defined their previous relationship ceased to hold good. French conquest was therefore, as it were, a process of rewriting those equations. France invaded because the prime minister of Imerina was unable to give the guarantees of security, freedom of trade and control of foreign policy which Paris demanded. When the French government did eventually impose first a protectorate and then a colony, on terms satisfactory to itself, the arrangement proved unacceptable to the mass of the people represented by the *menalamba*.

European demands upon Madagascar became overwhelming only after 1861 when Britain and France insisted on free trade, the right to evangelize and the right to hold property in the island. The rulers of Imerina, unable to resist these demands without the risk of a war which they could not afford and could not win, in turn required of their people forced labour, military service, taxes and the consumption of imported goods. But a glance at the main causes of popular discontent on the eve of the French conquest reveals that they date back to a period before European governments were demanding radical change. Military service was a burden for the Merina even in the 1820s. Forced labour was heavy and destructive of harmony in many villages by the middle of the century. Even the pace and mode of Christian conversion were dictated more by the enthusiasm of the Merina government than by the endeavour of the missionaries. Throughout the century the adoption of institutions of a European type or on an enlarged scale of operation pressed ahead faster than any European government demanded. This is even true of the period of Queen Ranavalona I, despite what the missionaries wrote about her. The changes enforced by the government of Imerina before 1861 were intended to have a modernizing effect in strengthening central government, especially by creating a literate civil service and a standing army. Although many of these innovations were inspired by European models they were done at the behest of an indigenous ruling class which saw in them a means of constructing a nation-state under its own control. A new type of state was arising in Imerina and colonizing Madagascar from within from about 1810. The considerable changes in the structure and scale of Merina government which occurred in the earlier nineteenth century derived from policies initiated in Antananarivo, not in Paris or London. They were the result of an internal dynamic.

But Merina society, rapidly changing though it was, was unsuited to the demands put upon it first by Imerina's rulers and later by the French. Its character was such that certain aspects of the modernization carried out in the nineteenth century were self-destructive, notably in regard to labour. It was a civilization based on the intensive cultivation of rice without machinery or significant capital investment, but with a great investment of time and labour by generations of freemen who had built the irrigation works. Kings before 1810 had encouraged the development of a society which consisted as nearly as possible of free demes fixed on the land of their ancestors. The kings thus promoted prosperity by establishing strong government over the settled and hard-working population which maintained dykes and canals. It is a measure of the success of royal government that Imerina has maintained the highest concentration of population in Madagascar for several centuries although it does not have the most fertile land in the island.

The innovations of the nineteenth century were paradoxical in the sense that mobility of labour was destructive of the fabric of this society and of its agricultural system. Freemen were the cultural and economic backbone of old Imerina. But they were also the people least disposed to accept the principle of labour mobility which threatened the way of life which had been evolved by their ancestors and which had ensured their collective survival in the face of hardships natural and man-made. The freemen would submit to almost any imposition except leaving their land and their ancestral tombs. For their part the magnates of the kingdom could not accept the introduction of wage labour which, though a vital component of economic development, would have undermined their own authority. Freemen had to travel to work, but they also identified with their ancestral villages. They had to work for others, but they were not to be paid.

Strangely enough, the defeat of the *menalamba* and the establishment of a colonial state which tried to create a modern labour force by taxes, education and a dozen other means have not destroyed what the Merina call the customs of the ancestors. The way of life which was normal in old Imerina has become an abstraction for the many who are nowadays obliged to earn their living other than in their ancestral villages. But far from becoming less important, the cult of the ancestors has become the means by which demes retain their identity in changed circumstances.[31] Merina villages are physically dominated more than ever by the large stone-built tombs where the forefathers of their inhabitants lie.

Some Europeans allowed themselves a moment of sentimentality when they saw a colonial government attempt the systematic destruction of the society of the ancestors. 'Today this curious Malagasy society lies in the dust', wrote a French administrator. 'We have destroyed it as a child breaks a toy, for

165

pleasure, and, on the place where it stood, we have constructed a house of paper, all façade and with no foundations.'[32] The thousands of Merina who followed Andrianampoinimerina's coffin from Ambohimanga to Antananarivo one March night in 1897 were obsessesd with the same thought, from a real terror of what the future would bring in a world where the customs of the ancestors were no longer respected. But if Andrianampoinimerina were to rise from his tomb in the citadel at Antananarivo, and to walk once more through the villages of Imerina, he might be surprised at how much was familiar to him in the lives of the inhabitants.

Appendix 1 Chronology of events

?Early 14th century	Early kingdoms in south-east Imerina
?16th century	Reign of King Ralambo
c.1675–c.1710	Reign of King Adriamasinavalona
c.1783–1810	Reign of King Andrianampoinimerina
1810–28	Reign of King Radama I
1828–61	Reign of Queen Ranavalona I
1861–63	Reign of King Radama II
1863–68	Reign of Queen Rasoherina
1868	Coronation of Queen Ranavalona II
1869	Baptism of Ranavalona II and Prime Minister Rainilaiarivony. Destruction of the talismans
1873	First appointments of Palace Church evangelists
1876	Compulsory education
1877	Liberation of Mozambique slaves
1883	Death of Ranavalona II. Coronation of Queen Ranavalona III
1883–85	Franco-Merina war
1885	Creation of French protectorate over Madagascar. Imerina to pay an indemnity of 10 million francs, plus interest on a French loan of a further 5 million francs
1890	Anglo-French agreement recognizes French rights over Madagascar
1891–2	Commercial crisis in Madagascar
October 1894	Le Myre de Vilers's ultimatum rejected
13 November 1894	French Chamber votes war credits of 65 million francs for an expedition to Madagascar
January 1895	French landings in Majunga; growth of religious revival in Imerina
July 1895	Death of Andrianony, nationalist Merina pastor
30 September 1895	Fall of Antananarivo
1 October 1895	Establishment of full French protectorate
October–November 1895	Disarmament of Merina officials; anti-European and anti-Christian movements in Imerina. Anti-Merina risings on the east coast
22 November 1895	Feast of *fandroana*. Death of Johnson family

167

December 1895	Alliance of Rainibetsimisaraka, Ratsizehana and Rambinintsoa in south Imerina
January 1896	Rabezavana, Rabozaka, Rafanenitra and Ratsimamanga meet at Analaroa; arrival of Laroche and General Voyron
Early February 1896	Discovery of 'Ambohimanga letter'
14 March 1896	First day of Alahamady. Patriotic meetings in northern Imerina; northern *menalamba* advance on Ambatondrazaka and Antananarivo
29 March 1896	Death of three Frenchmen at Manarintsoa
22 April 1896	Rambinintsoa killed by French troops
May 1896	Siege of Antsirabe
Late May 1896	French intelligence service announces discovery of a plot in Antananarivo
June 1896	*Menalamba* attack suburbs of Antananarivo; rising spreads to Vonizongo
July 1896	Rising of Mamolakazo and western Imerina
6 August 1896	Madagascar becomes a French colony
12 September 1896	Rafiringa proclaimed King of Madagascar at Andrarakasina
26 September 1896	Abolition of slavery in Madagascar
27 September 1896	Arrival of General Gallieni, acting governor-general
10 October 1896	Departure of Laroche
15 October 1896	Execution of Rainandriamampandry and Prince Ratsimamanga for alleged treason
November 1896	Increase of sectarian disputes in Imerina and Betsileo-land
28 February 1897	Exile of Queen Ranavalona III; abolition of monarchy in Imerina
14 March 1897	Exhumation of royal coffins at Ambohimanga
17 April 1897	Abolition of fiefs and noble privileges
May 1897	Rising of Tanala at Ambohimanga-Atsimo. Société des Missions Evangéliques takes over some London Missionary Society districts in Imerina and Betsileo-land. Murder of pastors Escande and Minault
June 1897	Surrender of Rabezavana and Rainibetsimisaraka; rising of the Bara-be
July 1897	Escape and recapture of Rabezavana
30 August 1897	Death of King Toera of Menabe
September–October 1897	Gallieni tours Betsileo-land
October 1897	Risings in Menabe
20 February 1898	Surrender of Rabozaka
July 1898	Second escape of Rabezavana
September 1898	Ambush of French troops in Kamoro valley by militia deserters
26 October 1898	Massacres of French settlers in Sambirano. News of the Fashoda affair. Revival of Protestant nationalism
November–December 1898	Sambirano rising

Early 1899	Rumours of rising in Imerina
Mid-1899	Gallieni returns to France for consultations
13 November 1899	The end of the world predicted

Appendix 2 Glossary of Malagasy words, excluding most proper names

Alahamady	The first month of the traditional lunar calendar
Andafy-Avaratra	Principal *hova* family serving as generals and prime ministers from *c*.1790 to 1895
andevo	The lowest category of slave
andriana	One related to, or descended from, a sovereign
deka	A military retainer. Corruption of French term *aide-de-camp*
fahavalo	Enemy, especially a bandit. Often used by the French to refer to the *menalamba*
fandroana	The feast of the bath. Traditionally the first day of Alahamady, but fixed in 1883 on 22 November
fatidra	The brotherhood of blood
foko	A deme
fokon'olona	A village commune
hasina	Supernatural virtue or power
hova	A commoner; that is, a freeman unrelated to a sovereign. Often used by Europeans to denote all Merina
kabinetra	Cabinet
karazana	A deme
Kelimalaza, also Ikelimalaza, or Rakelimalaza	The premier royal talisman
komity	Committee
mainty	'Black'. The name applied to the ritually unfree
menabe	An area owing allegiance to no intermediary between itself and the sovereign
menakely	An area supervised by a fief-holder, who had the right to receive certain dues normally accorded to the sovereign
menalamba	'Red shawls'. Those who resisted France in the name of the kingdom of Imerina or the kingdom of Madagascar
menamaso	The counsellors of Radama II (1861–3)
mpitandrina	A pastor
olona marina	Just people, good citizens

orim-bato	A standing-stone, used to mark a boundary or to commemorate a special event
ramanenjana	A possession cult
sampy	A talisman
sivilizesona	Civilization, especially European styles and manners
tanindrazana	The land of the ancestors
tia-tanindrazana	A lover of the land of the ancestors, i.e. a patriot
tompo	Master
tompo-menakely	A fief-holder
valonjatolahy	Literally, 'the eight hundred men'. Name applied to the descendants of a group of military colonists settled on Imerina's north-eastern border by King Andrianampoinimerina
vazaha	A foreigner, especially a European
Vazimba	The first inhabitants of Imerina. After their conquest by *hova* and *andriana*, the Vazimbas' spirits were thought to haunt old sites

Appendix 3 Principal Malagasy figures

ANDRIANAIVORAVELONA, Joseph (1835–97). Noble, Andrianamboninolona. Born at Ambohitromby, son of an elder of the deme. 1845–6: learns to read and write. Converts to Christianity. 1853–6: travels in Betsileo-land and south Imerina on government business. 1869–73: student at LMS Theological College. 1883: pastor to Queen Ranavalona III. Influential in Palace Church organization and Christian revival movement. Feb. 1897: accused of complicity with the *menalamba* and exiled.

ANDRIANONY (d. July 1895). 1869–73: student at LMS Theological College. 1881: pastor of Friends' church at Ambohitantely. Known for his independent views and opposition to European missionaries, he nevertheless worked with many missionary committees. July 1895: attempts to incite revolt among royal troops. Murdered on orders of Rainilaiarivony (q.v.).

LAIMIZA. Sakalava-Mamindra. Member of a Sakalava group conquered by Radama I and settled in Valalafotsy. His father, Iariaria, was made governor of Fenoarivo in Valalafotsy. 1863: Iariaria joins anti-government rising. Flees to Ambongo, but later returns to Valalafotsy under amnesty. *c.*1880: Laimiza succeeds as chief of Sakalava-Mamindra of Fenoarivo. 1885: organizes tax-revolt. 1892–4: leads resistance to tax and conscription. Oct. 1895: gathers army deserters. July 1896: joins *menalamba* at the request of Rafanenitra (q.v.). Late 1897: surrenders, but remains in contact with Sakalava resisters in Ambongo.

RABEONY. 1889: appointed governor-general of Antsihanaka. 14 honours.* Sometime evangelist. Acquires a considerable reputation for use of forced labour and for extortion. Nov. 1895: orders Rabozaka to attack bandits on borders of Antsihanaka. Apparently known personally by Rabozaka. Jan.–Feb. 1896: clashes with forces of Rabezavana and Rabozaka. Mar.–Oct. 1896: successfully defends Ambatondrazaka against the *menalamba*. Oct. 1896: dismissed from his post because of his unpopularity.

RABEZAVANA, alias Ravaikafo (1852–1900). Marofotsy, *mainty*. Born at Ambodiamontana of a senior family of the Marofotsy. Late 1880s: gathers a private army for the protection of his district. 1892: created 10 honours, governor of Antsatrana, and later 12 honours, for his success against bandits. 1895: refuses to join main army against the French, but fights with his own contingent. Sept. 1895–Feb. 1896: organizes army deserters and prepares national rising. Aug. 1896: spreads pro-British propaganda after his son's escape from French custody. Nov.

* The honours system, usually graded from 1 honour to 16 honours, was used to denote military rank. Thus '14 honours' indicated a very senior officer.

172

1896: attacks and occupies Ambohimanga. June 1897: surrenders, escapes and is recaptured. July–Aug. 1898: second escape and recapture. Exiled to Réunion. Returns in 1899 at French request. Apr. 1900: suspected murdered by French officer.

RABOZAKA, alias Ramasoandromahamay (*c.*1870–1920). Commoner, Zafimamy/ Zanakandriambe. Born of a political marriage. Educated Friends' High School, Antananarivo. Becomes pastor and hymn-writer. *c.*1894: governor of Mandanja. Apr.–July 1895: tours north with official recruiting party. Nov. 1895: refuses to disarm. Takes cattle from Ramahafinaritra (q.v.). Nov. 1895–Feb. 1896: prepares national rising. Feb. 1896: defeats troops of Governor Rabeony. 14–15 Mar. 1896: declares *menalamba* rising. 20 Feb. 1898: surrenders. Exiled to Réunion. Later returns from exile and reverts to Christianity.

RADANIELA. Commoner, of a senior family of the Zanakantitra. Educated in SPG schools. *c.*1890: governor of Isaha district and SPG schoolteacher. 1893–4: administers gold-*corvée* among Zanakantitra. Nov. 1895: leads opposition to local *menalamba*. Promoted by French, becomes a leading official in Ambodirano.

RAFANENITRA, alias Ramampanenitra, Ratsimametra. Noble, Zanadralambo. Born Andranomasina. Early 1890s: trades on east coast. Nov. 1895: leaves Andranomasina to organize anti-French resistance. Contacts Rabezavana (q.v.). Emerges in 1896 as the leading *menalamba* tactician. Late 1897: surrenders. Spared in exchange for information about Rabezavana and alleged 'British connection'. Exiled to Réunion.

RAFIRINGA. Noble. Fief-holder of Ambohipaniry. Important family connections among the nobles of the Mantasoa region. ?Apr. 1896: joins *menalamba*. 12 Sept. 1896: elected king of Madagascar by the *menalamba* of Vakinisisaony.

RAINANDRIAMAMPANDRY (1836–96). Commoner, Tsimiamboholahy. Born of a leading family of the oligarchy, destined to high office from birth. Educated at court by Raombana, under Queen Ranavalona I. Reads the Bible in secret. 1847: officer of the palace. 1869–73: LMS Theological College. 1874: teacher at Ambohidratrimo. Begins work on a history of Madagascar, still in progress at his death. 1881: foreign minister. Sends his son for education in Britain. 1883–95: governor of Tamatave. Oct. 1895: minister of the interior. Oct. 1896: falsely accused of treachery and shot.

RAINIANJANORO, *mainty*. Born of a powerful family of royal slaves. 1886–94: influential royal administrator. Travels widely in the administration of the gold-*corvée*. Oct. 1895: native director of the intelligence service. Allies with Rasanjy (q.v.). Nov. 1895: his father killed in French service at Amboanana. May 1897: negotiates surrender of Rabezavana (q.v.). Subsequently a leading French collaborator. 1915: leading role in destruction of VVS nationalist secret society.

RAINIBETSIMISARAKA (d. 1902). Born Ambohimirary, Vakinankaratra, of a long-established local family. Rich peasant farmer. *c.*1886: imprisoned after dispute with Pastor Robena (q.v.). 1886–95: operates as a bandit-chief in Voromahery and eastern Vakinankaratra, often paying protection-money to the family of Rainit-simbazafy. Dec. 1895: swears oath of brotherhood with Rambinintsoa (q.v.). Feb. 1896: kills 2 Europeans. 29 Mar. 1896: kills 3 Frenchmen at Manarintsoa. Declares southern rising. May 1896: lays siege to Antsirabe. June 1897: surrender. Exiled to Réunion. 1900: amnestied, returns to Madagascar. Sept. 1902: executed for alleged armed robbery.

RAINIJAONARY (1849–1919). Born of a family of military chiefs of Vakinankaratra. *c.* 1869: joins Lutheran Church. 1889: created 12 honours, governor of Inanatonana and military governor of Vakinankaratra. Successful in fighting bandits. 1894: created 14 honours. Jan. 1896: refuses to join *menalamba*. Apr.

173

1896: created governor-general of Vakinankaratra. May 1896: relieves siege of Antsirabe. Most successful of military collaborators of France. Jan. 1897: transferred because of threat to French power.

RAINIJIRIKA. *Andevo*, of Ambohitrimilahy in Vonizongo. Leaves his master *c*.1892 to trade on west coast. Acquires fortune, possibly in slave trade. 1896–7: leading *menalamba*.

RAINILAIARIVONY (1828–96). Commoner, Tsimiamboholahy. Son of Rainiharo, Andafy-Avaratra prime minster. 1864: prime minister and commander-in-chief of the army. Effective ruler of Imerina until 1895. Oct. 1895: arrested by French. Jan. 1896: exiled to Algiers.

RAINIMANGANORO. *Andevo*? Tanala. Nov. 1896: organizes pro-Merina rising at Antonjomanga. Allies with Rainibetsimisaraka (q.v.).

RAINISINGOMBY, alias Rainizafivoavy (*c*.1870–96). Commoner, Zanakantitra, cadet branch of the family of Andrianjaza. Pupil at FFMA school. 1895: conscripted to fight the French. Returns to Amboanana and organizes robber-band. Oct.– Nov. 1895: organizes Zanakantitra rising. Flees to the west. Aug. 1896: raises western Imerina in new revolt. 4 Oct. 1896: killed in battle, by Radaniela (q.v.).

RAINITAVY (d. 1898). Commoner, Antehiroka. Born Ambohimanarina. Fights against French in 1883–5. 1886: created 11 honours, governor of Mampikomy. Becomes second officer of province of Boina. Recruits for gold-*corvée*. July 1896: organizes supplies for northern *menalamba*. 1897: raises Sakalava and northern Merina garrisons in revolt. Nov. 1897: surrenders. Early 1898: executed.

RAJAMARIA (d. 1896). Sakalava-Mamindra. Hereditary chief at Tsiarofarana. Educated in Catholic schools. 1893–4: organizes tax-revolts with Laimiza (q.v.), and collaborates with bandits. Oct. 1895: organizes army deserters. July 1896: joins *menalamba* at request of Rafanenitra (q.v.). Aug. 1896: killed in battle.

RAMAHAFINARITRA (d. 1899). Commoner, Tsimahafotsy. Rich landowner of Analaroa, highly unpopular on account of his methods of enrichment. Nov. 1895: arrested. *c*.1896: escapes or released from prison having lost all his money. 1897–9: operates with remnants of northern *menalamba*. Late 1899: killed in action.

RAMAHATRA (1858–1938). Noble, Andriamasinavalona. Member of leading court faction. 1895: leader of pro-French party. Mar. 1896: receives letter from Rabezavana, which he shows to the French. Apr.–Oct. 1896: aids repression of northern rising. Oct. 1896: testifies at trial of Rainandriamampandry (q.v.). Native governor-general of military district of Ambatomanga. Nominates native officials of Vakinisisaony. Leading French collaborator until 1920s.

RAMAROKOTO. Noble, of Lazaina. Probably a relative of Rafiringa (q.v.). Leader of *menalamba* in Vakinampasina.

RAMBININTSOA (d. 1896). Degraded noble, of Ambohimanambola. Relative of the leading guardian of Kelimalaza. After the burning of the talismans in 1869, restores Kelimalaza in southern Vakinisisaony. Sept. 1895: reappears with Kelimalaza in Antananarivo. Sept. 1895 – Mar. 1896: organizes southern rising. Dec. 1895: allies with Rainibetsimisaraka (q.v.). 22 April. 1896: killed in battle.

RAMENAMASO, alias Ramandimby (1863–?). Marofotsy, *mainty*. Chief of Ampandrana. Mar. 1896: joins *menalamba*. Leads Marofotsy contingent at siege of Ambatondrazaka.

RAMIEBA. Noble, Zafimanely, king of Bara-be. Nov. 1896: joins anti-French conspiracy at Ihosy. Jan. 1897: deposed by French. Escapes; leads anti-French resistance, June 1897.

RANDRIAMISAODRAY, alias Ramialanenina (*c*.1845–?). Noble, Andrianamboninolona. Born Antenombe. *c*.1862: promoted to 8 honours. Stationed as army officer at Ankarana. 1867–76: military client of General Rainigory, and 1877–87 of his son Rainimiadana. 1888–91: military client of Rainilaiarivony, in charge of telegraph line to Tamatave. 1894: evangelist of Moramanga. 1895: serves against the French at Tamatave. ?June 1896: joins the *menalamba*. Son of Z. J. Andriamanantsiety, Protestant pastor and writer.

RANDRIANTSIMATAHOTRA (d. 1899). Governor of Ambohitrera. Nov. 1895: leads pagan revival among Mandiavato. Arrested. His arrest provokes great unrest among northern governors.

RASAMBA. Son of Ihasina, guardian of the principal talisman at Ankadimanga. 1896: *menalamba* leader.

RASANJY (1851–1918). Commoner, Tsimahafotsy. Son of the then governor of Betsileo. 1866: secretary to the prime minister. 1881: cabinet minister. 1886: member of embassy to Europe. Promoted to 14 honours. 1894–5: leads pro-French party. Oct. 1895: government chief secretary. Oct. 1896: chief prosecution witness at trial of Rainandriamampandry. Feb. 1897: native governor-general of Imerina. Jan. 1898: chevalier de la légion d'honneur. Leading French collaborator.

RATAIZAMBAHOAKA. Sakalava, noble. Hereditary fief-holder of Ambohitrondrana. Educated by Catholic mission. Jan. 1896: in dispute with local evangelist, a relative. July 1896: raises revolt in Valalafotsy, in league with Rafanenitra (q.v.).

RATSIMAMANGA. Noble, Andriamasinavalona. Hereditary fief-holder of Analaroa. Nov. 1895–Feb. 1896: plans northern rising in conjunction with Rabozaka and others. June 1897: surrenders.

RATSIMAMANGA, Prince (c.1820–96). Noble, Zanak'andriana. Uncle of Queen Ranavalona III. Leading member of noble faction at court. Renowned for his financial exactions, he was extremely unpopular. Falsely accused of revolt and executed Oct. 1896.

RATSIZEHENA, alias Ramampanjaka. Tsidingana, noble(?). 1887: leads revolt against gold-*corvée*. Flees and becomes bandit-chief in Voromahery. 1895: alliance with Rainibetsimisaraka confirmed by marriage of Ratsizehena's sister with Rainibetsimisaraka (q.v.). Self-proclaimed king.

RAZAFINDRAINIBE, Jean-Baptiste (1862–?). Noble, Andriantompokoindrindra of Ambohimalaza. Roman Catholic. Educated Jesuit school, Antananarivo. 1894: leader of Catholic Union. 1896: *sous-gouverneur* of Ambohimalaza. Nov. 1896–July 1897: leads attacks on Protestants in Vakinampasina. Feb. 1897: native governor-general of Ambatomanga military district.

REVANARIVO (1839–97). Tanala. Hereditary king of Ambohimanga-Atsimo. 1895: in dispute with his brother, the latter wishing to resist the French, Revanarivo in favour of collaboration. Late 1896: Revanarivo reconciled with his brother, and approached by Rainibetsimisaraka (q.v.). Apr. 1897: leads anti-French rising. July 1897: commits suicide on board a ship taking him to exile in Réunion.

ROBENA. Hereditary fief-holder of Ambohiponana. Sometime governor of Ambatofangehana. Lutheran pastor. 1886: arrests Rainibetsimisaraka (q.v.). 1888–90: persecutes Catholics at Ambohimirary, Rainibetsimisaraka's native village. Nov. 1895: fights Rainibetsimisaraka's followers at Ambohimirary. Leads pro-French party in eastern Vakinankaratra. May 1897: negotiates surrender of Rainibetsimisaraka. 1902: reported as in alliance with Rainibetsimisaraka in case of armed robbery!

TOERA (1862–97). Noble, Sakalava-Zafimbolamena. King of Menabe, in dispute with his brother who also claims the throne. c.1880–94: builds powerful anti-Merina alliance. 1895–6: negotiates with Rainijaonary (q.v.) to establish relations with France. 1897: receives embassy from Rainibetsimisaraka. 30 Aug. 1897: killed in French ambush.

Notes

Introduction

1 Andriamena, *A Madagascar. Souvenirs d'un soldat d'avant-garde* (Paris, n.d.), 208.

1. The decline of Imerina

1 M. E. F. Bloch, *Placing the Dead* (London and New York, 1971), 41–50.
2 J. Sibree, *The Great African Island* (London, 1880), 326.
3 G. Condominas, *Fokon'olona et collectivités rurales en Imerina* (Paris, 1960), 119–30.
4 W. Ellis, *History of Madagascar* (2 vols., London, 1838), I, 397.
5 F. Callet (trans. G. S. Chapus and E. Ratsimba), *Histoire des rois* (rev. edn, vols. I–III, V, plus index, Antananarivo, 1974–8), III, 775. All references to this collection of Merina traditions in the present text refer to the marginal page-numbers of the translation, which correspond to the Malagasy original. It will henceforth be abbreviated to *TA*, i.e. *Tantaran' ny Andriana*.
6 *Ibid.*, II, 531–2.
7 Andriamifidy, 'Andriana', *Mpanolo-tsaina*, new series, V (1908), 46.
8 Figures calculated by contemporaries. C. Caillon-Filet, 'Jean Laborde et l'Océan Indien' (Univ. of Aix-en-Provence, thèse de 3e cycle, 1978), 287–94; de Lastelle quoted in C. Buet, *Six mois à Madagascar* (Paris, 1894), 262; G. S. Chapus and G. Mondain, 'Le tanguin', *Bulletin de l'Académie malgache*, new series, XXVII (1946), 176; Rainandriamampandry, 'Tantarany Madagascar', multi-volume ms., 1874–96, Archives de la république malgache, royal archives, SS12, f.97.
9 J. Sibree, *Madagascar and its People* (London, 1870), 481–3; 'Ikelimalaza', in *Ny Boky Firaketana ny Fiteny sy ny Zavatra Malgasy* (unfinished publication in instalments, Antananarivo, 1937–).
10 My use of the words 'pagan' and 'paganism' is not pejorative. It is intended to describe the cult of the ancestors, and the customs of the ancestors, which stood in opposition to Christianity in the later 19th century. I have avoided calling the cult of the ancestors 'traditional' because in the 19th century it included many innovative elements, some of them borrowed from Christianity. In particular the cults of the royal talismans were a fairly recent introduction.
11 J. C. Thorne, 'Elementary Education in Madagascar', *Antananarivo Annual*, III (1885), 35–7.
12 Statistics quoted in F. Koerner, 'L'échec de l'éthiopianisme dans les églises protestantes malgaches', *Revue française d'histoire d'outre-mer*, LVIII, ii (1971), 220.
13 J. Sewell, quoted in P. Doncaster (ed.), *Faithful Unto Death: a Story of the Missionary Life in Madagascar of William and Lucy S. Johnson* (London, 1896), xi.

176

14 J. Pearse, 'LMS Churches and Congregations and Christian Life in Madagascar', *Ant. Ann.*, V (1895), 316–29.
15 J. Sharman, 'Memorandum on Native Leadership in Madagascar', *c.* 1929, archives of the London Missionary Society, Madagascar series, Odds, box 1.
16 LMS Reports, box 5, folder 1: Vonizongo (W. Huckett), 1895.
17 Thorne, 'Elementary Education', 29.
18 There are many references in the archives to such abuses during the war of 1883–5. See for example the journal of the Rev. J. A. Houlder, 1884, in LMS Odds, box 3; also, *The Madagascar Times*, 30 Apr., 11 June 1884.
19 ARM HH3, ff. 76–7, 87: Bishop Kestell-Cornish to Rainilaiarivony, 16 Jan. 1888, 30 May 1889.
20 London Missionary Society, *Ten Years' Review of Mission Work in Madagascar 1870–1880* (Antananarivo, 1880), 137–40.
21 *Ibid*. For similar descriptions of lay preachers, R. Dumeray, 'Boutou-kely. Souvenirs de la vie malgache', *Revue des deux mondes*, cxxix (May 1895), 175–6; and J. H. Haile, 'Malagasy Village Life: Pen and Ink Sketches of the People of Western Imerina', *Ant. Ann.*, V (1893), 7, 19.
22 LMS, *Ten Years' Review, 1870–1880*, 139.
23 Letter from Pastor Vig, 30 Dec. 1887, in *Norsk Missionstidende*, XLIII (1888), 253–62; letter from Père Campenon, n.d., *Lettres d'Uclès*, 2nd ser., I (1890), 195–219.
24 Diaire d'Ambohidratrimo, entry for 14 June 1880, archives of the archbishopric of Antananarivo at Andohalo, séries Diaires, no. 98.
25 J. Rasamimanana and L. Razafindrazaka, *Contribution à l'histoire des malgaches: ny Andriantompokoindrindra* (2nd edn, Antananarivo, 1957), 34.
26 C. Le Myre de Vilers, 'Situation économique et financière', 14 Dec. 1888, Ministère des affaires étrangères, Paris, Madagascar (old series), correspondance politique, vol. 30, f. 43.
27 Cited in B. A. Gow, 'The British Protestant Missions in Madagascar, 1818–1895' (Dalhousie Univ. Ph.D. thesis, 1975), 460–1.
28 B. A. Gow, *Madagascar and the Protestant Impact* (London, 1979), 94–9; H. E. Clark, 'Where We Are', *Ant. Ann.*, II (1882), 95–105. Series HH of the Merina royal archives in the Archives de la république malgache is also rich in descriptions of troubles of this sort.
29 LMS Reports 5/2: Ambatonakanga (T. T. Matthews), 1895.
30 W. D. Cowan, *The Bara Land: a Description of the Country and People* (Antananarivo, 1881), 67.
31 Archives nationales, section outre-mer, Paris, Madagascar series, MAD 438(1201): Giraudet to Gallieni, 3 Jan. 1897, encl. with Gallieni's report of 13 Jan. 1897.
32 C. M. Le Myre de Vilers, 'Le traité hova', *Revue de Paris* (15 Nov. 1895), 225–41.
33 H. Lacaze, 'Rapport politique et administratif 1896–1904, province de l'Imerina centrale', Dépôt des archives d'outre-mer, Aix-en-Provence, Madagascar series, 2 D 117.
34 Sharman, 'Memorandum on Native Leadership', LMS Odds, 1.
35 Letter from Père Camperon, n.d., *Uclès*, 2nd ser., I (1890), 208–9.
36 *Ibid*.
37 LMS Incoming 24b/2/A: Baron to Thompson, 31 Jan. 1894.
38 R. Delval, *Radama II, prince de la renaissance malgache* (Paris, 1972), 52.
39 Archives of the United States' consulate at Tamatave (original in Washington DC, microfilm in Archives nationales, Paris), vol. II (microfilm 253 Mi 34): Robinson to Hunter, 21 July 1879; J. Sibree, 'A Quarter Century of Change and Progress: Antananarivo and Madagascar Twenty-Five Years Ago', *Ant. Ann.*, III (1888), 405–6.
40 US Cons. II (253 Mi 34): Finkelmeier to sec. of the treasury, 5 Jan. 1870, and Robinson to Hunter, 11 Aug. 1876; vol. III (253 Mi 35): Robinson to Stanwood, 27 Oct. 1880.
41 MAE, series Mémoires et Documents, vol. 144, fols. 349–50: Ranchot's commercial report for 1886.

42 *Ny Gazety Malagasy*, lxxxi (5 Feb. 1887); 'Fanasaovam-bahoaka', anon. ms. of 6 pp., *c*.1903, Berthier papers, Académie des sciences d'outre-mer, Paris; J-P. Raison, 'Utilisation du sol et organisation de l'espace en Imerina ancienne', *Etudes de géographie tropicale offertes à Pierre Gourou* (Paris, The Hague, 1972), 423.

43 J. S. Sewell, *Remarks on Slavery in Madagascar, with an Address on that Subject, Delivered at Antananarivo* (London, 1876), 10; letter from Louis Street in the *English Independent*, 15 and 22 Nov. 1877.

44 V. F. Stanwood, 'Commerce of the West Coast of Madagascar in the hands of white men', 1 Dec. 1880, US Cons. III (253 Mi 35). In using these figures I have followed the usual convention of the time in assuming one US dollar to be equivalent to one piastre. 'Tableau des importations et exportations de la côte est de Madagascar', 1881, DAOM 4 Z 111; US Cons. III (253 Mi 35): Robinson to Payson, 2 Oct. 1880; C. de la Vaissière, *Vingt ans à Madagascar* (Paris, 1885), 23 and 330–1.

45 J. and S. Chauvicourt, 'La monnaie coupée et les poids monétaires de Madagascar', *Numismatique malgache*, fascicule IV (Antananarivo, 1967), and *idem*, 'Les premières monnaies introduites à Madagascar', *Numismatique malgache*, fascicule III (Antananarivo, 1968), 37–40.

46 S. D. K. Ellis, 'The Merina Background, from Andrianampoinimerina to the French Conquest', in J. Simensen and F. Fuglestad (eds.), *Norwegian Missions in South Africa and Madagascar* (Norwegian Universities Press, in press).

47 LMS, *Ten Years' Review, 1870–1880*, 139.

48 ARM IIICC 148: Rabesoaroy *et al.* to Rainilaiarivony, 11 Adijady/8 Feb. 1892.

49 ARM HH1, ff. 78–9: Baron to Rainilaiarivony, 22 Dec. 1891.

50 ARM HH4, Dahle to same, 8 Jan. 1885.

51 Arch. And., C.9(c): draft memorandum by Père Campenon(?), May 1890, pp. 23–5.

52 Statistics in A. Martineau, *Madagascar en 1894* (Paris, n.d.), 136–75; P. Boiteau, *Madagascar: contribution à l'histoire de la nation malgache* (Paris, 1958), 188–9; Public Record Office, Kew, Foreign Office papers, series 48, vol. 85, f. 371: enc. with Awdry to Undersec., 27 Aug. 1895. For the Europeans' distribution and occupations, see *Annuaire de Madagascar pour 1892* (Antananarivo, 1891). The best work on European relations with Madagascar in the 19th century is probably P. M. Mutibwa, *The Malagasy and the Europeans* (London, 1974).

53 ANSOM MAD 212(434): Larrouy to min. des cols., 28 Aug. 1893; 'Renseignements sur le commerce de Madagascar', MAE, M&D, Africa vol. 144, f. 459.

54 Archives départementales de l'Orne, Alençon, Le Myre de Vilers papers, dossier 20: Le Myre de Vilers to min. of foreign affairs (draft), n.d.

55 A. d'Anthouard, 'Rapport commercial sur Madagascar en 1890', MAE, M&D Africa 144, ff. 360–5, 377–463.

56 W. C. Pickersgill, 'The Trade and Commerce of Madagascar', *Ant. Ann.*, III (1886), 179, note 1; A. Cabaret, 'Un an à Madagascar', *Revue politique et littéraire. Revue bleue*, 4th ser., IV, xvii (Oct. 1895), 521.

57 DAOM 2 Z 265: *passim*, and esp. Delhorbe to resident-general, 8 Jan. 1894.

58 *TA*, III, 879–83; J. J. Freeman and D. Johns, *A Narrative of the Persecution of the Christians in Madagascar* (London, 1840), 45–6.

59 This is based on analysis of prices gleaned from numerous sources, but also from contemporary descriptions of prices such as that in FO 48/1: Baker to Sir W. Nicaulay, 1836.

60 Sibree, *Madagascar and its People*, 230.

61 For example, I. Wilks, *Asante in the Nineteenth Century* (Cambridge, 1975), 444–5. There are many stimulating parallels described in K. Polanyi, *Dahomey and the Slave Trade, an Analysis of an Archaic Economy* (Seattle and London, 1966). Polanyi's work has been demonstrated to be based on insufficient reading of Dahomeyan history, but his ideas remain stimulating nonetheless.

62 Letter to the editor, *The Madagascar Times*, 5 Feb. 1887.
63 Rabenjamina, 'Histoire d'Ambohimanga', mss. 1671, Bibliothèque nationale, Antananarivo. The second couplet is a reference to a famous speech by King Andrianampoinimerina, recorded in *TA*, III, 707.

2. The Provinces of Madagascar

1 M. Mahatsanga, 'L'évolution de la société Bara dans la deuxième moitié du XIXe siècle' (Univ. of Madagascar, mémoire de maîtrise, 1977); R. K. Kent, *Early Kingdoms in Madagascar 1500–1700* (New York, 1970), 116–58.
2 G. Ferrand, 'Les tribus du sud', 6 pp. typescript, c.1890, Archives de l'académie malgache, unclassified.
3 C. Razafimbelo, 'Les origines de l'implantation chrétienne en pays sihanaka: contribution à l'histoire des mentalités locales' (Univ. of Madagascar, travail d'études et de recherches, 1978), *passim*.
4 The higher figure is in Bibliothèque nationale, Antananarivo, mss. 106 (Rafanoharana papers), pp. 83–5: enc. with Rafanoharana to Ranavalona III, 1 Asombola/3 Nov. 1888. The lower figure is in ANSOM Gallieni papers, 5(32): Gallieni to Dr Besson, 9 Dec. 1896.
5 Dr Besson, 'Rapport sur la situation générale du pays des Betsileo au 20 Mars 1889', MAE, CP 32, ff. 2–23.
6 E. Escande, *Les disciples du seigneur* (Paris, 1926), 20 *et seq.*
7 Mahirilanja, 'Ny foko Vorimo', oral tradition transcribed at Masomelaka, 22 June 1921, 6 pp., Berthier papers.
8 M. Esoavelomandroso, 'La province maritime orientale du "Royaume de Madagascar" à la fin du XIXe siècle (1882–1895)' (2 vols., Univs. of Madagascar and Paris, thèse de 3e cycle, 1976), *passim*.
9 C. Le Myre de Vilers, 'Note sur la situation politique et morale', 14 Dec. 1888, MAE, CP 30, ff. 23–32.
10 DAOM 2 Z 356: Gautier to Laroche, 19 Aug. 1896.
11 J. Richardson, *A new Malagasy–English Dictionary* (republished Farnborough, Hants, 1967), entry on 'Imerina'.
12 *TA*, I, 19–20; G. Ralaimihoatra, 'Les premiers rois d'Imerina et la tradition vazimba', *BAM*, n.s., L, ii (1972), 25–32.
13 Rainianjanoro, *Tantara nataon' dRainianjanoro* (no place or date), 8–9.
14 J-P. Domenichini, *Histoire des palladium de l'Imerina d'après les manuscrits anciens* (roneotyped, Musée d'art et d'archéologie de Tananarive, documents inédits no. VIII, Antananarivo, 1971), 2–91; *TA*, I, 205, and II, 411.
15 M. Gendronneau, 'Etude détaillée des diverses régions de Madagascar', *Notes, reconnaissances et explorations*, I (1897), 159.
16 J. Randriamandimby Ravoahangy-Andrianavalona, 'Critique d'un texte de Rabenjamina Androvakely à propos de la généalogie des Andriamasinavalona d'Andramasina', *BAM*, n.s., LV, i–ii (1977), 61–4.
17 Sibree, *Madagascar and its People*, 481–3.
18 Domenichini, *Histoire des palladium*, 91.
19 LMS Reports 3/1: Vonizongo (J. A. Houlder), 1885.
20 On the history of Rambinintsoa, see the record of interrogations attached to the report of Gen. Oudri, 8 May 1896, DAOM 2 Z 361.
21 LMS Reports 5/1: Tsiafahy (W. J. Edmonds), 1894, written 23 Feb. 1895.
22 LMS Reports 5/1: Ankadibevava (C. Jukes), 1895; letter from Père Labaste, n.d., *Uclès*, 2nd ser., I, iii (1891), 336.
23 Père Taix, 'Mémorial sur la fondation et le développement du district Atsinanana', c.1914, Arch. And. D.101. I am also indebted to Jean-Pierre and Bakoly Domenichini for reporting

to me some of the oral traditions of Ambohimalaza. Madame Domenichini-Ramiaraman-
ana is herself a descendant of the first Catholic family of the village.

24 Père Finaz, 'Diaire d'Ambohitsoa', entry for 2 Apr. 1869, Arch. And. D.121.

25 A. Boudou, *Les jésuites à Madagascar au XIXe siècle* (2 vols., Paris, 1940–2), II, 66–8.

26 'Diaire d'Ambohitsoa', Arch. And. D.121.

27 H. E. Clark, 'The Zanakantitra Tribe', *Ant. Ann.*, V (1896), 450–4; J. Ranaivo, 'Tantaran'
Andrefankaratra', 26 July 1905, ms. of 7 pp., Berthier papers.

28 E. O. MacMahon, *Christian Missions in Madagascar* (London, 1914), 127–43.

29 Doncaster, *Faithful Unto Death*, 243–5.

30 *Review of the Work of the Friends' Foreign Mission Association in Madagascar, 1876–1880*
(Antananarivo, 1880), 45–6.

31 *TA*, II, 536–54.

32 G. Julien, *Institutions politiques et sociales de Madagascar* (2 vols., Paris, 1909), I, 445.

33 W. Ellis, *The Martyr Church: a Narrative of the Introduction, Progress, and Triumph of
Christianity in Madagascar* (London, 1870), 346–7.

34 DAOM 6(2) D 3: court case of Ramialy v. Rabedasy.

35 *TA*, III, 710.

36 'Notice concernant la région d'Andriamena', incomplete typescript *c.*1906, DAOM 6(9) D
27.

37 E. Ramilison, *Ny Loharanon' ny Andriana Nanjaka teto Imerina, etc.* (2 vols.,
Antananarivo, 1951–2), II, 124–39.

38 *Ireo Voninahitrao ry Vonizongo* (no place, 1949).

39 LMS Reports 5/3: Ambatonakanga (T. T. Matthews), 1896.

40 J. Ravelomanana, 'La vie religieuse à Ambositra, 1880–1895' (Univ. of Madagascar, travail
d'études et de recherches, 1971), *passim.*

41 Dr Fontoynont, 'Tsinjoarivo', *BAM*, n.s., XXIV (1941), 186–9; *Nor. Miss.*, LI (1896),
315.

42 ARM IIICC189: note of 12–13 May 1896; Pourrat, 'Le cercle d'Anjozorobé ou pays des
Mandiavato', *NRE*, IV (1898), 1455–6.

43 Chef de bat. Reynes, 'Perceptions des tomponmenakelys sur les marchés', Sept. 1896,
DAOM 2 D 54/A.

44 M. Massiot, *L'administration publique à Madagascar* (Paris, 1971), 36–7.

45 *TA*, IV, 345.

46 J-P. Raison, 'Perception et réalisation de l'espace dans la société merina', *Annales*, XXXII,
iii (1977), 412–32.

47 'Filazana ny tantaran' iMamolakazo', anon. ms. 12 pp., Berthier papers; E-F. Gautier,
'Atlas of Ambongo', *Ant. Ann.*, VI (1899), 345.

48 'Brief Summary of Important Events in Madagascar', *Ant. Ann.* (1889), 124–6.

49 Lt Vacher, 'Renseignements sur l'Ambongo', Jan. 1898, Service historique de l'armée,
Vincennes, Madagascar series, n.f. box 15, folder 28(4), piece 4.

50 W. D. Cowan, 'Geographical Excursions in South Central Madagascar', *Proceedings of the
Royal Geographical Society*, n.s., IV, iv (1882), 528.

51 ANSOM MAD 140(196): Savaron to Larrouy, 15 Sept. 1893.

52 *Journal officiel de Madagascar et dépendances*, 27 Apr. and 13 May 1897, pp. 407, 461;
ARM IIICC 6: Rainisoamody to Rainilaiarivony, 2 Adijady 1893; ARM IIICC 193:
Rainiseheno *et al.* to same, 25 Asombola 1891 and 13 Adimizana 1892.

53 *The Mission Field*, ccclii (1 Apr. 1885).

54 G. Jacob, 'Fahavalisme et troubles sociaux dans le Boina à la fin du XIXe siècle', *Annales de
l'Université de Madagascar*, série lettres, vi (1967), 21–32.

55 *TA*, II, 428; J. Rainizanajafy, 'Tantaran' ny Niorenan' ny Fiangonana teto Ambatomainty
(1873–1922)', 42 pp. ms., copied by his son. Archives of the Society of Jesus, Antananarivo,
unclassified.

56 A. Delivré, *L'histoire des rois d'Imerina: interprétation d'une tradition orale* (Paris, 1974), *passim*.
57 Rasamimanana and Razafindrazaka, *Ny Andriantompokoindrindra*, i.
58 *TA*, II, 647.
59 Gow, *The Protestant Impact*, 86–99.
60 Doncaster, *Faithful Unto Death*, xiv, 174–86; LMS Reports 5/1: Faravohitra (J. Wills) 1894, and 5/2: Antsihanaka (A. W. Wilson) 1895.

3. The fall of Imerina

1 G. Jacob, 'Les intérêts économiques lyonnais à Madagascar de la conquête à la première guerre mondiale', *Bulletin du centre d'histoire économique et sociale de la région lyonnaise*, iv (1971), 2–3.
2 E. F. Knight, *Madagascar in War Time* (London, 1896), 160–6, 208–9, 275, 305.
3 FO 48/87: Porter to Souzier, 22 July 1895; LMS Incoming, 25/2/A: Baron to Matthews, 22 July 1895; on Andrianony's background, Gow, *The Protestant Impact*, 54, 152, 219.
4 Knight, *Madagascar in War Time*, 192.
5 LMS Incoming 25/1/B: Baron to Thompson, 18 Mar. 1895.
6 L. Brunet, *L'oeuvre de la France à Madagascar* (Paris, 1903), 92.
7 DAOM 2 Z 342: Ranchot to min. des aff. étr., 15 Nov. 1895.
8 R. Pascal, 'Les rapports de quinzaine d'Hippolyte Laroche', pt I, *Bulletin de Madagascar*, ccxlv (Oct. 1966), 942, note 4; 'Notice historique sur l'armement de l'armée hova aux diverses périodes de l'intervention française', 20 May 1896, SHA, NF 8/5/103.
9 C. Borchgrevink, *Fire Foredrag om de sidste Begivenheder på Madagascar og Missionens naervaerende Udsigter* (Chicago, 1900), 19.
10 *Beatificationis seu declarationis martyrii servi dei Jacobi Berthieu, sacerdotis e societate iesu in odium fidei, ut fertur, interfecti* (Rome, 1940), 90–1. cf. *TA*, III, 775.
11 Friends' Foreign Mission Association archives, London, Madagascar papers: committee of missionaries, minutes (field original), vol. IV, p. 172.
12 W. J. Edmonds, 'Charms and Superstitions in South-East Imerina', *Ant. Ann.*, VI (1897), 62.
13 'The Report of Ranaivojaona, the Evangelistic-School Master at Andranomiantra, Anativolo, Madagascar, for 1895', LMS Reports, 5/2.
14 Knight, *Madagascar in War Time*, 187–8. My italics.
15 LMS Incoming 26/2/B: Baron to Thompson, 26 Nov. 1895.
16 ARM IIICC 34: Rafaralahiboana to Rainitsimbazafy, 14 Alakarabo/31 Oct. 1895; ARM IIICC 113: Radaoro to same: 27 Alakarabo/13 Nov. 1895.
17 'The Report of Rakotovao the Evangelist at Andraopasika, Anativolo, for 1895', written Jan. 1896, LMS Reports 5/2.
18 LMS Reports 5/2: Antsihanaka (A. W. Wilson) 1895, written 8 Nov. 1895, and Imerimandroso (Miss Foxall) 1895, written Nov. 1895.
19 Some examples may be found in LMS Reports 5/2: Tsiafahy (W. J. Edmonds) 1895; DAOM 2 Z 356: Revanarivo to Rainitsimbazafy, 9 Mar. 1896; ARM NN86: Rainandriamampandry to Peake, 25 Nov. 1895; ARM HH3, ff. 457–8: Gregory to Rainitsimbazafy, 25 Nov. 1895; ARM IIICC 36: Roben to Rainitsimbazafy, 18 Nov. 1895; ARM HH6: Borchgrevink to Rainandriamampandry, 22 Nov. 1895.
20 *TA*, cited by Delivré, *L'histoire des rois*, 382, note 65.
21 C. Borchgrevink and L. Gulbrandsen, 'Filazana any Pastor Rapanoela', Jan. 1896, ARM HH6, ff. 308–11. Another version is Capt. Lamy, 'Notice sur les districts d'Ilempona et d'Ankisatra', 26 Nov. 1896, DAOM 2 D 5(A). A published copy of Lamy's account, omitting the crucial manuscript passage on Rapanoela's death, is in *NRE*, I (1897), 25–32.

For other published versions, *Det Norske Missionsselskabs* (Stavanger, 1896), 29; and A. Siegriest, *Des rois, des reines, des brigands, des héros* (Antananarivo, 1940), 209–13.

22 ARM IIICC 17: Rahamefy to Rainilaiarivony, 13 Oct., 17 Nov. 1892 and 8 Apr. 1893.

23 LMS Incoming 25/2/D: Matthews to Thompson, 27 Nov. 1895.

24 The following account of the rising is based on the three main published accounts in Doncaster, *Faithful Unto Death*; M. Rasamuel, *Ny Menalamba tao Andrefan' Ankaratra 1895–1896 sy ny Zanakantitra* (6 pts, Antananarivo, 1948–52); and Rajaobelina, *Ilay Tabataba tany Arivonimamo tamin' ny Taona 1895* (reprinted edn, Antananarivo, 1956).

25 Rasamuel, *Ny Menalamba*, 49–50.

26 ARM, col. series D – cab. civ. – box 278, folder 3, ff. 74–8: MacMahon to Herqué, 3 Mar. 1896.

27 MacMahon, *Christian Missions*, 136–41.

28 Rajaobelina, 'Ankaratra', pt I, *Mp-ts.*, n.s., XXI (1924), 132–4.

29 SHA, AF 9: Ganeval to Duchesne, 6, 17–20, 28 Dec. 1895; DAOM 2 Z 332: Capt. Aubé to Duchesne, 24 Dec. 1895.

30 MacMahon in *The Mission Field* (1896), 123; *idem, Christian Missions*, 140.

31 SHA, AF 9: Ganeval to Duchesne, 17–20 Dec. 1895.

32 *Ibid.*: same to same, 17 Dec. 1895.

33 DAOM 6(2) D 1: 'Affaire Johnson,' fragment of anon. ms. This important account forms part of the evidence brought at the trial in October 1896 of some of the Johnsons' murderers, although it may have been composed earlier.

34 ARM IIICC 258: Ratsimanohatra *et al.* to Rainitsimbazafy, 10 Alakaosy/25 Nov. 1895.

35 S-V. Duruy, 'De Tsaratanana à nossi-bé', *NRE*, II (1897), 437–8; B. Magnès, 'Essai sur les institutions et la coutûme des Tsimihety', *B. de M.*, lxxxix (Oct. 1953), 13–18.

36 La. p.: Gautier to Laroche, 11 March 1896.

37 *Ibid.*, 29 May 1896.

38 LMS Incoming 26/5/B: Jones to Thompson, 20 Mar. 1896.

39 G. Grandidier, *Histoire politique et coloniale* (3 vols., Paris and Antananarivo, 1942–57), II, 259; G. L., *Notice sur le district d'Andevorante* (Antananarivo, 1901), 5; La. p.: Besson to Laroche, 22 Jan. 1896.

40 La. p.: Besson to Laroche, 22 Jan. 1896.

41 ARM IIICC 81: anon. undated note; cf. SHA, AF 15: Contre-amiral Bienaimé to Duchesne, 6 Dec. 1895.

42 'Renseignements recueillis pendant la réunion du 9 février 1896', SHA, NF 8/6/6.

43 SHA, AF 9: Sous-lt Grammont to Lt-col. Belin, 26 and 28 Jan. 1896; NF 8/6/5: Belin to Gen. Voyron, 5 Feb. 1896; DAOM 2 Z 358: vice-rés. Ponty to Laroche, 11 Apr. 1896; Père Fontanié to Capt. Lacarrière, 6 Jan. 1896, *Uclès*, 2nd ser., II, iii (1896), 508.

44 DAOM 6(6) D 19: interrogation of Botopelaka and Ihafo at Tamatave, 4 Feb. 1896.

45 La. p.: Ferrand to Laroche, 25 Feb. 1896.

46 Pascal, 'Les rapports de quinzaine', pt I, 956–7.

47 *Ibid.*; SHA, AF 44: Lebon to Gen. Billot, 25 Mar. 1896; ANSOM MAD 216(447): 'Affaires Freystatter et Ganeval: exécution de fahavalos'. The Laroche papers contain a private dossier kept by Laroche on the Freystatter affair. For Freystatter's own account, SHA, AF 9: rapport du capitaine Freystatter, 17 Feb. 1896.

4. The rising of the *Menalamba*

1 Père H. de Villèle to Père provincial, 1 Dec. 1895, *Uclès*, 2nd ser., III, iii (1896), 485–7.

2 Letter from Père Fourcadier, Dec. 1895, *Uclès*, 2nd ser., III, iii (1896), 488. Fourcadier's italics.

3 DAOM 2 Z 332: Aubé to Duchesne, 11 Dec. 1895; J. Rasoanasy, *Menalamba sy Tanindrazana* (Antananarivo, 1976), 82.

4 Rainianjanoro, *Fampandrian-tany sy Tantara Maro Samy Hafa* (Antananarivo, 1920), 5–9.
5 DAOM 2 Z 332: Aubé to Duchesne, 22 Dec. 1895.
6 LMS Incoming 25/2/D: Wilson to Thompson, 6 and 21 Dec. 1895.
7 LMS Reports 5/1: Ambatonakanga (T. T. Matthews) 1895, written 24 Feb. 1896.
8 DAOM 2 Z 332: Aubé to Duchesne, 21 Dec. 1895.
9 LMS Incoming 26/2/A: Sibree to Thompson, 22 Apr. 1896.
10 *Beatificationis Jacobi Berthieu*, 92.
11 DAOM 6(2) D 3: Ramampanenitra to Ramasoandromahamay (Rabozaka),
19 Alakarabo 1896.
12 SHA, NF 8/3/11: Aubé to chef d'état-major, 4 Jan. 1896.
13 e.g. DAOM 6(2) D 3: Ravaikafo (Rabezavana) to Ramasoandromahamay (Rabozaka), 13 Alakarabo/18 Oct. 1896, calling Rabozaka '*havako*' and '*zaondahiko*'.
14 'Note . . . dictée par M. Doerrer', La. p.
15 *Ibid.*; La. p.: Paillant to Laroche, 25 Mar. 1896.
16 DAOM 2 Z 364: Aubé to Voyron, 5 Jan. 1896.
17 *TA*, I, 31.
18 Until 1883 the feast of *fandroana* had always taken place on the first day of Alahamady. The Christian Queen Ranavalona III, using the Gregorian calendar, fixed it on 22 November, which was her birthday. This is in fact a good example of how Christian monarchs tried to use old rituals in a new context. By 1895 the *fandroana* was associated both with 22 November and with the first of Alahamady in the minds of many Merina.
19 DAOM 2 Z 342: Ranchot to min. des aff. étr., 16 Jan. 1896.
20 DAOM 2 Z 365: Gen. Voyron to min. de la guerre, 1 Feb. 1896.
21 ANSOM MAD 216 (447): Laroche to min. des cols., 25 Feb. 1896. Enclosed is a French translation of the letter dated 1 Feb. 1896.
22 E. Blavet, *Au pays malgache. De Paris à Tananarive et retour* (Paris, 1897), 96–104.
23 DAOM 6(6) D 19: de Sardelys to Laroche, 26 Mar. 1896.
24 Anon. (trans. T. T. Matthews), 'Among the Fahavalo: Perils and Adventures of a Prisoner for Fourteen Months in the Rebel Camp', *Ant. Ann.*, VI (1897), 81.
25 ARM NN91: the wrongly attributed 'régistre de Rabezavana'. Entry for 2 Alahamady 1896. Extracts from this letter-book are published in 'Sombin-tantaran'ny Menalamba', *Tantara*, vii–viii (1979), 29–57.
26 F. Hellot, *La pacification de Madagascar (Opérations d'Octobre 1896 à Mars 1899)* (Paris, 1900), 10.
27 LMS Incoming 26/2/A: Sibree to Thompson, 22 Apr. 1896.
28 H. Laroche, 'Le Nord de l'Imerina', p. 32 of typed draft. La. p.
29 ANSOM Gallieni papers 5(29): Gonard to Gallieni, 5 Feb. 1897.
30 LMS Incoming 26/2/C: Huckett to Thompson, 3 July 1896.
31 H. Berthier, 'Rapport politique et administratif' for Itasy province, 1896–1904, Berthier papers.
32 Bourde to Lebon, 10 June 1896, in A. Lebon, *La pacification de Madagascar* (Paris, 1928), 204.
33 Matthews (trans.), 'Among the Fahavalo', 83.
34 J. Sibree, 'Missionary Heroes and Heroism in Madagascar', p. 44, LMS Personal 2/6.
35 ANSOM MAD 216(447): Ravaikafo (Rabezavana) to Ramahatra, 2 Alohotsy/7 Mar. 1896 (French trans.), enc. with Laroche to min. des cols., 28 Mar. 1896.
36 cf. *TA*, III, 707, quoted on p. 55 above.
37 Quoted in 'Le pays sihanaka ou cercle d'Ambatondrazaka', *NRE*, IV (1898), 1048.
38 La. p.: memorandum by rés-inspecteur Pradon, 5 Sept. 1896.
39 *Beatificationis et canonizationis seu declarationis martyrii servi dei Jacobi Berthieu sacerdotis* (Antananarivo, 1933), 19–22.
40 Berthier papers: Penel to Laroche, 3–4 Aug. 1896.

41 DAOM 2 Z 361: letter from Père Malzac, 11 Jan. 1896, and Père Delpuech to Père Malzac, 17 Jan. 1896.
42 DAOM 2 Z 361: interrogation of Ingahimandranto, attached to report of Gen. Oudri, 8 May 1896; J. D. Lentonnet, *Carnet de campagne en Madagascar* (Paris, 1897), 185–7.
43 DAOM 2 Z 361: Col. Oudri to Voyron, 8 Apr. 1896, and 'rapport du Gén. Oudri', 8 May 1896.
44 DAOM 2 Z 361: Capt. Bordeaux to Voyron, 8 May 1896. Cf. above, p. 22.
45 LMS Incoming 26/6/A: Johnson to A. Huckett, 11 June 1896, enc. with A. Huckett to Thompson, 12 June 1896.
46 L. Vig in *Missions luthériennes à Madagascar* (15 Feb. 1903), 219.
47 DAOM 2 Z 387: Alby to Laroche, 20 and 26 July 1896.
48 *Ibid.*, 28 Sept. 1896.
49 C. Savaron, *Mes souvenirs à Madagascar avant et après la conquête* (Mémoires de l'Académie malgache, no. XIII, Antananarivo, 1932), 297.
50 *Idem*, 'Rainibetsimisaraka', article no. VI in a series of eight cuttings from an unknown newspaper, AAM unclassified.
51 'Diaire de la Mission d'Ambositra', vol. II, entries for 23–5 Jan. 1888, archives of the Catholic mission, Ambositra.
52 LMS Incoming 26/2/C: Peake to Thompson, 9 July 1896.
53 LMS Incoming 26/2/B: Wills to Thompson, 9 May 1896.
54 Berthier papers: Ramahatra to Lt-col. Borbal-Combret, 7 Oct. 1896; SHA, NF 8/8/47: Noel to Voyron, 18 Sept. 1896; SHA, NF 8/8/46: note by Lt Mahéas, same date; letter from Père Gardes, 20 Sept. 1896, *Uclès*, 2nd ser., IV, ii (1897), 203.
55 'Rapport de l'émissaire Raharijaona', 20 Mar. 1897, SHA, NF 12/21/73.
56 A. Cahuzac, *Essai sur les institutions et le droit malgaches* (Paris, 1900), 29.
57 Borchgrevink, *Fire Foredrag*, 18–19.
58 *Beatificationis seu declarationis*, 14.
59 DAOM 6(2) D 3: anon. to Gallieni, 28 Alakarabo/2 Nov. 1896.
60 Razanakinimarina, 'Inona no mety atao mba hampiadana ny vahoaka malagasy?', 2 pp. ms., *c*.1900, Berthier papers.
61 '1ère proclamation de Rabezavana' (French trans.), ARM F.124.
62 'Proclamation d'un chef rebelle du Cercle d'Ambatomanga', no date, annexe no. 2 to Gallieni's report of 13 Dec. 1896, ANSOM MAD 215(445).
63 DAOM 6(10) D 1: decree of Ranavalona III, 22 Aug. 1896, and chef de bat. Gouttenègre to Gallieni, 27 July 1897; DAOM 2 Z 361: list of objects found in Rambinintsoa's house, 22 Apr. 1896.
64 LMS Incoming 26/2/C: Peake to Thompson, 9 July 1896. Peake's italics.
65 Bourde to Lebon, 10 June and 10 Aug. 1896, in Lebon, *La pacification*, 200, 243–4; LMS Incoming 26/2/A: Sibree to Thompson, 22 Apr. 1896; LMS Incoming 26/2/C: Peake to same, 9 July 1896.
66 LMS Incoming 26/3/B: Matthews to Thompson, 19 Aug. 1896

5. The war of the sects

1 Berthier papers: Ramahatra to Gallieni, 19 Oct. 1896; La. p.: same to Rasanjy, 19 Mar. 1896 (French trans.); SHA, NF 8/3/15: same to Bourde, same date, and 'Déclaration du messager qui a porté la lettre au Prince Ramahatra . . .', Mar. 1896.
2 Laroche to Lebon, 14 June 1896, in Lebon, *La pacification*, 163–4.
3 SHA, AF 26: Oudri to min. de la guerre, 25 Aug. 1896.
4 ANSOM MAD 215(445): Gallieni's report no. 1 *bis*, 10 Oct. 1896.
5 G. Talvas, *Madagascar depuis l'occupation française* (Paris, 1939), 118.
6 S. D. K. Ellis, 'The Political Elite of Tananarive and the Revolt of the *Menalamba*: the

Creation of a Colonial Myth in Madagascar, 1895–1898', *Journal of African History*, XXI, ii (1980), 221–3.

7 J. Sibree, 'Odd and Curious Experiences of Life in Madagascar', *Ant. Ant.*, III (1887), 374.

8 Ly. p., a.cl.445: 'Randriantavy' to Rabozaka *et al.*, 31 Aug. 1896 (French trans.).

9 Ly. p., a.cl.445: 'Mr Pillin' to Rafanenitra, 15 Aug. 1896 (French trans.).

10 DAOM 6(4) D 16, 'Affaire Peill'; ANSOM MAD 359(979), 'L'affaire Peill'. This version was confirmed by the boy himself, who in old age reported it to the Reverend J. T. Hardyman. I am grateful to Mr Hardyman for passing on the anecdote.

11 Société des Missions Evangéliques, Paris, series Madagascar local 1897: B. Escande to Boegner, 9 Dec. 1896.

12 LMS Reports 5/3: Isandra (J. Pearse) 1896.

13 Mgr Cazet to recteur d'Uclès, 16 June 1896, *Uclès*, 2nd ser., IV, i (1897), 53, 57.

14 LMS Incoming 26/3/B: Sibree to Thompson, 25 Aug. 1896.

15 La. p.: Besson to Laroche, n.d.

16 Archives of the Society of Jesus, Antananarivo, unclassified: Cazet to Berthieu, 3 Apr. 1896.

17 La. p.: Gautier to Laroche, 11 Mar. 1896; Alby to Laroche, 19 Aug. 1896; Père Félix to Alby, 20 Aug. 1896.

18 Letter from Père Labaste, 22 Aug. 1896, *Uclès*, 2nd ser., III, ii (1897), 189–98.

19 Letter from S. Delord, *Journal des Missions Evangéliques* (1897), 693.

20 ARM IIICC 23: govs. of Ambohimanambola and Tsarahonenana to Rainitsimbazafy, 26 Alahamady/8 Apr. 1896; ARM IIICC 23: Jukes to Rainitsimbazafy, 17 Apr. 1896.

21 DAOM 6(4) D 51: Père Delpuech to Gallieni, 2 Nov. 1896.

22 Letter from Père Gardès, 20 Sept. 1896, *Uclès*, 2nd ser., IV, ii (1897), 203.

23 Letter from Père Fourcadier, 25 Oct. 1896, *Uclès*, 2nd ser., IV, ii (1897), 215.

24 SME (local 1897): B. Escande to Boegner, 21 Oct. 1896.

25 Letter of 5 Dec. 1896 in B. Escande, *Neuf mois à Madagascar* (Paris and Geneva, 1898), 104.

26 DAOM 4 B 25: Gallieni to Besson, 30 Sept. 1896.

27 SME (local 1897): Johnson to Lauga, 15 Nov. 1896.

28 DAOM 6(4) D 52: note by Dr Besson, n.d.; DAOM 6(4) D 50: Boegner to Col. Houry, 19 Aug. 1898.

29 LMS Reports 5/3: Ambohimandroso (D. M. Rees and Chas. Collins), 1898.

30 LMS Incoming 27/4/B: A. Huckett to Cousins, 17 Apr. 1897, and Haile to Cousins, 12 Apr. 1897.

31 SME (local 1897): E. Escande to Boegner, 30 Dec. 1897; LMS Incoming 27/3/D: Thompson to Cousins, 28 Dec. 1897.

32 SME (intérieur 1896–7): extracts of letters from Dr Borchgrevink to Gallieni, n.d.

33 SHA, NF 10/15/53: Capt. Durand to Lt-col. Sucillon, 3 Mar. 1897.

34 SME (local 1897): E. Escande to directors, 17 Oct. 1897.

35 SME (local 1898): report by M. Gaignaire, 26 Oct. 1898.

36 DAOM 6(4) D 50: Durand to Sucillon, 26 Jan. 1898.

37 DAOM 6(4) D 51: Père Delpuech to Gallieni, 2 Nov. 1896.

38 LMS Incoming 26/4/D: Rainiketamanga to Briggs, 13 Dec. 1896, enc. with Briggs to Thompson, 26 Dec. 1896.

39 SME (local 1897), anon. note, n.d.; letter from B. Escande, 8 Nov. 1896, in *Neuf mois*, 83–5.

40 LMS Incoming 26/4/D: Jukes to Thompson, 28 Dec. 1896; Escande, *Neuf mois*, 135.

41 Letter from Père Fourcadier, 6 Jan. 1897, *Uclès*, 2nd ser., IV, ii (1897), 219; LMS Incoming 27/1/A: Jukes to Thompson, 13 Jan. 1897.

42 Missionaires' letters in *Uclès*, 2nd ser., IV, i (1897), 48–50, and IV, ii (1897), 223, 227–38.

43 *JME* (1897), 228.

44 'Examen des pièces justificatives . . .', n.d., ARM D – cab. civ. – 280/2.
45 SME (local 1897): Peake to Boegner, 18 Nov. 1897.
46 DAOM 6(4) D 16: 'Affaire Edmonds', esp. Comte to Dubreuil, 4 Mar. 1897.
47 ARM D – cab. civ. – 40/2: Rasanjy to Ramahatra, 27 Nov. 1896.
48 Personal communication by J-P. and B. Domenichini. cf. *Norsk Missionstidende*, LI (1896), 15.
49 DAOM 6(10) D 1: *arrêté* of 29 Apr. 1901.
50 P. Lupo, 'Les laics pendant la guerre de 1894–1895 d'après l'*Histoire-Journal* de Paul Rafiringa' (Travail d'études et de recherches, Univ. of Madagascar, 1978).

6. The spread of resistance

1 Vallois, 'Souvenirs', 119.
2 '1ère proclamation de Rabezavana', found on 18 Nov. 1896, ARM F.124.
3 ANSOM MAD 438(1202): Ravaikafo *et al.*, to Rainivelo *et al.*, 26 Alohotsy/27 Feb. 1897.
4 ANSOM MAD 438(1201): Gallieni's report of 13 Feb. 1897.
5 C. Delhorbe, 'La colonisation à Madagascar depuis la conquête française', *Madagascar au début du XXe siècle* (Paris, 1902), 346–7.
6 DAOM 2 Z 415: Alby to Gallieni, 18 Nov. 1896; DAOM 4 B 66: Rançon's report of 30 Mar. 1899.
7 Delhorbe, 'La colonisation', 346–7.
8 SHA, NF 10/15/53: Capt. Durand to Col. Sucillon, 25 Apr. 1897.
9 DAOM 6(2) D 3: Rainitavy to Ramasoandromahamay, 26 Adijady 1896.
10 Magnès, 'Essai sur les institutions', 15–16; La. p.: Pradon to sec-gen., 6, 20, 28 Dec. 1896.
11 La. p.: Pradon to sec-gen., 28 Dec. 1896.
12 ARM NN 142: Raselelambo to Rainilaiarivony, 10 Nov. 1895.
13 Capt. de Bouvié, 'Marches et reconnaissances dans le Bouéni', *NRE*, I (1897), 235–47.
14 Letter of 21 March 1897, Escande, *Neuf mois*, 214–15; SME (local 1897): Durand to Boegner, 7 Apr. 1897; 'Rapport concernant la translation des restes des anciens rois . . .', Mar. 1897, ARM SS 30.
15 Borchgrevink, *Fire Foredrag*, 25; Boiteau, *Madagascar*, 216.
16 SHA, NF 14/25/39: anon. list.
17 Berthier papers: Ramahatra to Gallieni, 19 Oct. 1896.
18 S. D. K. Ellis, 'The Political Elite', 225.
19 Ly. p., a.cl.455: Lyautey to Gallieni, 14 June 1897; ARM D – cab. civ. – 153/5: Lebon to Gallieni, 9 Jan. 1897; ARM D – aff. pol. – 469: Rémond to Lyautey, 27 Oct. 1897.
20 S. D. K. Ellis, 'The Political Elite', 223–5.
21 ARM D – aff. pol. – 469: Rainivotsotra to Lyautey, n.d., and Ratsimametra to Lyautey, n.d.
22 Ly. p., a.cl.455: Lyautey to Rémond, 18 Nov. 1897. Lyautey's italics.
23 SHA, NF 15/28(2)/2: 'Rapport sur le cercle-annexe d'Andriamena', Feb. 1899.
24 SHA, NF 25: Lyautey to Gallieni, 9 Apr. 1899.
25 DAOM 2 D 36: rapports politiques, cercle-annexe d'Anjozorobé, Mar. and Apr. 1899, by Capt. Leblanc.
26 Ly. p., a.cl.453/6: Lyautey to Gallieni, 15 Apr. 1899; and a.cl.31: Rémond to Lyautey, 3 Feb. 1899.
27 DAOM, unclass.: Lt Laporte to comm. du cercle de Tsiafahy, 28 Mar. 1899.
28 SME (local 1899): dossier 'conférence'.
29 'Cercle de Miarinarivo, rapport politique et administratif', Oct. 1899, by Capt. Morel, DAOM 2 D 159 – Morel's italics. cf. J. H. Haile, 'Some Betsileo Ideas', *Ant. Ann.*, VI (1900), 16.
30 Ly. p., a.cl.31: Comm. d'Arivonimamo to Lyautey, 22 Feb. 1898; DAOM 4 B 63: Capt.

Durand to Comm. d'Antsirabe, 13 July 1897, and same to Comm. d'Inanatonana, 20 July 1897; statistics in DAOM 6(3) D 31.

31 ARM D – aff. pol. – 469: fiche de renseignements by Raybaud, 11 Oct. 1898.

32 Ly. p., a.cl.35: Besson to Lyautey, 26 June 1903.

33 Gallieni to Lebon, 27 Feb. 1898, in Lebon, *La pacification*, 105–6.

34 LMS Reports, 6/1: Ambohipotsy (W. E. Cousins), 1898.

35 Boin and Mouveaux, 'Les Baras et les Tanalas des districts d'Ivohibé et d'Ihosy', *NRE*, II (1897), 452–3.

36 DAOM 6(2) D 5: Rahanetra *et al.* to Ramieba, 27 Nov. 1896.

37 R. Decary, 'Une année de l'histoire des Bara', in *Perspectives nouvelles sur le passé de l'Afrique noire et de Madagascar. Mélanges offertes à Hubert Deschamps* (Paris, 1974), 117–28.

38 *Ibid.*, 118–23; E-J. Bastard, 'Inapaka', pt I, *R. de M.*, 1st ser. (1907), 275–6.

39 DAOM 2 Z 358: Ponty to Laroche, 11 Apr. 1896.

40 DAOM 2 Z 356: Revanarivo to Rainitsimbazafy, 9 Mar. 1896, and Gautier to Laroche, 15 Sept. 1896.

41 Vergnes papers, Paris: Rainimanganoro *et al.* to Ratsiarahina, 15 Alakarabo 1896; and same to Rasifa, Alohotsy 1897.

42 Vergnes papers: dossier 'Sahavato 1897'; *JOMD* (3 Apr. 1897), p. 314; ANSOM MAD 215(446): Comm. Gérard to Gallieni, 22 May 1897.

43 ANSOM MAD 438(1202): Gallieni's report of 27 June 1897, with annexes; DAOM 6(2) D 1: 'Dossier Paty'; ANSOM MAD 438(1204): Gallieni's report of 11 Nov. 1897, p. 69.

44 ARM D – aff. pol. – 469: report by Ranamahatsara, 8 Mar. 1898.

45 ANSOM MAD 65(82), 'Réclamation Andersen Moinet': Andersen to Gallieni, n.d.

46 Rainianjanoro, *Fampandrian-tany*, 25–34; P. Vigné d'Octon, *La gloire du sabre* (4th edn, Paris, 1900), 183–224; Capt. Condamy, *Une méthode de guerre coloniale. La conquête du Menabe à Madagascar* (Paris, n.d.), *passim*.

47 La. p.: Alby to Laroche, 21 Apr. 1897; SHA, NF 16/29/11: notes by Capt. Laverdure, 1899; Chef de bat. Lamolle, 'Rapport sur l'insurrection du Nord-Ouest à Madagascar', 13 Feb. 1899, DAOM 6(2) D 7.

48 DAOM 6(2) D 7: letter from M. Chauvot, 16 Dec. 1898.

49 Gallieni to de Mahy, 28 Nov. 1898, in P-B. Gheusi, *Gallieni et Madagascar* (Paris, n.d.), 175.

50 DAOM 6(2) D 7: Ikarija to Imandanona *et al.*, 1 Alakarabo/16 Sept. 1898 (French trans.).

51 DAOM 6(2) D 7: Comm. Mondon to Gallieni, 27 Dec. 1898.

52 Chef de bat. Lamolle, 'Renseignements sur les agissements des Mpanjakas . . .', 14 Feb. 1899, DAOM 6(2) D 7.

53 DAOM 6(2) D 7: letter from Chauvot, 16 Dec. 1898.

54 'Rapport du Capitaine Briand sur la période qui a précédé l'insurrection dans la région du Cercle d'Analalava', 17 Feb. 1899, DAOM 6(2) D 7.

55 Lamolle, 'Rapport sur l'insurrection . . .', 13 Feb. 1899, DAOM 6(2) D 7.

56 DAOM 6(2) D 7: Chauvot to Gallieni, n.d.

57 Ly. p., a.cl.445: Capt. de Bouvié to Lyautey, 1 Dec. 1898.

58 H. Deschamps, *Histoire de Madagascar* (4th edn, Paris, 1972), 238.

59 DAOM 6(2) D 7: Gallieni to min. des cols., 15 Apr. 1899.

60 DAOM 6(2) D 7: letter from Chauvot, 16 Dec. 1898. Chauvot's italics.

61 ANSOM MAD 202(397): Gallieni to min. des cols., 7 Dec. 1898.

62 Le Myre de Vilers papers, 29: Gallieni to Le Myre de Vilers, 8 and 25 Aug. 1898.

63 Père Dupuy to Mgr Cazet, n.d., *Uclès*, 2nd ser., IV, iii (1897), 439–44.

64 B. Martin, 'Rapport fait au nom de la commission du budget . . .', 1901, SHA, NF 21/43/8; *Madagascar de 1896 à 1905*, II, 364–9; P. Leroy-Beaulieu, *De la colonisation chez les peuples modernes* (6th edn, 2 vols., Paris, 1908), II, 152.

65 C. Basset, *Madagascar et l'oeuvre du Général Gallieni* (Paris, 1903), 93; Tourtet, 'Gallieni et le chemin de fer malgache' (Mémoire du diplôme des études supérieures, no place, 1967 – copy in ARM E.284), 83.
66 SPG Reports 1898, vol. B, no. 93: J. Fuller (Mahandro), 9 Oct. 1898.
67 FO 27/3490: Willis to O' Conor, 1 June 1899.
68 M. Olivier, *Six ans de politique sociale à Madagascar* (Paris, 1931), 70–1.
69 SHA, NF 25: Gallieni to min. des cols. (draft), 16 Jan. 1899.
70 ARM D – cab. civ. – 54/1: Pennequin to min. des cols., 26 June 1899.
71 ARM D – cab. civ. – 77/2: Pennequin to Col. Borbal-Combret, 8 Feb. 1900.
72 SHA, NF 25: Gallieni to Prud'homme, 31 July 1900.
73 'Note relative à la réglementation du transport des corps dans l'intérieur de la colonie', *c.* Jan. 1902, DAOM 6(5) D 10.
74 Comm. Bourgeon, *Souvenirs d'un soldat français* (Paris, 1955), 33–4.
75 Report of the Picquié mission of 1902–3, cited in Y-G. Paillard, 'Victor Augagneur: socialisme et colonisation', *BAM*, n.s., LII, i–ii (1974), 68.
76 Hixe, *La crise économique de Madagascar* (Paris, 1904), *passim*.
77 Paillard, 'Victor Augagneur', 68–9; Le Hérissé, 'Madagascar et le rapport de M. Le Hérissé, *R. de M.*, 1st ser. (1906), 12–20.

7. Conclusion

1 ARM IIICC 18: Razaka to Rabezavana, 26 Feb. 1894.
2 Sibree, *Madagascar and its People*, 101.
3 LMS Incoming 26/3/A: Wills to Thompson, 9 Aug. 1896.
4 Condominas, *Fokon'olona*, 91, note 3.
5 The tentative remarks I have made here are based on statistics gleaned from over a dozen sources covering various periods of the 19th century. But there is a pressing need for further research on the changing pattern of Imerina's population at that time. As far as I am aware, the subject has never been analysed in any depth. The most complete statistics, covering the later 19th century, are in A. Grandidier, *Ethnographie de Madagascar* (2 vols., Paris, 1908), I, 234–312.
6 Boudou, *Les jésuites*, II, 439.
7 Y. Talmon, 'Millenarian Movements', *Archives européennes de sociologie*, VII, ii (1966), 181–92.
8 H. A. Landsberger, 'Peasant Unrest: Themes and Variations', in *idem* (ed.), *Rural Protest: Peasant Movements and Social Change* (London, 1974), 44.
9 M. Gluckman, *Order and Rebellion in Tribal Africa. Collected Essays* (London, 1963), 144.
10 Talmon, 'Millenarian Movements', 159–200; N. Cohn, 'Medieval Millenarianism: its Bearing on the Comparative Study of Millenarian Movements', in S. L. Thrupp (ed.), *Millenial Dreams in Action* (Comparative Studies in Society and History, supplement no. II, The Hague, 1962), 31–43; G. Shepperson, 'The Comparative Study of Millenarian Movements', *ibid.*, 44–52.
11 Talmon, 'Millenarian Movements', 177–8.
12 J. J. Freeman and D. Johns, *Persecution of the Christians in Madagascar*, 91–7; F. Raison, 'Radama II, ou le conflit du réel et de l'imaginaire dans la royauté merina', *Les Africains* (vol. VIII, Paris, 1977), 279–310.
13 T. O. Ranger, *Revolt in Southern Rhodesia* (London, 1963).
14 G. Balandier, 'Les mythes politiques de colonisation et de décolonisation en Afrique', *Cahiers internationaux de sociologie*, xxxiii (1962), 85–96.
15 Rasamimanana and Razafindrazaka, *Ny Andriantompokoindrindra*, i.
16 Balandier, 'Les mythes politiques', 93.
17 It is generally agreed that the first work to set out the theoretical territory of this debate was

T. O. Ranger, 'Connexions Between "Primary Resistance" Movements and Modern Mass Nationalism in East and Central Africa', *JAH*, IX (1968), 437–53, 631–41. Since then Terence Ranger and others have continued to write on the subject. It has been enriched by many monographs examining 'primary resistance' to colonial rule in different places. However, the theoretical debate has remained rather static.

18 J. Fremigacci, 'L'administration coloniale: les aspects oppressifs', *Omaly sy anio*, vii–viii (1978), 212.

19 Ranger, 'Connexions'; J. Iliffe, 'The organization of the Maji-Maji Rebellion', *JAH*, VIII, iii (1967), 495–512.

20 Gallieni, Lyautey, Gautier and Berthier may all be said to have purposely distorted the history of the rising, in particular by falsifying the role of Rainandriamampandry and by obscuring the conditions on which *menalamba* leaders surrendered. The relevant works are cited in the bibliography. Laffaye, writing under the pseudonym Carol, published a more accurate account. Laroche too attempted a more honest account but his memoirs remain unpublished.

21 Rasamuel, *Ny Menalamba tao Andrefan' Ankaratra.*

22 'Ny Menalamba', *Réalités malgaches*, xvii (27 Sept. 1972), 2.

23 J. Tronchon, *L'insurrection malgache de 1947* (Paris, 1974).

24 J. Randriamandimby Ravoahangy-Andrianavalona, *La VVS, Vy Vato Sakelika (Fer, Pierre, Ramification). Contribution à l'étude sur l'origine du nationalisme malgache* (Paris, 1978).

25 *Maty ve Ratsimandrava?* (Antananarivo, n.d.).

26 Deschamps, *Histoire de Madagascar*, 273–4.

27 G. Althabe, 'Les luttes sociales à Tananarive en 1972', *Cahiers d'études africaines*, XX, iv (1980), 407–47.

28 cf. T. O. Ranger, 'The People in African Resistance: a Review', *Journal of Southern African Studies*, iv (1977), 125–46.

29 M. E. F. Bloch, 'Modes of Production and Slavery in Madagascar: Two Case Studies', in J. L. Watson (ed.), *Asian and African Systems of Slavery* (London, 1979), 100–34.

30 R. E. Robinson, 'Non-European Foundations of European Imperialism: Sketch for a Theory of Collaboration', in W. Roger Louis (ed.), *Imperialism: the Gallagher and Robinson Controversy* (New York and London, 1976), 128–52.

31 Bloch, *Placing the Dead.*

32 J. Carol (pseud. Laffaye), *Chez les Hovas (au pays rouge)*, (Paris, 1898), 45–6.

Bibliography

A. MANUSCRIPT SOURCES

a. Archive collections

I. Great Britain

i. Foreign Office records, Public Record Office, London
Series 27: general correspondence: France. Includes reports from the British consulate in Antananarivo after 1895, and from the British consulate in Réunion.
Series 48: general correspondence: Madagascar. 87 volumes of consular reports from the British consulate in Antananarivo up to 1895.
Series 710: consular archives of British consulates and vice-consulates in Madagascar, from 1888.

ii. Colonial Office records, Public Record Office, London
Series 167: correspondence, Mauritius. Includes information on Madagascar, especially for the period 1817–50.

iii. The British Museum, London
Farquhar papers, add. mss. 18117–18140. Essential for the history of Madagascar c.1760–1820.

iv. Archives of the Society for the Propagation of the Gospel, 15 Tufton Street, London
Series D: letters received, Africa.
Series E: reports, Africa.

v. Archives of the Friends' Foreign Mission Association, Friends' House, Euston Road, London
Most of the archives relating to Madagascar have been destroyed, but there remain a couple of packets of letters and a series of minute-books.

vi. Archives of the London Missionary Society, School of Oriental and African Studies, London
Madagascar Incoming series: letters classified by box, folder and jacket.
Madagascar Reports series: letters classified by box and folder.
Madagascar Journals series: journals classified by box and folder.
Madagascar Odds series: includes private correspondence, diverse manuscripts etc.
Madagascar Personal series: private letters and manuscripts from missionary collections.
Madagascar Miscellanies: 19 vols. of rare pamphlets and reports collected by Rev. J. Sibree. Catalogued under WCCM G4/72–4; G5/1–17.
Unclassified material: includes the scrap-books of Rev. J. Sibree.

190

vii. The National Library of Wales, Aberystwyth
NLW 14643E: papers of David Griffith. Includes letters from Madagascar, c.1830.
NLW 19157E: Neuaddlwyd and Aberaeron papers. Private letters from missionaries in Madagascar, 1821–32.

II. France

i. Archives nationales, section outre-mer, rue Oudinot, Paris
Madagascar, série moderne. Documents on every aspect of colonial administration. Some valuable reports of travellers and diplomats before 1895.
Gallieni papers. A small collection of official papers. The bulk, including private material, remains with the Gallieni family and is not available for consultation.
Réunion series. Includes material on trade with Madagascar, notably the slave trade and the recruitment of *engagés*.

ii. Archives nationales, rue des francs-bourgeois, Paris
Series F^{12}, commerce. Includes material on pre-colonial trade with Madagascar.
Series F^{30} 244, finances. Includes material on loans by the Malagasy government, before and after 1895.
Microfilms of US archives, 253 Mi 34–43 (see below).

iii. Archives du ministère des affaires étrangères, quai d'Orsay, Paris
Mémoires et documents series. Includes six volumes on Madagascar.
Correspondance politique: Madagascar old series. 61 volumes of reports from consuls, ambassadors and residents-general, pre-1895.

iv. Laroche papers and Vergnes papers, private, Paris
All unclassified.
The unpublished memoirs of H. Laroche. Mostly typescript, with some early and unfinished drafts. Written c.1904.
Copies of administrative correspondence by Laroche, 1896. Includes copies of some records in ANSOM.
Official and private letters from colleagues in Madagascar. A very rich source.
Vergnes papers include material on Tanala revolts, 1897–8.

v. Lyautey papers, private, Paris
An exceptionally rich archive of private and official papers. *Ancien classement* refers to the classification made by the Lyautey family. *Nouveau classement* refers to the small quantity of material which has been reclassified by archivists at the Archives nationales, rue des francs-bourgeois.

vi. Archives of the Société des Missions Evangéliques, Boulevard Arago, Paris
Madagascar series includes incoming letters and reports.
Also miscellaneous correspondence concerning Madagascar.

vii. Berthier papers, Académie des sciences d'outre-mer, rue Lapérouse, Paris
Unclassified. Includes manuscripts collected by H. Berthier, and some administrative correspondence relating to his work as an administrator in Madagascar.

viii. Musée de l'armée, hôtel des Invalides, Paris
J. Vallois, 'Souvenirs et impressions d'un marsouin', 169 pp. ms. in 2 examples, 1902.

191

Bibliography

Invaluable diary and reflections of a private soldier, on his part in the campaigns against the *menalamba*.

ix. Ecole nationale de la France outre-mer, avénue de l'Observatoire, Paris
Theses by student administrators. Some are useful secondary studies; some contain original primary material, including transcriptions of oral traditions.

x. Archives départementales de l'Orne, Alençon
Le Myre de Vilers papers. 1 box of correspondence.
Includes dossier 29: 60 letters from Gallieni, 1896–1905.

xi. Service historique de l'Armée, chateau de Vincennes
Madagascar *ancien fonds*: 75 boxes chiefly on the 1895 expedition and on administrative affairs.
Madagascar *nouveau fonds*: 40 boxes on military administration in Madagascar. Boxes 5–25 are one of the best sources on the *menalamba*.

xii. Dépôt des archives d'outre-mer, Aix-en-Provence
Madagascar series 1 Z: general material on Madagascar.
Madagascar series 2 Z: records of the French consulate and residence-general in Antananarivo, 1830–98.
Madagascar series 3 Z: records of the French consulate at Tamatave, 1830–97.
Madagascar series B: archives of the government-general.
Madagascar series D, in course of classification: archives of local administration in Madagascar. 6(2) D 3 includes the most complete series of papers emanating from the *menalamba*, consisting mostly of letters captured from Rabozaka in late 1896.

III. United States of America

i. The National Archives, Washington DC
11 volumes of reports from the US consulate at Tamatave, 1853–1906. These may be consulted on microfilm at the French Archives nationales (see above).

IV. Madagascar

i. Archives de la république malgache, Antananarivo
Merina royal archives. Records of the Merina government at Antananarivo from 1820 to 1896.
Colonial period. Archives of French administration from 1896.

ii. Archives de l'Académie malgache, Antananarivo
Classified manuscripts: identified by their library call-numbers. Unclassified manuscripts: a rich collection, including Rabozaka's 'Notes d'histoire malgache'.

iii. Bibliothèque universitaire, Antananarivo
Classified manuscript collection.

iv. Archives of the Society of Jesus, Antananarivo
Volumes series.
Cartons series.
Unclassified: includes selection of mss. on the death of Père Berthieu, an invaluable source on the *menalamba*.
Boudou papers, unclassified.

192

v. Bibliothèque nationale, Antananarivo
A manuscript collection catalogued separately from the main library. Includes the papers of Rafanoharana, governor of Betsileo-land.

vi. Archives de l'archevêché d'Antananarivo, Andohalo
Cartons series.
Diaries series.

vii. Archives of the Norwegian Missionary Society, Antananarivo
Boxes numbered and divided into districts of origin: Antananarivo; nord-synod; mid-synoden; west-synod.

viii. Institut de la recherche scientifique malgache, Antananarivo
Books and manuscripts from the Grandidier collection. Includes a valuable selection of mss. classified by library call-numbers.

ix. Rasanjy papers, private, Antananarivo
Disappointing, but includes an exercise-book with some details of Rasanjy's property interests.

x. Martin papers, private, Antananarivo
Includes the account-books of Razanabelo of Andramasina, 1888–91.

xi. Papers of M. Razafy, private, Ambatomanga
2 manuscripts written by M. Razafy describing the history of Ambatomanga.

xii. Archives of the Society of Jesus, Ambositra
Includes local histories and church records. Copies by Père Boudou in the archives of the Society at Antananarivo.

b. Unpublished manuscripts and theses

Andrianarisandy, J., 'Rainipiana'. Typescript of 84 pp., 1971. Bib. Nat. Tana., mss. 1465.

Baron, R., 'Political and Social Review of the Last Decade'. Prepared for the LMS *Ten Years' Review, 1890–1900*, but never published. Copy annexed to *Ant. Ann.*, VI (1900), Rhodes House Library, Oxford.

Belrose-Huyghues, V., 'Historique de la pénétration protestante à Madagascar jusqu'en 1827' (2 vols., Univs. of Paris and Madagascar, thèse de 3e cycle, 1978).

Berg, G. M., 'Historical Traditions and the Foundations of Monarchy in Imerina' (Univ. of California, Berkeley, Ph.D. thesis, 1975).

Caillon-Filet, C., 'Jean Laborde et l'Océan Indien' (Univ. of Aix-en-Provence, thèse de 3e cycle, 1978).

Chapus, G. S., 'Nouveaux documents sur l'époque de Radama Ier et Ranavalona Ière', typescript of 315 pp., extracts from archives in London and Mauritius. AAM (AM 325).

Chastanier-Atger, J., 'Le Madagascar Times d'Anthony Tacchi, 1882–1890' (Univ. of Paris VII, travail d'études et de recherches, 1977).

Ellis, S. D. K., 'Collaboration and Resistance in Madagascar, 1895–9, with Special Reference to the Kingdom of Imerina' (D.Phil., Oxford Univ., 1981).

Esoavelomandroso, M., 'La province maritime orientale du "Royaume de Madagascar" à la fin du XIXe siècle (1882–1895)' (2 vols., thèse de 3e cycle, Paris/Antananarivo, 1976).

Finaz, le Père, 'Mémoires sur les commencements de la Mission dans la Province du Betsileo', ms. of 139 pp., 1876, SJ Tana., volumes, 1/4.

Bibliography

Fremigacci, J., 'La fin des protectorats intérieurs', paper presented to the colloquium on Malagasy history, Tuléar, April 1979.

Gow, B. A., 'The British Protestant Missions in Madagascar, 1818–1895' (Ph.D., Dalhousie Univ., 1975).

Handfest, C., 'Histoire de la région d'Ambositra', 16 pp., typescript, 1950, AAM, unclass.

'Histoire du Vonizongo', 12 pp. ms., 1921, ARM D – cab. civ. – 113/7.

Jacob, G., 'Sur les origines de l'insurrection du Sud-Est de Madagascar (Novembre–Décembre 1904)', paper presented to the colloquium on Malagasy history, Tuléar, April 1979.

Keating, Sir H. S., 'Travels in Madagascar, Greece and the United States', typescript, 1825, includes 127 pp. on Madagascar. Bodleian Library, Oxford, Ms. Eng. misc. C.29.

Laikera, Janoa, 'Menalamba', typescript of 122 pp., 1970, Bib. Nat. Tana., mss. 1549.

Lamy, Capt., 'Notice sur les districts d'Ilempona et d'Ankisatra', 26 Nov. 1896. DAOM 2 D 5(A). Printed in part in *NRE*, I (1897), 25–32.

Laroche, H., Memoirs. Includes the following drafted chapters: ch. I: 'Le lendemain de la conquête', 12 pp. ms.; ch. II: 'Période tranquille', 80 pp. ms.; ch. III: 'L'implantation française'; ch. IV: 'Les cultes et l'instruction publique'; ch. V: 'Prodromes d'insurrection'; ch. VI: 'Duret de Brie et ses compagnons', 57 pp. ms.; ch. VII: 'Les indigènes et la reine'; ch. VIII: 'Les hommes de proie'; ch. IX: 'Fahavalos et insurgés'; ch. X: 'Les 53 heures d'Antsirabé', 34 pp. ms.; ch. XI: 'Le nord de l'Imerina', 46 pp. typescript; ch. XII: 'Le service des renseignements militaires', 57 pp. typescript; ch. XIII: 'Le commandement et le pouvoir civil'; ch. XIV: 'L'insurrection impuissante'; ch. XV: 'Exécution du ministre de l'intérieur et du Prince Ratsimamanga', 67 pp.; ch. XVI: 'L'écrasement de l'Imerina'; ch. XVII: 'Les provinces. Menabé', 12 pp. typescript; ch. XVIII: 'Les prestations militaires'; ch. XIX: 'Lettres et récits de la grande île'; ch. XX: conclusion. Plus over forty packets of rough drafts.

Laube, 'Histoire locale des habitants du district de Loholoka', typescript of 15 ff. Bib. U. Tana., FL 18198.

'La liberté religieuse à Madagascar. Réponse de Mgr. Cazet, vicaire apostolique, aux attaques protestantes', printed but unpublished, Archives de la Propaganda, Rome. Notes on this were kindly made available to me by Françoise Raison.

Lupo, P., 'Les laïcs pendant la guerre de 1894–1895 d'après l'*Histoire-Journal* de Paul Rafiringa' (travail d'études et de recherches, Univ. of Madagascar, 1978).

Mahatsanga, M., 'L'évolution de la société Bara dans la deuxième moitié du XIXe siècle' (mémoire de maîtrise, Univ. of Madagascar, 1977).

'Notice concernant la région d'Andriamena', incomplete typescript, DAOM 6(9) D.

Peetz, E. A. O., 'Friends' Mission Work in Madagascar up to 1927 and its Doctrinal Implications' (B.Litt. thesis, Univ. of Oxford, 1960).

Philippe, Y., 'La colonisation de peuplement à Madagascar. Etude historique, géographique et économique' (ENFOM mémoire no. 75, 1941–2).

Rabenjamina, 'Histoire d'Ambohimanga, la ville sainte. Histoire du roi Andriamasinavalona. Le rôle des descendants d'Andriamasinavalona sous les gouvernements malgache et français', 10 pp. typescript, Bib. Nat. Tana., mss. 1671.

Rabozaka, 'Notes d'histoire malgache'. Translation, *c*.1914, in 2 exercise-books, AAM, unclass. In December 1979 I was unable to locate the second of the two exercise-books.

Rainandriamampandry, 'Tantarany Madagascar'. Several ms. drafts of a multi-volume work, 1874–96, ARM SS4–14, SS20–26.

Rainizanajafy, J., 'Ny nasehoan' ny fikomiana tao Avaratra (Menalamba)', ms. of 16 ff., *c*.1908, SJ Tana. unclass. A modified version was translated and published by Père Krol.

Randriamahaleo, 'Tantaran' ny Marofotsy', *c*.1945, 7 pp. typescript, with French translation. By the son of Rabezavana. ARM unclass. Second copy in ARM D – cab. civ. – 114/11.

Rantoandro Andriamiarintsoa, G., 'Le gouvernement de Tamatave de 1845 à 1865: développement économique' (travail d'études et de recherches, Univ. de Madagascar, 1973).

194

Raombana, (ed. Ayache), 'Histoires'. Edition by S. Ayache prepared for forthcoming publication. Provisional copy in AM 412.

'Annales'. Edition by S. Ayache prepared for forthcoming publication. Provisional copy in AM 413.

Rasoamiaramanana, M., 'Aspects économiques et sociaux de la vie à Majunga entre 1862 et 1881' (travail d'études et de recherches, Univ of Madagascar, 1974).

Ratrimoharinosy, H., 'La société malgache et la crise de 1883–5 à travers le journal de Rainilaiarivony' (2 vols., thèse de 3e cycle, Univ. of Paris I, 1972).

Ravelomanana, J., 'La vie religieuse à Ambositra, 1880–1895' (travail d'études et de recherches, Univ. of Madagascar, 1971).

Ravonintsoa, J., 'Gouverneurs merina et gouvernement de la province de Tamatave de 1829 à 1845' (travail d'études et de recherches, Univ. of Madagascar, 1971).

Razafimbelo, C., 'Les origines de l'implantation chrétienne en pays sihanaka: contribution à l'histoire des mentalités locales' (travail d'études et de recherches, Univ. of Madagascar, 1978).

Richard, C., 'Le gouvernement de Victor Augagneur à Madagascar (1905–1910)' (thèse de 3e cycle, Paris, n.d.).

Savaron, C., speech to the Académie malgache reviewing Chapus and Mondain's *Rainilaiarivony*. Typescript of 11 pp., n.d., AAM unclass.

Sibree, J., 'Missionary Heroes and Heroism in Madagascar'. Ms. including a chapter on the *menalamba*. LMS Personal, box 2.

Tourtet, 'Gallieni et le chemin de fer malgache' (mémoire du diplôme des études supérieures, no place, 1967). Copy in ARM E.284.

Vallois, J., 'Souvenirs et impressions d'un marsouin', 169 pp. ms. in 2 examples, 1902. Musée de l'armée, hôtel des Invalides, Paris, M1028.

Vassé, J., 'Journal de mon intendance près de S. E. Rainilaiarivony, ancien Premier Ministre de la reine de l'Ile de Madagascar', 552 pp. ms., 1896–7, IRSM 2300.

Vogel, C., 'Chroniques du Vakiniadiana' (roneotyped, no place, 1975). Copy in Bib. Nat. Tana. 908 (691.111) CHR.

B. PUBLISHED SOURCES

a. Primary sources

I. Government and official publications

i. French government

d'Anthouard, A., 'Rapport commercial sur Madagascar en 1890', *Journal officiel de la république française*, 21 June 1891.

Bartholomé, 'Le régime de la propriété foncière à Madagascar', *NRE*, V (1899), 215–39.

Boin and Mouveaux, 'Les Baras et les Tanalas des districts d'Ivohibé et d'Ihosy', *NRE*, II (1897), 446–56.

du Bois de la Villerabel, Capt., 'Etude sur le secteur des Bara Imamono', *NRE*, V (1899), 523–8.

'La tradition chez lez Baras', *NRE*, VI (1900), 263–73.

Boussand, M., 'Notice sur les tribus Tanalas et Sakalaves', *NRE*, I (1897), 80–2.

de Bouvié, Capt., 'Marches et reconnaissances dans le Bouéni', *NRE*, I (1897), 235–47.

'De Marovoay à la Mahajamba', *NRE*, II (1897), 240–50.

Brun, Capt., 'Note sur le secteur de l'Ikongo', *NRE*, IV (1898), 1631–46.

Bulletin du comité de Madagascar (monthly, Paris, 1895–9).

Bulletin économique de Madagascar (government quarterly, Antananarivo, 1901–32).

Bibliography

de Cointet, Lt, 'De Tananarive à Ankavandra', *NRE*, I (1897), 59–68.

Durand, A., 'Etude sur les Tanalas d'Ambohimanga du Sud', *NRE*, IV (1898), 1261–97.

Duruy, S-V., 'De Tsaratanana à Nossi-bé', *NRE*, II (1897), 413–45.

Gendronneau, M., 'Etude détaillée des diverses régions de Madagascar', *NRE*, I (1897), 150–62, 271–302.

Gouvernement-general de Madagascar, *Rapport d'ensemble sur la pacification, l'organisation et la colonisation de Madagascar* (Antananarivo, 1899).

    Madagascar de 1896 à 1905. Rapport du Général Gallieni, gouverneur général, au ministre des colonies, 30 Avril 1905, et annexes au rapport (2 vols., Antananarivo, 1905).

Guillain, C., *Documents sur l'histoire, la géographie et le commerce de la partie occidentale de Madagascar* (Paris, 1845).

Hanotaux, G., *L'affaire de Madagascar* (Paris, 1896). Collection of speeches and official documents.

Hellot, F., *La pacification de Madagascar (Opérations d'octobre 1896 à mars 1899)* (Paris, 1900).

'Historique des troubles du Nord-Ouest', *Bulletin du comité de Madagascar*, V, vi (1899), 242–57.

Houry, Col., and Taupin, Comm., 'Rapports sur l'organisation militaire et administrative des cercles de l'Imerina centrale et d'Arivonimamo', *NRE*, V (1899), 1–50.

Jouannetaud, Lt, 'Notes sur l'histoire du Vakinankaratra', *NRE*, VI (1900), 275–87.

Journal Officiel de Madagascar et Dépendances.

Lamy, Capt., 'Notice sur les districts d'Ilempona et d'Ankisatra', *NRE*, I (1897), 25–35.

Lebon, André, *La pacification de Madagascar* (Paris, 1928). Includes official texts.

Le Hérissé, 'Madagascar et le rapport de M. Le Hérissé', *R. de M.*, 1st ser. (1906), 12–20.

Lepreux, C., 'Les impôts indigènes et le budget de Madagascar', *R. de M.*, 1st ser. (1904), 97–119.

Merleau-Ponty, Dr, 'Le pays sihanaka', *NRE*, I (1897), 344–54.

Noël, Comm., 'Le pays bezanozano', *NRE*, II (1897), 1–27.

Notes, reconnaissances et explorations (monthly and quarterly, Antananarivo, 1897–1900). Organ of the French government-general in Madagascar.

Pascal, R., 'Les rapports de quinzaine d'Hippolyte Laroche', *B. de M.*, ccxlv (Oct. 1966), 927–68; ccxlvi (Nov. 1966), 1063–93; ccxlvii (Dec. 1966), 1157–70; ccxlvii *bis* (Jan. 1967), 73–93; ccxlviii (Feb. 1967), 135–70.

    'Le pays sihanaka ou cercle d'Ambatondrazaka', *NRE*, IV (1898), 1016–51.

Pourrat, 'Le cercle d'Anjozorobé ou pays des Mandiavato', *NRE*, IV (1898), 1397–459.

Prud'homme, Lt-Col., 'Considérations sur les Sakalaves', *NRE*, VI (1900), 1–43.

Revue de Madagascar. 1st ser., 1899–1911: monthly organ of the comité de Madagascar; 2nd–5th ser., 1933–69: organ of the government of Madagascar.

Sénèque, Lt, 'Les Mandiavatos', *NRE*, IV (1898), 862–9.

ii. Malagasy government

Bibliographie nationale de Madagascar (Antananarivo, annually from 1964).

Gamon, A., 'Le code de Ranavalona Ière (1828)', *BAM*, o.s., V (1907), 2–22.

    Ny Gazety Malagasy (Antananarivo, occasional, 1883?–94?).

Julien, Gustave, 'L'institution des sakaizambohitra', *NRE*, V (1899), 557–82.

    'Le code des 305 articles', *NRE*, VI (1900), 93–186.

    'Les réformes de 1889 – l'autonomie des *fokon'olona* et les règlements des gouverneurs de l'Imerina', *BAM*, o.s., I, i (1902), 23–46.

iii. British government

Parliamentary papers. Esp. 1873 vol. LXI; 1887 vol. LXXXV; 1890–1 vol. LXXXVII.

196

iv. Missionary
Beatificationis et canonizationis seu declarationis martyrii servi dei Jacobi Berthieu sacerdotis (Antananarivo, 1933).
Beatificationis seu declarationis martyrii servi dei Jacobi Berthieu, sacerdotis e societate iesu in odium fidei, ut fertur, interfecti (Rome, 1940).
FFMA, *Review of the Work of the Friends' Foreign Mission Association in Madagascar, 1867–1880* (Antananarivo, 1880).
LMS, *A Brief Review of the LMS Mission in Madagascar from 1861 to 1870* (Antananarivo, 1871).
Ten Years' Review of Mission Work in Madagascar 1870–1880 (Antananarivo, 1880).
Det Norske Missionsselskabs (Stavanger, 1896).
SPG, *The Church in Madagascar, SPG Mission, Second Report, 1877–8* (Winchester, n.d.).
Thompson, R. W., and Spicer, E. *Report of the Deputation to Madagascar* (London, n.d.). Copy in LMS library, Madagascar Miscellanies V/31.

v. International
International Council on Archives, *Guide to the Sources of the History of Africa*, vol. III (2 pts, Zug, 1971, 1976).

II. Newspapers and periodicals

Antananarivo Annual (quarterly, Antananarivo, 1875–1900). Includes a chronicle of current events, plus scholarly articles listed below.
Chronicle of the London Missionary Society.
Church Missionary Intelligencer.
The Friend.
Journal des Missions Evangéliques.
Lettres d'Uclès.
The Madagascar Times (occasional, Antananarivo, 1882–90).
The Mission Field.
Ny Mpanolo-Tsaina (monthly, old series Antananarivo 1877–1903; new series, 1904–). Includes a chronicle of current events, plus scholarly articles listed below.
Norsk Missionstidende (monthly, Stavanger, 1845–).
Le Progrès de l'Imerina (weekly, Antananarivo, 1887–94).
Teny Soa (monthly, Antananarivo, 1866–).

III. Contemporary works, memoirs and secondary editions of contemporary works

Ader, R-L., 'Note sur le commerce du Sud de Madagascar vers les années 1860', *B. de M.*, cclxxix (Aug. 1969), 689–92.
Andriamena, *A Madagascar. Souvenirs d'un soldat d'avant-garde* (Paris, n.d.).
Andrianaivoravelona, J. (trans. Clark), 'The Ancient Idolatry of the Hovas', *Ant. Ann.*, III (1885), 78–82.
Annuaire de Madagascar pour 1892 (Antananarivo, 1891).
d'Anthouard, A., and Ranchot, M., *L'expédition de Madagascar 1895. Journaux de route* (Paris, 1930).
Baron, R., 'Ranavalona II, the Late Queen of Madagascar', *Ant. Ann.*, II (1883), 1–12.
'Over New Ground: a Journey to Mandritsara and the North-West Coast', *Ant. Ann.*, III (1887), 261–82.
Bastard, E-J., 'Inapaka', *R. de M.*, 1st ser. (1907), 269–81, 317–27.
Bennett, N. R. (ed.), *The Zanzibar Letters of Edward D. Ropes, Jr, 1882–1892* (Boston, 1973).

and Brooks, George, E. (eds.), *New England Merchants in Africa: a History through Documents, 1802–1865* (Boston, 1965).

Berthier, H., 'Le protectorat du ler octobre 1895 au 18 janvier 1896', *BAM*, n.s., XXIV (1941), 115–31.

Besson, L., 'Madagascar: pays Betsileo et sud de l'île', *Bulletin de la société de géographie de Marseilles* (1902).

'Situation économique du Betsileo', *R. de M.*, 1st ser. (1906), 789–800.

Blavet, E., *Au pays malgache. De Paris à Tananarive et retour* (Paris, 1897).

Bonnard, P., *Madagascar après la conquête* (Paris, 1895).

Bourgeon, Comm., *Souvenirs d'un soldat français* (Paris, 1955).

Brockway, T., 'A Visit to Ambohimanga in the Tanala Country', *Ant. Ann.*, I (1876), 58–64.

Brunet, L., *La France à Madagascar, 1815–1895* (Paris, 1895).

L'oeuvre de la France à Madagascar (Paris, 1903).

Buet, C., *Six mois à Madagascar* (Paris, 1894).

Cabaret, A., 'Un an à Madagascar', *Revue politique et littéraire. Revue bleue*, 4th ser., IV, xvii (Oct. 1895), 513–22.

Callet, F. (trans. G. S. Chapus and E. Ratsimba), *Histoire des rois* (revised edn, vols. I–III, V, Antananarivo, 1974–8).

Cameron, J., Letter from Antananarivo, in the London *Standard*, 15 May 1883.

de Cantilly, L.,'En pleine brousse malgache', *R. de M.*, 1st ser. (1909), 243–9.

Carol, J. (pseud. Laffaye), *Chez les Hovas (au pays rouge)* (Paris, 1898).

Catat, L., *Voyage à Madagascar (1889–90)* (Paris, 1895).

Caustier *et al.*, *Ce qu'il faut connaître de Madagascar* (2nd edn, Paris, 1896).

Chabaud, M., *Madagascar. Impressions de Voyage* (Paris, 1893).

'A Chapter on Antsihanaka, its People and Superstitions', *Ant. Ann.*, IV (1890), 212–18.

Chapus, G. S., 'Lettre du Révérend J. Richardson au sujet de la libération des Mozambiques', *BAM*, n.s., XVIII (1935), 79–83.

(trans.) 'Journal du Rév. Baron (du 23 Septembre au 1er Octobre 1895)', *BAM*, n.s., XVIII (1935), 69–78.

Clark, H. E., 'Where We Are', *Ant. Ann.*, II (1882), 95–105.

'The Zanakantitra Tribe', *Ant. Ann.*, V (1896), 450–6.

Condamy, Capt., *Une méthode de guerre coloniale. La conquête du Menabe à Madagascar* (Paris, n.d.).

Cousins, W. E., 'The Ancient Theism of the Hovas', *Ant. Ann.*, I (1875), 5–11.

'The Abolition of Slavery in Madagascar, with some Remarks on Malagasy Slavery Generally', *Ant. Ann.*, V (1896), 446–50.

Cowan, W. D., *The Bara Land: a Description of the Country and People* (Antananarivo, 1881).

'Geographical Excursions in South Central Madagascar', *Proceedings of the Royal Geographical Society*, n.s., IV, iv (1882), 521–37.

Davidson, A., 'The Ramanenjana or Dancing Mania of Madagascar', *Ant. Ann.*, IV (1889), 19–27.

Dawson, E. W., *Madagascar, its Capabilities and Resources* (London, 1895).

Decary, R., 'Ankazobe avant Lyautey. Le journal du Capitaine Nicard', *RFHOM*, LIV (1967), 151–70.

Domenichini, J-P., *Histoire des palladium de l'Imerina d'après les manuscrits anciens* (roneotyped, Musée d'art et d'archéologie de Tananarive, documents inédits no. VIII, Antananarivo, 1971).

'Une tradition orale: l'histoire de Ranoro', *ASEMI*, VIII, iii–iv (1977), 99–150.

Doncaster, P. (ed.), *Faithful Unto Death: a Story of the Missionary Life in Madagascar of William and Lucy S. Johnson* (London, 1896).

Dumeray, R., 'Boutou-kely. Souvenirs de la vie malgache', *Revue des deux mondes*, cxxix (May 1895), 163–88.

Durand, A., *Les derniers jours de la cour hova* (Paris, 1933). An officer's diary.

Edmonds, W. J., 'The "Mohara" or War-Charm of Imerina', *Ant. Ann.*, V (1896), 421–5.

'Charms and Superstitions in South-East Imerina', *Ant. Ann.*, VI (1897), 61–7.

Ellis, W., *History of Madagascar* (2 vols., London, 1838).

Three Visits to Madagascar (London, 1859).

Madagascar Revisited (London, 1867).

The Martyr Church: a Narrative of the Introduction, Progress, and Triumph of Christianity in Madagascar (London, 1870).

Escande, B., *Neuf mois à Madagascar* (Paris and Geneva, 1898).

Foucart, G., *Le commerce et la colonisation à Madagascar* (Paris, 1894).

Foulonneau, F. E., 'Etude commerciale sur Tamatave (Madagascar)', *Bulletin de la société de géographie commerciale de Bordeaux*, 2nd ser., XVI (1893), 417–38.

Freeman, J. J., and Johns, D., *A Narrative of the Persecution of the Christians in Madagascar* (London, 1840).

G. L., *Notice sur le district d'Andevorante* (Antananarivo, 1901).

Gallieni, J. S. *Neuf ans à Madagascar* (Paris, 1908).

Lettres de Madagascar, 1896–1905 (Paris, 1928). Introduction by G. Grandidier and J. Chailley-Bert.

Gardey, P., *Anglophilie gouvernementale: manoeuvres des protestants à Tahiti et à Madagascar* (Paris, 1897).

Gautier, E-F., 'Atlas of Ambongo', *Ant. Ann.*, VI (1899), 338–49.

Trois Héros (Paris, 1931). pp. 67–139: on Rainandriamampandry, by the man who betrayed him.

Grandidier, A., 'Le commerce de Madagascar', *Bulletin de la société de géographie de Paris*, III (1872), 208–13.

(trans. Sibree), 'Property and Wealth among the Malagasy', *Ant. Ann.*, VI (1898), 224–33.

Voyage à Madagascar. Notes et souvenirs (document manuscrit inédit) (roneotyped, Musée d'art et d'archéologie de Tananarive, documents anciens sur Madagascar no. VI, Antananarivo, 1970).

Grosclaude, E., *Un parisien à Madagascar* (2nd edn, Paris, 1898).

Haile, J. H., 'Malagasy Village Life: Pen and Ink Sketches of the People of Western Imerina', *Ant. Ann.*, V (1893), 1–20.

'Some Betsileo Ideas', *Ant. Ann.*, VI (1900), 1–16.

Hixe, *La crise économique de Madagascar* (Paris, 1904).

Johnson, W., 'Farahantsana, Itasy and Ankaratra: Scraps from a Notebook', *Ant. Ann.*, I (1875), 56–63.

Jully, A., 'La politique des races à Madagascar', *R. de M.*, 1st ser. (1907), 3–17.

Knight, E. F., *Madagascar in War Time* (London, 1896).

Kruger, F. H. 'The Siege of Antsirabe', *Ant. Ann.*, V (1896), 484–90.

Lacaze, H., *Souvenirs de Madagascar* (Paris, 1881).

Le Myre de Vilers, C. M., 'Le traité hova', *Revue de Paris* (15 Nov. 1895), 225–41.

Lentonnet, J. D. *Carnet de campagne en Madagascar* (Paris, 1897). pp. 173–211: on operations against the *menalamba*.

Leroy-Beaulieu, P., *De la colonisation chez les peuples modernes* (6th edn, 2 vols., Paris, 1908).

Lord, T., 'The Early History of Imerina Based upon a Native Account', *Ant. Ann.*, VI (1900), 451–74.

Lux, *La vérité sur Madagascar* (Paris, 1896).

Lyautey, H., *Lettres du Tonkin et de Madagascar* (2nd edn, Paris, 1921).

Mackay, J. G., 'Some Amusing Reminiscences of Mission Work among the Sihanaka', *Ant. Ann.*, IV (1892), 402–6.

MacMahon, E. O., 'First Visit of an European to the Betsiriry Tribe', *Ant. Ann.*, IV (1891), 273–80.

'The Population of Madagascar: Does it Increase or Decrease?', *Ant. Ann.*, V (1893), 90–4.

Christian Missions in Madagascar (London, 1914).

Mager, H. *La vie à Madagascar* (Paris, n.d.).

Martineau, A., *Madagascar en 1894* (Paris, n.d.).

Matthews, T. T. (trans.), 'Among the Fahavalo: Perils and Adventures of a Prisoner for Fourteen Months in the Rebel Camp', *Ant. Ann.*, VI (1897), 80–93.

Thirty Years in Madagascar (2nd edn, London, 1904).

Maty ve Ratsimandrava? (Antananarivo, n.d.).

Maude, F. C., *Five Years in Madagascar* (London, 1895).

Mayeur, N., 'Voyage dans le sud et dans l'intérieur des terres et particulièrement au pays d'Hancove (janvier à décembre 1777)', *BAM*, o.s., XI (1913), 139–76.

'Voyage au pays d'Ancove (1785)', *BAM*, o.s., XII (1913), 13–42.

Les missions et la question religieuse à Madagascar (Merlin–Hardricourt, 1907).

Moss, C. F. A., 'Over Swamp, Moor and Mountain', *Ant. Ann.*, I (1876), 3–19.

'Hindrances to the Progress of the Gospel', *Ant. Ann.*, I (1877), 347–60.

Peake, P. G., 'The Bezanozano or Bush People', *Ant. Ann.*, I (1877), 431–45.

Pearse, J., 'LMS Churches and Congregations and Christian Life in Madagascar', *Ant. Ann.*, V (1895), 316–29.

Pickersgill, W. C., 'The Trade and Commerce of Madagascar', *Ant. Ann.*, III (1886), 177–84.

Piolet, J-B., *Madagascar et les Hova* (Paris, 1895).

Rabe (trans. Sibree), 'The Sihanaka and their Country', *Ant. Ann.*, I (1877), 309–29.

Rainianjanoro, *Fampandrian-tany sy Tantara Maro Samy Hafa* (Antananarivo, 1920).

Rainivelo (trans. Sibree), 'The Burning of the Idol Ramahavaly', *Ant. Ann.*, I (1875), 107–10.

Rainizanajafy, J. (trans. Krol), 'Origine de la révolte dans le nord. Mort du R. P. Berthieu', *Lettres de Gémert*, IV, i (1911), 528–46. See above for a fuller original version in manuscript.

Rajaobelina, *Ilay Tabataba tany Arivonimamo tamin' ny Taona 1895* (reprinted edn, Antananarivo, 1956).

Reibell, Comm., *Le commandant Lamy, d'après sa correspondance et ses souvenirs de campagne (1858–1900)* (Paris, 1903), pp. 265–371 on Madagascar.

Romanet, A., Letter in *Les débats*, 27 July 1936.

Sardelys, le comte de, 'Trois mois chez les Antsihanaka', *NRE*, I (1897), 69–79.

Savaron, C., *Mes souvenirs à Madagascar avant et après la conquête* (mémoires de l'Académie malgache, no. XIII, Antananarivo, 1932).

Sewell, J. S., *Remarks on Slavery in Madagascar, with an Address on that Subject, Delivered at Antananarivo* (London, 1876).

Shaw, G. A., *Madagascar and France* (London, 1885).

Shervinton, K., *The Shervintons, Soldiers of Fortune* (London, 1899). pp. 91–233 on Madagascar.

Sibree, J., *Madagascar and its People* (London, 1870).

'The Arts and Commerce of Madagascar, its Recent Progress, and its Future Prospects', *Journal of the Society of Arts* (4 June 1880), 623–31.

The Great African Island (London, 1880).

'Odd and Curious Experiences of Life in Madagascar', *Ant. Ann.*, III (1887), 367–78.

'A Quarter Century of Change and Progress: Antananarivo and Madagascar Twenty-Five Years Ago', *Ant. Ann.*, III (1888), 397–420.

'A Curious Burial Custom in North Imerina', *Ant. Ann.*, V (1896), 497–8.

Madagascar Before the Conquest (London, 1896).

'The Malagasy Custom of "Brotherhood of Blood"', *Ant. Ann.*, (1897), 1–6.

Fifty Years in Madagascar (London, 1924).

Smith, G. H., *Among the Menabe – Thirteen Months in Madagascar* (London, 1896).

Solofo, P., *Hitako ny Nitifirana an-dRainandriamampandry sy Ratsimamanga* (Antananarivo, 1959).

'Sombin-tantaran' iMadagasikara nosoratan' ny ombiasin-dRanavalona I', *Documents historiques de Madagascar*, xx–xxiii (Fianarantsoa, 1970). The first part of the manuscript usually called 'Le manuscrit de l'ombiasy', written 1864–70.

'Sombin-tantaran' ny Menalamba', *Tantara*, vii–viii (1979), 29–57. Edition of the first register of Rabozaka in ARM.

Standing, H. F., 'The Tribal Divisions of the Hova Malagasy', *Ant. Ann.*, III (1887), 354–65.

Street, L., *Journal of a Missionary Tour in the Betsileo* (no place or date).

Letter on slavery in Madagascar in *The English Independent*, 15 and 22 Nov. 1877.

Talvas, G., *Madagascar depuis l'occupation française* (Paris, 1939).

Thorne, J. C., 'Elementary Education in Madagascar', *Ant. Ann.*, III (1885), 27–39.

de la Vaissière, C., *Vingt ans à Madagascar* (Paris, 1885).

Valette, J., 'Une lettre de Kingdon à Le Myre de Vilers (23 janvier 1895)', *B. de M.*, ccxxiv (Jan. 1965), 73–84.

Vig, L., Article on the siege of Antsirabe, in *Missions luthériennes à Madagascar*, 15 Feb. 1903, reprinted from *Nordisk Missionstidsskrift*.

Vigné d'Octon, P., *La gloire du sabre* (4th edn, Paris, 1900).

b. Secondary sources

Abrams, L., and Miller, D. J., 'Who were the French Colonialists? A Re-assessment of the Parti Colonial 1890–1914', *Historical Journal*, XIX, iii (1976), 685–726.

Alpers, E. A., *Ivory and Slaves in East Central Africa: Changing Patterns of International Trade to the Later Nineteenth Century* (London, 1975).

Althabe, G., *Oppression et libération dans l'imaginaire. Les communautés villageoises de la côte orientale de Madagascar* (Paris, 1969).

'Les luttes sociales à Tananarive en 1972', *Cahiers d'études africaines*, XX, iv (1980), 407–47.

André, E-C., *De l'esclavage à Madagascar* (Paris, 1899).

Andrew, C. M., and Kanya-Forstner, A. S., 'The French "Colonial Party": its Composition, Aims and Influence, 1885–1914', *Historical Journal*, XIV, i (1971), 99–128.

Andriamanantsiety, Z. J., *Tantaran' Andrianamboninolona* (no place or date).

'Ny tafik' Andrianampoinimerina nandrava an' Ambohibeloma', *Mp-Ts.*, n.s., IX (1912), 1–9.

Andriamanjato, R. M., *Le tsiny et le tody dans la pensée malgache* (Paris, 1957).

and Rabemanahaka, J. W., *Ilay Mahery Fo* (Antananarivo, 1976).

Andriamifidy, 'Andriana', *Mp-Ts.*, n.s., V (1908), 45–8.

Andrianampoinimerina: Mpanjakan' i Madagasikara Zafin' Andriamamilaza (Antananarivo, 1960).

Andriantseheno, 'Ny Nandoroana ny Sampy tao Antananarivo sy Imerina', *Mp-Ts.*, n.s., XXVI (1929), 207–11.

Arbousset, F., *Le Fokon'olona à Madagascar* (Paris, 1950).

Archer, R., *Madagascar depuis 1972* (Paris, 1976).

Augagneur, V., *Erreurs et brutalitès coloniales* (Paris, 1927).

Augustins, G., 'Esquisse d'une histoire de l'Imamo', *B. de M.*, ccci (June 1971), 547–58.

Ayache, S., 'Introduction à l'oeuvre de Rainandriamampandry', *Ann. Univ. Mad.*, X (1969), 11–50.

Raombana l'historien, 1809–1855 (Fianarantsoa, 1976).

and Richard, C., 'Une dissidence protestante malgache: l'église Tranozozoro', *Omaly sy Anio*, vii–viii (1978), 133–84.

Balandier, G., 'Les mythes politiques de colonisation et de décolonisation en Afrique', *Cahiers internationaux de sociologie*, xxxiii (1962), 85–96.

Bibliography

Basset, C., *Madagascar et l'oeuvre du général Gallieni* (Paris, 1903).

Baubérot, J., 'L'antiprotestantisme politique à la fin du XIXe siècle. 1. Les débuts de l'antiprotestantisme et la question de Madagascar', *Revue d'histoire et de philosophie religieuse*, LII, iv (1972), 449–84.

Berg, G. M., 'Royal Authority and the Protector System in Nineteenth Century Imerina', in R. K. Kent (ed.), *Madagascar in History* (1979), 102–22.

'Riziculture and the Founding of Monarchy in Imerina', *JAH*, XXII, iii (1981), 289–308.

Binoche, J., 'Le rôle des parlementaires d'outre-mer dans la conquête de Madagascar (1871–1897)', *Revue d'histoire moderne et contemporaine*, XXII, iii (1975), 416–32.

Bira, M., *Jao, mpanazary Tsimihety* (Antananarivo, 1949).

Birkeli, F., 'Sur les projets maritimes de l'ancien gouvernement hova', *BAM*, n.s., XXVII (1946), 147–56.

Bloch, M. E. F., *Placing the Dead* (London and New York, 1971).

'Property and the End of Affinity', in *idem* (ed.), *Marxist Analyses and Social Anthropology* (London, 1975), 203–28.

'The Disconnection Between Power and Rank as a Process: an Outline of the Development of Kingdoms in Central Madagascar', *Archives européennes de Sociologie*, XVIII, i (1977), 107–48.

'Modes of Production and Slavery in Madagascar: Two Case Studies', in J. L. Watson (ed.), *Asian and African Systems of Slavery* (London, 1979), 100–34.

'Social Implications of Freedom for Merina and Zafimaniry Slaves', in R. K. Kent (ed.), *Madagascar in History* (1979), 269–97.

'Hierarchy and Equality in Merina Kinship', *Ethnos*, i–ii (1981), 5–18.

Boiteau, P., *Madagascar: contribution à l'histoire de la nation malgache* (Paris, 1958).

'Les droits sur la terre dans la société malgache précoloniale', in *Sur le 'mode de production asiatique'* (Paris, 1969), 135–68.

Ny Boky Firaketana ny Fiteny sy ny Zavatra Malagasy (unfinished publication in instalments, Antananarivo, 1937–).

Borchgrevink, C., *Fire Foredrag om de sidste Begivenheder på Madagascar og Missionens naervaerende Udsigter* (Chicago, 1900).

Boudou, A., *Le Père Jacques Berthieu (1838–96)* (Paris, 1935).

Les jésuites à Madagascar au XIXe siècle (2 vols., Paris, 1940–2).

Bouillon, A., *Madagascar, le colonisé et son 'âme'* (Paris, 1981).

Braudel, F., *Ecrits sur l'histoire* (Paris, 1969).

Brown, M., *Madagascar Rediscovered* (London, 1978).

Brunschwig, H., *French Colonialism* (English edn, New York, 1966).

'L'empire français de l'Afrique noire', *JAH*, X (1970), 401–17.

'De la résistance africaine à l'impérialisme européen', *JAH*, XV, i (1974), 47–64.

'Afrique noire (impérialisme)', *Revue historique*, dxxiv (Oct.–Dec. 1977), 457–84.

Cahuzac, A., *Essai sur les institutions et le droit malgaches* (Paris, 1900).

Campbell, G., 'Labour and the Transport Problem in Imperial Madagascar, 1810–1895', *JAH*, XXI, iii (1980), 341–56.

'Madagascar and the Slave Trade, 1810–1895', *JAH*, XXII, ii (1981), 203–27.

Chaigneau, P., 'Le système de partis à Madagascar', *Penant*, dcclxxxi–dcclxxxii (Aug.–Dec. 1983), 306–45.

Chapus, G. S. and Mondain, G., 'Le tanguin', *BAM*, n.s., XXVII (1946), 157–88.

Rainilaiarivony, un homme d'état malgache (Paris, 1953).

Chauliac, G., 'Contribution à l'étude médico-militaire de l'expédition de Madagascar en 1895', *B. de M.*, ccxl (May 1966), 411–41; ccxli (June 1966), 507–51; ccxlii (July 1966), 624–40.

Chauvicourt, J. and S., 'La monnaie coupée et les poids monétaires de Madagascar', *Numismatique malgache*, fascicule IV (Antananarivo, 1967).

'Les premières monnaies introduites à Madagascar', *Numismatique malgache*, fascicule III (Antananarivo, 1968).

Chauvin, J., 'Le prince Ramahatra', *Revue d'histoire des colonies*, XXVII, ii (1939), 33–46.

Cohen, W. B., *Rulers of Empire: the French Colonial Service in Africa* (Stanford, 1971).

Cohn, N., 'Medieval Millenarianism: its Bearing on the Comparative Study of Millenarian Movements', in S. L. Thrupp (ed.), *Millenial Dreams in Action* (Comparative Studies in Society and History, supplement no. II, The Hague, 1962), 31–43.

The Pursuit of the Millenium (revised edn, London, 1970).

Condominas, G., *Fokon'olona et collectivités rurales en Imerina* (Paris, 1960).

'La situation coloniale à Madagascar (la société Merina)', *Cahiers internationaux de sociologie*, xxx (Jan.–June 1961), 67–74.

Dama-Ntsoha, *Histoire politique et religieuse des Malgaches depuis les origines jusqu'à nos jours* (Antananarivo, 1952).

Dambreville, E., 'Aspects de l'économie de la société réunionnaise. La fin de la période esclavagiste. Naissance d'une société de classes', *Les cahiers de la Réunion et de l'Océan Indien*, IV (1974), 56–81.

Danielli, M., 'The State Concept of Imerina, Compared with the Theories found in Certain Scandinavian and Chinese Texts', *Folk-Lore*, LXI (1950), 186–202.

David-Bernard, E., *La conquête de Madagascar* (Paris, 1943).

Decary, R., 'Les Marofotsy, coutumes et croyances', *BAM*, n.s., XXVII (1946), 124–35.

'L'ancien régime de l'or à Madagascar', *BAM*, n.s., XL (1962), 83–96.

'Contribution à l'histoire du sud-est de Madagascar', *R. de M.*, 5th ser., xxx (1965), 36–50.

Coutumes guerrières et organisation militaire chez les anciens malgaches (2 vols., Paris, 1966).

'Une année de l'histoire des Bara', in *Perspectives nouvelles sur le passé de l'Afrique noire et de Madagascar. Mélanges offertes à Hubert Deschamps* (Paris, 1974), 117–28.

Delhorbe, C., 'La colonisation à Madagascar depuis la conquête française', in *Madagascar au début du XXe siècle* (Paris, 1902), 333–95.

Delivré, A., *L'histoire des rois d'Imerina: interprétation d'une tradition orale* (Paris, 1974).

'Oral Tradition and Historical Consciousness: the Case of Imerina', in R. K. Kent (ed.), *Madagascar in History* (1979), 123–47.

Delord, R., 'Limites et contenu de l'idée de patrie à Madagascar, avant l'époque moderne', *BAM*, n.s., XXXV (1957), 135–8.

'Un document inestimable sur la dynastie royale d'Ambositra', *BAM*, n.s., XXXVIII (1960), 69–77.

Delval, R., *Radama II, prince de la renaissance malgache* (Paris, 1972).

Deschamps, H., *Les Antaisaka* (Antananarivo, 1936).

Les migrations intérieures à Madagascar (Paris, 1959).

'La notion de "Peuples", l'exemple malgache', *B. de M.*, clxxvii (Feb. 1961), 95–8.

Histoire de Madagascar (4th edn, Paris, 1972).

Dez, J., 'Considérations sur les prix pratiqués à Tananarive en 1870', *BAM*, n.s., XL (1962), 42–61.

'Le Vakinankaratra – esquisse d'une histoire régionale', *B. de M.*, cclvi (Sept. 1967), 657–702.

'Eléments pour une étude de l'économie agro-sylvo-pastorale de l'Imerina ancienne', *Terre Malgache*, viii (1970), 9–60.

'Eléments pour une étude sur les prix et les échanges de biens dans l'économie Merina ancienne', *BAM*, n.s., XLVIII, i (1970), 41–90.

'La légende de l'Ankaratra', *Ann. Univ. Mad.*, xi (1970), 93–126.

Domenichini, J-P., 'Antehiroka et Vazimba: contribution à l'histoire de la société du XVIe au XIXe siècle', *BAM*. LVI, i–ii (1978), 11–27.

'Jean Ralaimongo (1884–1943) ou Madagascar au seuil du nationalisme', *RFHOM*, LVI, iii (1969), 236–87.

Bibliography

Donque, G., 'Le zoma de Tananarive. Etude géographique d'un marché urbain', *Madagascar. Revue de géographie*, VII (July–Dec. 1965), 93–227.

Dousset, R., *Colonialisme et contradictions: études sur les causes socio-historiques de l'insurrection de 1878 en Nouvelle-Calédonie* (Paris, 1970).

Dubois, H., *Monographie des Betsileo* (Paris, 1938).

Duffy, J., *A Question of Slavery* (Oxford, 1967). Chs. III and IV include material on the Madagascar slave trade.

Ellis, S. D. K., 'The Political Elite of Tananarive and the Revolt of the *Menalamba*: the Creation of a Colonial Myth in Madagascar, 1895–1898', *JAH*, XXI, ii (1980), 219–34.

'Les traditionalistes *menalamba* et les rois d'Imerina', in F. Raison (ed.), *Les souverains de Madagascar* (Paris, 1983), 373–89.

'The Merina Background, from Andrianampoinimerina to the French Conquest', in J. Simensen and F. Fuglestad (eds.), *Norwegian Missions in South Africa and Madagascar* (Norwegian Universities Press, forthcoming).

Escande, E. *Les disciples du seigneur* (Paris, 1926).

Esoavelomandroso, F. V., 'Les Sadiavahé: essai d'interprétation d'une révolte dans le Sud (1915–1917)', *Omaly sy Anio*, i/ii (1975), 139–71.

'Rainilaiarivony and the Defence of Malagasy Independence at the End of the Nineteenth Century', in R. K. Kent, *Madagascar in History* (1979), 228–51.

Review of S. D. K. Ellis, 'Collaboration and Resistance in Madagascar 1895–8', in *Omaly sy anio*, xii (1980), 139–56.

Esoavelomandroso, M., 'Le Mythe d'Andriba', *Omaly sy Anio*, i/ii (1975), 43–73.

'Religion et politique: l'évangélisation du pays betsimisaraka à la fin du XIXe siècle', *Omaly sy Anio*, vii–viii (1978), 7–42.

Falck, K., 'Norsk handel, sjøfart og kolonisasjon på Madagaskar, 1865–1880', *Sjøfartshistorisk Arbok* (Oslo, 1965), 95–141.

Fenard, G., *Les indigènes fonctionnaires à Madagascar* (Paris, 1939).

Filliot, J-M., *La traite des esclaves vers les Mascareignes au XVIIIe siècle* (Paris, 1974).

Fontoynont, Dr, 'Tsinjoarivo', *BAM*, n.s., XXIV (1941), 186–9.

and Nicol, *Les traitants français de la côte est de Madagascar, de Ranavalona I à Radama II* (mémoires de l'Académie malgache, fascicule XXXIII, Antananarivo, 1940).

and Raomandahy, 'Les Andriana du Vakinankaratra', *BAM*, n.s., XXIII (1940), 33–56.

François, E., 'L'économie malgache en 1895 et aujourd'hui', *R. de M.*, série de la libération, xxiv (Oct. 1945), 29–33.

Fremigacci, J., 'L'administration coloniale: les aspects oppressifs', *Omaly sy Anio*, vii–viii (1978), 209–37.

Fuglestad, F., '*Tompon-tany* and *tompon-drano* in the History of Western and Central Madagascar', *History in Africa*, IX (1982), 61–76.

Gheusi, P–B., *Gallieni et Madagascar* (Paris, n.d.).

Gluckman, M., *Order and Rebellion in Tribal Africa. Collected Essays* (London, 1963.

Gontard, M., 'La politique religieuse de Gallieni à Madagascar pendant les premières années de l'occupation française (1896–1900)', *RFHOM*, LVIII, ii (1971), 183–214.

Gow, B. A., *Madagascar and the Protestant Impact* (London, 1979).

Grandidier, A., *Ethnographie de Madagascar* (2 vols., Paris, 1908). Pt IV of the massive *Histoire physique, naturelle et politique de Madagascar*.

and Grandidier, G., *Bibliographie de Madagascar* (3 vols., Paris, 1905, 1933, 1956). Updated and continued as the *Bibliographie nationale de Madagascar* (Antananarivo, 1956–).

Grandidier, G., *Le Myre de Vilers, Duchesne, Gallieni: quarante années de l'histoire de Madagascar 1880–1920* (Paris, 1923).

Histoire politique et coloniale (3 vols., I, Paris, 1942; II, Antananarivo, 1956; III, Antananarivo, 1957). Pt V of the *histoire physique, naturelle et politique de Madagascar*.

204

Handfest, C., *Histoire du Fisakana (Betsileo du Nord)* (Antananarivo, 1950).

Hébert, J-C., 'Madagascar et Malagasy: histoire d'un double nom de baptême', *B. de M.*, cccii–ccciii (July–Aug. 1971), 583–613.

Hempenstall, P. J., 'Resistance in the German Pacific Empire: Towards a Theory of Early Colonial Response', *Journal of the Polynesian Society*, LXXXIV, i (1975), 5–24.

Hieke, E., *Zur Geschichte des deutschen Handels mit Ostafrika* (Hamburg, 1939), pp. 178–89 on Madagascar.

Hommes et destins (dictionnaire biographique d'outre-mer) (vol. III, Paris and Nice, 1979).

Hopkins, A. G., *An Economic History of West Africa* (London, 1973).

Iliffe, J., 'The Organization of the Maji-Maji Rebellion', *JAH*, VIII, iii (1967), 495–512.

Ireo Voninahitrao ry Vonizongo (no place, 1949).

Isaacman, A. F., with Isaacman, B., *The Tradition of Resistance in Mozambique. Anti-Colonial Activity in the Zambezi Valley, 1850–1921* (London, 1976).

Isnard, H., 'Les bases géographiques de la monarchie Hova', in *Eventail de l'histoire vivante: hommage à Lucien Fèbvre* (2 vols., Paris, 1953), I, 195–206.

Jacob, G., 'Léon Suberbie et les relations franco-malgaches de 1882 à 1887', *RFHOM*, LII, iii–iv (1965), 315–51.

'Fahavalisme et troubles sociaux dans le Boina à la fin du XIXe siècle', *Ann. Univ. Mad.*, vi (1967), 21–32.

'Les intérêts économiques lyonnais à Madagascar de la conquête à la première guerre mondiale', *Bulletin du centre d'histoire économique et sociale de la région lyonnaise*, iv (1971), 1–18.

'Influences occidentales en Imerina et déséquilibres économiques avant la conquête française', *Omaly sy anio*, v–vi (1977), 223–32.

and Koerner, F., 'Economie de traite et bluff colonial: la Compagnie Occidentale de Madagascar (1895–1934)', *Revue historique*, div (1972), 333–366.

Jacquier, L., *La main d'oeuvre locale à Madagascar* (Paris, 1904).

Julien, G., *Institutions politiques et sociales de Madagascar* (2 vols., Paris, 1909).

Kanya-Forstner, A. S., *The Conquest of the Western Sudan* (Cambridge, 1969).

Kasanga, F., *Tantaran' ny Antemoro Anakara teto Imerina tamin' ny andron' Andrianampoinimerina sy Ilaidama* (Antananarivo, 1956).

Kent, R. K., *Early Kingdoms in Madagascar, 1500–1700* (New York, 1970).

(ed.), *Madagascar in History. Essays from the 1970s* (Albany, Calif., 1979).

Koerner, F., 'L'échec de l'éthiopianisme dans les églises protestantes malgaches', *RFHOM*, LVIII, ii (1971), 215–38.

Kottak, C. P., *The Past in the Present. History, Ecology and Cultural Variation in Highland Madagascar* (Ann Arbor, 1980).

Landsberger, H. A., 'Peasant Unrest: Themes and Variations', in *idem* (ed.), *Rural Protest: Peasant Movements and Social Change* (London, 1974).

Lavau, G., 'Les pierres commémoratives de Betafo', *R. de M.*, 2nd ser., iii (1933), 31–50.

Le Révérend, A., *Lyautey* (Paris, 1983).

Lombard, J., *La royauté sakalava. Formation, développement, et effondrement, du XVIIe au XXe siècle. Essai d'analyse d'un système politique* (roneotyped, ORSTOM, Antananarivo, 1973).

Magnès, B., 'Essai sur les institutions et la coutume des Tsimihety', *B. de M.*, lxxxix (Oct. 1953), 1–95.

Mair, L., *African Kingdoms* (Oxford, 1977).

Malzac, V., *Histoire du royaume Hova* (Antananarivo, 1912).

Mamelomanana, E., 'Les principaux facteurs de la religiosité du peuple malgache', *BAM*, n.s., LII, i (1974), 35–55.

Mannoni, O., *Prospero and Caliban: the Psychology of Colonization* (English edn, London, 1956).

205

Bibliography

Mantaux, C., and Verin, P., 'Traditions et archéologie de la vallée de la Mananara (Imerina du Nord)', *B. de M.*, cclxxxiii (Dec. 1969), 966–85.

Marchal, J-Y., 'Contribution à l'étude historique du vakinankaratra – évolution du peuplement dans la cuvette d'Ambohimanambola, sous-préfecture de Betafo', *B. de M.*, ccl (Mar. 1967), 241–80.

Massiot, M., *L'administration publique à Madagascar* (Paris, 1971).

Masson, P., *Marseilles et la colonisation française* (Marseilles, 1906), pp. 302–32 on Madagascar.

'Ny Menalamba', *Réalités malgaches*, xvii (27 Sept. 1972), 2.

Miers, S., and Kopytoff, I., *Slavery in Africa* (Madison and London, 1977).

Mottet, G., 'L'Itasy à la fin du XIXe siècle. Essai de géographie historique', *Madagascar. Revue de géographie*, xv (July–Dec. 1969), 53–80.

Mutibwa, P. M., 'Trade and Economic Development in Nineteenth-Century Madagascar', *Transafrican Journal of History*, II, i (1972), 33–63.

The Malagasy and the Europeans (London, 1974).

Olivier, M., *Six ans de politique sociale à Madagascar* (Paris, 1931).

Paillard, Y-G., 'Problèmes de pacification et d'organisation de l'Imerina en 1896–7', *Ann. Univ. Mad.*, xii (1971), 27–91.

'Victor Augagneur: socialisme et colonisation', *BAM*, n.s., LII, i–ii (1974), 65–79.

and Boutonne, J., 'Espoirs et déboires de l'immigration européenne à Madagascar sous Gallieni: l'expérience de colonisation militaire', *RFHOM*, LXV, iii (1978), 333–51.

Petit, M., and Jacob, G., 'Un essai de colonisation dans la baie d'Antongil', *Ann. Univ. Mad.*, iii (1965), 33–55.

Poirier, C., 'Un "menabé" au coeur de la forêt de l'Est', *BAM*, n.s., XXV (1942–3), 96–136; XXVI (1944–5), 1–26.

'Prise de possession de Mananjara (Masindrano)', *BAM*, n.s., XXIV (1941), 152–70.

Polanyi, Karl, *Dahomey and the Slave Trade* (Seattle and London, 1966).

Profita, P., 'Les responsables Betsileo de la vallée d'Imerina-Imady sous la monarchie Merina', *BAM*, n.s., XLVI, ii (1968), 273–80.

Purcell, V., *The Boxer Uprising: a Background Study* (Cambridge, 1963).

Rabary, *Rainandriamampandry, na Ilay Maritioran' ny Tanindrazany tamin' ny Taona 1896* (Antananarivo, 1957).

Ny Daty Malaza (reprinted, vols. I and II, Antananarivo, 1975, 1978).

Rafamantanantsoa-Zafimahery, G., 'Le conseil du roi dans l'ancienne organisation du royaume de l'Imerina', *BAM*, n.s., XLIV, ii (1966), 137–45.

Rainianjanoro, *Tantara nataon-dRainianjanoro, 16Vtra* (no place or date).

Rainihifina, J., *Tantara Betsileo* (Fianarantsoa, 1975).

Rainitovo, 'Ny Mpikomy tamin' ny Niambohoan-dRasoherina', *Mp-Ts.*, n.s., XXIII (1926), 166–71.

Raison, F., Le catholicisme malgache: passé et présent', *Revue française d'études politiques africaines*, liii (1970), 78–99.

'Un tournant dans l'histoire religieuse merina du XIXe siècle: la fondation des temples protestants à Tananarive entre 1861 et 1869', *Ann. Univ. Mad.*, xi (1970), 11–56.

'Spiritualité et ecclésiologie protestantes en Imerina sous la colonisation', *Revue d'histoire de la spiritualité*, XLIX, ii (1973), 165–97.

'Les Ramanenjana', *ASEMI*, VII, ii–iii (1976), 271–93.

'Radama II, ou le conflit du réel et de l'imaginaire dans la royauté merina', *Les Africains* (vol. VIII, Paris, 1977), 279–310.

(ed.). *Les souverains de Madagascar* (Paris, 1983).

Raison, J-P., 'Utilisation du sol et organisation de l'espace en Imerina ancienne', in *Etudes de géographie tropicale offertes à Pierre Gourou* (Paris, The Hague, 1972), 407–25.

206

'Perception et réalisation de l'espace dans la société merina', *Annales*, XXXII, iii (1977), 412–32.
Rajaobelina, 'Andriantoarivo sy Vonizongo', *Mp-ts.*, n.s., VI (1909), 173–8, 207–17.
'Ankaratra', *Mp-ts.*, n.s., XXI (1924), 127–35, 175–9; XXII (1925), 21–5.
Rajaobelina, J., 'Portraits et anecdotes: gouverneurs du sud: Rarivo, gouverneur à Ambositra de 1885–1889', *BAM*, n.s., XLI (1963), 25–6.
Ralaimihoatra, E., *Histoire de Madagascar* (2 vols., Antananarivo, 1965).
Ralaimihoatra, G., 'Les premiers rois d'Imerina et la tradition vazimba', *BAM*, n.s., L, ii (1972), 25–32.
Ramanantsialonina, J-B., *Histoire de l'occupation du Betsileo par les Hovas* (Fianarantsoa, 1922).
Ramilison, E., *Ny Loharanon' ny Andriana Nanjaka teto Imerina, etc.* (2 vols., Antananarivo, 1951–2).
Randriamandimby Ravoahangy-Andrianavalona, J., 'Critique d'un texte de Rabenjamina Androvakely à propos de la généalogie des Andriamasinavalona d'Andramasina', *BAM*, n.s., LV, i–ii (1977), 61–4.
La VVS, Vy, Vato, Sakelika (Fer, Pierre, Ramification). Contribution à l'étude sur l'origine du nationalisme malgache (Paris, 1978).
Randriamiseza, 'Tantara fohifohy, ny Fiangonana Ambatomanga etc.', *Ny Mpamafy*, vii–viii (1925), 101–4, 117–23.
Randrianarisoa, P., *La diplomatie malgache face à la politique des grandes puissances (1882–95)* (Antananarivo, n.d.).
Ranger, T. O., *Revolt in Southern Rhodesia* (London, 1963).
'Connexions between "Primary Resistance" Movements and Modern Mass Nationalism in East and Central Africa', *JAH*, IX (1968), 437–53, 631–41.
'African Reactions to the Imposition of Colonial Rule in East and Central Africa', in L. H. Gann and P. Duignan (eds.), *Colonialism in Africa 1870–1960* (vol. I, Cambridge, 1969), 293–324.
'The People in African Resistance: a Review', *Journal of Southern African Studies*, iv (1977), 125–46.
Rasamimanana, J., and Razafindrazaka, L., *Contribution à l'histoire des malgaches: ny Andriantompokoindrindra* (bilingual text, 2nd end, Antananarivo, 1957).
Rasamuel, M., 'Ny Vazimba', *Mp-ts.*, n.s., XXIV (1927), 246–54; XXV (1928), 59–64.
Ny Menalamba tao Andrefan' Ankaratra 1895–1896 sy ny Zanakantitra (6 pts, Antananarivo, 1948–52).
Rasoanasy, J., *Menalamba sy Tanindrazana* (Antananarivo, 1976).
Razafintsalama, A., *Les Tsimahafotsy d'Ambohimanga, organisation familiale et sociale en Imerina – Madagascar* (roneotyped, Cahiers du centre de sociologie et d'anthropologie sociale no. I, Antananarivo, 1973).
Razi, G. M., *Sources d'histoire malgache aux Etats-Unis (1792–1882)* (Antananarivo, 1978).
Renault, F., *Lavigerie, l'esclavage africain et l'Europe* (2 vols., Paris, 1971).
Renel, C., *La coutume des ancêtres* (Paris, 1913). An attempt to describe the *menalamba* movement in the form of a novel.
'Les amulettes malgaches, ody et sampy', *BAM*, n.s., II (1915), 31–279.
'Ancêtres et dieux', *BAM*, n.s., V (1920–1), 1–256.
Richardson, J., *A New Malagasy–English Dictionary* (republished Farnborough, Hants, 1967).
Robinson, R. E., 'Non-European Foundations of European Imperialism: Sketch for a Theory of Collaboration', in W. Roger Louis (ed.), *Imperialism: the Gallagher and Robinson Controversy* (New York and London, 1976), 128–52.
'European Imperialism and Indigenous Reactions in British West Africa, 1880–1914', in H. L. Wesseling (ed.), *Expansion and Reaction* (Leiden, 1978).

and Gallagher, J., with Denny, A., *Africa and the Victorians* (London, 1961).

Savaron, C., 'Notes sur le Farihin-dRangita (marais de Rangita), Nord d'Imerimanjaka', *BAM*, o.s., X (1912), 373–7.

'Contribution à l'histoire de l'Imerina', *BAM*, n.s., XI (1928), 61–81, XIV (1931), 57–66.

'Note sur les Antankaratra et la forêt de l'Ankaratra (Manjakatompo)', *BAM*, n.s., XIV (1931), 67–73.

'Rainibetsimisaraka (1889–1901)', a series of 8 cuttings from an unidentified newspaper, *c.*1936, AAM unclass.

'Les Andriana Betsileos (Vakin'Ankaratra)', *BAM*, n.s., XXIII (1940), 57–64.

Scherer, A., *Histoire de la Réunion* (Paris, 1965).

La Réunion (Paris, 1980).

Schlemmer, B., 'Ethnologie et colonisation. Le moment de la conquête et le moment de la gestion. Eléments de réflexion à partir du cas du Menabe', in D. Nordman and J-P. Raison (eds.), *Sciences de l'homme et conquête coloniale* (Paris, 1980), 115–34.

Segre, D. A., 'Madagascar: an Example of Indigenous Modernization of a Traditional Society in the Nineteenth Century', in K. Kirkwood (ed.), *St Antony's Papers XXI* (London, 1969), 67–91.

Shepperson, G., 'The Comparative Study of Millenarian Movements', in S. L. Thrupp (ed.), *Millenial Dreams in Action* (Comparative Studies in Society and History, supplement no. II, The Hague, 1962), 44–52.

Siegriest, A., *Des rois, des reines, des brigands, des héros* (Antananarivo, 1940).

Simensen, J., and Fuglestad, F. (eds.), *Norwegian Missions in South Africa and Madagascar* (Norwegian University Press, forthcoming).

Spacensky, A., *Madagascar – cinquante ans de vie politique* (Paris, 1970).

Stokes, E., 'Traditional Resistance Movements and Afro-Asian Nationalism: the Context of the 1857 Mutiny Rebellion in India', *Past and Present*, xlviii (1970), 100–18.

Talmon, Y., 'Millenarian Movements', *Archives européennes de sociologie*, VII, ii (1966), 159–200.

Tantaran' Amboatany (Antananarivo, 1976).

Toussaint, A., *History of the Indian Ocean* (English edn, Chicago, 1966).

Tresoret, J., *La question minière à Madagascar depuis la conquête* (Paris, 1912).

Tronchon, J., *L'insurrection malgache de 1947* (Paris, 1974).

Valette, J., 'La vie économique à Tamatave en 1888–9', *B. de M.*, clvii (June 1959), 483–91.

'Eléments pour une biographie du Prince Ratovonony (1865–1914)', *B. de M.*, cclvi (Sept. 1966), 708–11.

'Eléments pour une biographie de Rafanoharana (1852–1927)', *B. de M.*, ccxlvii (Dec. 1966), 1247–8.

Vérin, P., 'Le commerce et l'activité économique des côtes nord-ouest de Madagascar au XIXe siècle', *Revue économique de Madagascar*, vi (1971), 137–45.

Vial, M., 'La royauté antankarana', *B. de M.*, xcii (Jan. 1954), 3–26.

Vidal, H., 'L'abolition de l'esclavage à Madagascar et l'arrêté du 26 Septembre 1896', *Penant*, dccxxii (Oct.–Dec. 1968), 525–35.

de Villars, Lt, *L'ancienne armée malgache* (Paris, n.d.), reprinted from the *Revue des troupes coloniales*.

Wilks, I., *Asante in the Nineteenth Century* (Cambridge, 1975).

Index

209

Index

Index